Female Body Image and Beauty Politics in Contemporary Indian Literature and Culture

EDITED BY SRIRUPA CHATTERJEE AND
SHWETA RAO GARG

Female Body Image and Beauty Politics in Contemporary Indian Literature and Culture

TEMPLE UNIVERSITY PRESS
Philadelphia • *Rome* • *Tokyo*

TEMPLE UNIVERSITY PRESS
Philadelphia, Pennsylvania 19122
tupress.temple.edu

Library of Congress Cataloging-in-Publication Data

Names: Chatterjee, Srirupa, 1979– editor. | Garg, Shweta Rao, 1982– editor.
Title: Female body image and beauty politics in contemporary Indian
literature and culture / edited by Srirupa Chatterjee and Shweta Rao
Garg.
Description: Philadelphia : Temple University Press, 2024. | Includes
bibliographical references and index. | Summary: "Using a Humanistic
Cultural Studies approach, this edited volume is the first book-length
study of its kind to offer insights on the myriad representations and
conceptualizations of women's body image in contemporary India"—
Provided by publisher.
Identifiers: LCCN 2023042568 (print) | LCCN 2023042569 (ebook) | ISBN
9781439922514 (cloth) | ISBN 9781439922521 (paperback) | ISBN
9781439922538 (pdf)
Subjects: LCSH: Body image in women—India. | Beauty, Personal—Political
aspects—India. | Women in popular culture—India. |
Physical-appearance-based bias—India. | BISAC: POLITICAL SCIENCE /
Public Policy / Social Policy | POLITICAL SCIENCE / Public Affairs &
Administration
Classification: LCC BF697.5.B63 F63 2024 (print) | LCC BF697.5.B63
(ebook) | DDC 306.4/6130954—dc23/eng/20240130
LC record available at https://lccn.loc.gov/2023042568
LC ebook record available at https://lccn.loc.gov/2023042569

9 8 7 6 5 4 3 2 1

Contents

Acknowledgments

This book is indebted to many people, experiences, and conditions. Even as it primarily originated in the personal experiences of the editors as well their overall understanding of Indian womanhood, it took its current shape from debates and discussions with many an Indian everywoman, activist, and scholar, some of whom have contributed chapters to this book. This project, then, is an outcome of years of engagement with and experiences of body image discourses, which the editors have encountered both as women and as academics.

Some of the earliest books that the editors read while studying feminist theory as undergraduate students, including Susie Orbach's *Fat Is a Feminist Issue*, Naomi Wolf's *The Beauty Myth*, and Susan Bordo's *Unbearable Weight: Feminism, Western Culture and the Body*, have been powerful tools for articulating body anxieties and formed the foundational ideas on which this project was built. While engaging with such works early in life, the editors realized that what the Western feminists were addressing had deep reverberations within Indian contexts as well where an ideal body image emerges from numerous intersectional forces to oppress and delimit women, just as it does in many other parts of the world. Subsequently, the editors found both familiarity and solace in the voices of Radhika E. Parameswaran, Jyotsna Vaid, Amali Phillip, and Vanita Reddy, among others, for variously challenging the hegemony of an ideal body image, specifically for Indian women. To these voices of resistance, the editors remain ever grateful.

In addition, the editors are grateful to Gurumurthy Neelakantan of the Indian Institute of Technology Kanpur, who was the thesis adviser of the lead editor, Srirupa Chatterjee, and provided many valuable insights on the problem of women's embodiment that this book builds on. Chatterjee is also grateful to Esther Rothblum of San Diego State University, who, while not being directly associated with this project, has been a huge source of inspiration for her enormous contribution to the field of fat studies and her scholarly resistance to body shaming. If this book has gained enormously from Chatterjee's brief academic interactions with her, Rothblum's nuanced articulations on issues of fat stigma and fat feminism deeply inform the spirit of this book.

This project was conceptualized during the COVID-19 pandemic when our worlds became unrecognizable in many ways. This book would not have seen the light of day—especially for being crafted through lockdowns, disease, and death—had it not been for the constant support from the editor of Temple University Press, Shaun Vigil. Shaun, your earnest and prompt help in all matters, academic and personal, is deeply appreciated. Likewise, the passionate engagement with which the various contributors not only designed their essays but also worked with the editors to revise and rework their material is commendable. We are grateful to these scholars and academics who, despite facing inconveniences, challenges, and even tragedies, persisted and provided their valuable interventions. The project is also indebted to graduate students working under Chatterjee's mentorship, Aswathi Velayathikode Anand and Shreya Rastogi, at the Indian Institute of Technology Hyderabad, for their help in compiling the various manuscript drafts of this volume.

This project could not have been successful without the tremendous encouragement and support of Sampa and Bhaskar Chatterjee, who are Srirupa Chatterjee's parents. Chatterjee would also like to say a heartfelt thanks her sister, Moumita Chatterjee, and her husband, Sayantan Chatterjee, for their unwavering faith in her efforts; especially Sayantan, for your support has been a blessing.

The coeditor of this volume, Shweta Rao Garg, would likewise wish to thank all those who saw beauty in her when she could not see it herself: her parents, Namdev and Veena Rao; her sisters, Swati and Trupti Rao; her aunts, Mala Rao and Anita Kudva; and many others. Garg also thanks her friend, Esha Mahajan, who introduced her to body positivity and self-love in praxis. She thanks all her students, especially Sayan Mukherjee for his inputs and Revathi P. M. for her insights on body image. Garg also thanks Swapnil Rai and Namrata Chaturvedi for their support. More important, she thanks her husband, Gagan Garg, who, regardless of the projects she undertakes, is always her sounding board. Garg also acknowledges Yash, Sharanya, and Yukta, who taught her to wonder at the world around her. Finally, Garg thanks all the feminist scholars, writers, and artists who helped her unravel her complex feelings about bodies in general and her own body in particular.

The editors are ever grateful to all the names mentioned here; you have together reaffirmed our faith in appreciating human bodies in all their naturalness.

Female Body Image and Beauty Politics in Contemporary Indian Literature and Culture

Introduction

Female Body Image and the Politics of Appearance in Contemporary India

Srirupa Chatterjee

A scholarly commentary on female body image in contemporary Indian literature and culture is long overdue. Since the politics of feminine appearance (across ages, classes, geographic regions, castes, sexual identities, and physical abilities, among others) represented in literature and popular culture has hardly received the critical and intellectual attention it deserves, our edited collection attempts to initiate a theoretically informed conversation on female body image and self-identity within contemporary neoliberal India's cultural paradigms.[1] In this book we therefore examine female body image vis-à-vis the politics of beauty, keeping in mind a few critical points. First, notwithstanding the biological essentialism associated with the term "female," we use it because, as a category, it includes people from all ages, communities, classes, body types, and sexual orientations and expressions who identify themselves as female. Second, while the politics of an ideal body image in the present times affects all genders, it is the female gender across the global spectrum that continues to be the most vulnerable target of the politics of appearance. And finally, we believe that this book, even as it speaks of female body image in India, will open up possible discursive paradigms for addressing body image problems faced by other genders, ethnic groups, and communities that have hitherto not received sufficient critical attention.

Notably, body image scholarship in the early twentieth century belonged exclusively to the global West and to the domain of neuropathology, with a focus on victims of the world wars who suffered grave wounds (or other injuries) and developed body dysmorphic disorders. It was Paul Schilder who used his expertise in neurology to first discuss body image in the 1930s as a physiological and sociocultural phenomenon.[2] Since then, much progress has been made in this area, and as Thomas Cash and Linda Smolak point out in *Body Image: A Handbook of Science, Practice, and Prevention*, the 1990s proved to be the most significant decade in the development of body image studies across global cultures. Simply put, body image today refers to one's own perceptions and beliefs toward one's physical appearance and sexual attractiveness. These beliefs are in turn shaped by innumerous sociocultural forces, both local and global, that one grows up with. If contemporary psychologists and cognitive theorists view body image as an experience of embodiment that often induces insecurities and anxieties with regard to one's appearance, feminists and body studies experts view it as a cultural imperative where "looking good" becomes an integral part of a woman's social and aesthetic capital.[3]

Hence, for contemporary Indian women, being normatively "beautiful," or having an ideal body image, largely refers to being young and able bodied, having a fair, tall, and curvaceous but slim and athletic form with sharp facial features and thick, lustrous hair. If this contemporary ideal developed largely as a result of colonial influences on twentieth-century India, it was massively augmented through the 1990s by Western forces of globalization and liberalization, the media and the Internet revolution, and a globally booming fitness, fashion, and aesthetic economy. Connecting the changing aesthetic contours of female embodiment to the opening up of the Indian market to global influences, Radhika Parameswaran aptly points out that "the tailoring of the government's liberalization package to suit the interests of multinationals" since the 1990s has "resulted in a shift in the emphasis of national policies from socialist modernity . . . to capitalist modernity—promoting the urban middle-class as a lucrative market for the sale of global consumer culture."[4] Under such neoliberal paradigms, a purportedly well-groomed body that subscribes to an ideal body image carries with it connotations of upward social mobility, progress, and empowerment that are tellingly supplied by the growing market of beauty, health, fitness, and fashion products. Ideals of female body image in India today are therefore appropriately modeled on globally dominant Eurocentric physical parameters whose prescriptive requirements have left millions of women anxious, insecure, and uncomfortable in their own skin.[5]

Our book takes into account how the globally celebrated Eurocentric ideal of female body image has beleaguered Indian women since the beginning of the twentieth century, but most palpably over the last thirty-odd years. It also takes into account the fact that where Indian women and their embodiment is concerned, issues such as "purity," virginity, sexual abuse, fertility, sexually transmitted diseases, menopause, aging, and malnutrition—to name a few—have garnered scholarly attention for supposedly being "serious" enough. However, when it comes to discourses of millions of women languishing under the everyday experience of beauty labor and the imperative of looking normatively beautiful, there hardly exists any substantial scholarly intervention. In fact, one of the most significant questions that inspires this project is why are there so many intellectual deliberations on Indian women's embodied experiences of poverty, lack of health care, casteism, domestic violence, sexual threats, unemployment, and lack of sanitation in general but none on the appearance bias that daily impacts their lives and fates in powerful ways?[6] It is for this reason that while this book deeply acknowledges and is informed by the contributions of many South Asian feminist intellectuals and theorists for engaging powerfully with women's condition and their troubled experiences of embodiment,[7] it aims to pick up from where most theoretical debates on Indian patriarchy, society, culture, economy, and politics leave off. More precisely, this book seeks to theorize issues of body image vis-à-vis Indian womanhood while connecting this to all other socioeconomic and cultural parameters.

Significantly, unlike Western intellectual traditions, where, since the advent of second-wave feminism, vastly diverse voices of feminist activists and writers ranging from Betty Friedan to Susie Orbach, from Naomi Wolf to Susan Bordo, from Esther D. Rothblum to Deborah L. Rhode, and from Sonya Renee Taylor to Nina Kullrich have compellingly debunked the beauty imperative propagated by the combined intersectional forces of patriarchy, racism, capitalism, consumer culture, and technology for enslaving women,[8] in India there hardly exists a unified body of scholarship contesting the cultural hegemony of an ideal body image unleashes anxieties and trauma on women. Hence, while powerful voices of resistance against the beauty myth, fat shaming, body shaming, colorism, ageism, and ableism abound in Western intellectual and academic circles, such voices lack coherent and collective theorizing as well as support within India. If the present project is an earnest attempt at developing such a body of scholarship customized specifically for Indian women—who most definitely do not form a homogenous category—it is also an endeavor to draw upon and diversify the arguments put forth by Western scholars and theorists on women's embodiment. Thus, even as this book is keenly mindful of the fact that Western feminist scholarship on body image speaks to women living under very different geographic, economic, and cultural specifications, it nonetheless draws upon these resistive voices because women's vulnerability to discourses of beauty and desirability is largely universal and as old as civilization itself. It is this ubiquity and immutability of the beauty imperative that this book seeks to examine and deconstruct. In sum, while this book is indebted to scholars both from the global West and South Asia for vocalizing its take on Indian women's embodiment, it is also driven by the ambition to outline the diverse, unique, and unheard voices of millions of women pining under discourses of normative feminine appearance.

Our edited volume therefore attempts to highlight the fact that while Indian women face distinct physical and mental challenges and experiences during childhood, adolescence, menarche, turning sexually active, or entering motherhood, menopause, and aging, all these stages are also intrinsically tied to their appearance, which often defines their place in society. We primarily view normative beauty as a matter of social value in line with Pierre Bourdieu's theories on capital to argue that a woman adhering to an ideal body image finds "credential" or "credit in the various senses of the word." In India, we therefore claim, the "volume of the social capital possessed" by normatively good-looking women creates a "multiplier effect" and garners "symbolic profits" to convert such women into "a rare, prestigious group"[9] such that the beauty ideology secures promises of social and economic benefits for them. While in no manner whatsoever do we claim that normatively beautiful women have it all or are free from the troubles experienced by their so-called unattractive counterparts, we definitely want to highlight the fact that every Indian woman, from the very moment of initiation into cultural codes, knows what beauty politics can do. They know that "beauty" refers to "biopower" and functions like "a discourse and concern about the vitality of the body . . . [and] the soul" and that it "can and does become an important site of signification, power, and knowledge about how to live."[10] As already discussed, while a number of psychologists, anthropologists, and medical practitioners have in the past examined how lived experiences of contemporary Indian women are governed by the beauty imperative,[11] a systematic study of this vexed issue as represented in contemporary Indian literature and culture is surprisingly missing.

Empirical and quantitative research (some of which is mentioned in endnote 11) demonstrates that many Indian women and girls continuously grapple with negative body perceptions owing to familial and sociocultural conditioning as well as the messages they receive from popular culture and mass media. Psychologists have recursively examined how a negative body image can lead to self-doubt and anxiety along with self-objectification and self-surveillance within an affected populace. In more serious cases, many women and girls develop eating disorders, such as anorexia nervosa and bulimia, that can have fatal consequences. Empirical research also demonstrates that Indian women, depending upon their purchasing power, are increasingly and willingly undergoing invasive aesthetic procedures to obtain the ever-elusive body ideal. Liposuctions, tummy tucks, lip jobs, rhinoplasty procedures, breast augmentations, vaginal tightening, skin lightening, and laser hair removal, among several others, are fads cultivated by many Indian women today. These medical procedures have no doubt helped some women regain their physical abilities and self-esteem after accidents or illnesses altered their natural bodies. And yet, for many regular women and girls, procedures that promise achievable and everlasting beauty often go wrong, leading to devastating outcomes. In addition to youthful, heterosexual, and able-bodied women, queer and trans women, women with special physical abilities, and aging women are often the most vulnerable targets of this overwhelmingly growing market for health, fitness, and aesthetic procedures. Empirical data thus demonstrates that a large proportion of Indian women and girls are in the thrall of the contemporary aesthetic market, which, in turn, is bolstered by mass media, consumerist ideologies, and health industries that together manipulate female body anxieties to create a powerful customer base.

With a keen awareness of the fact that ethnographers, empiricists, and scientists have already addressed the reality of Indian women's struggles with body image, this book attempts an analysis of body image as a cultural discourse and takes into account literary and popular culture representations of women across age groups, sexual identities, classes, castes, and bodily abilities, among others. This does not imply that the present volume is indifferent to the lived realities of Indian women; instead, it touches upon their experiences of embodiment by examining fictional and not-fictional accounts of both regular and nonnormative female bodies with the help of literary works, autobiographies, memoirs, interviews, films, advertisements, and popular magazines. The chapters in this book examine accounts of girls and women struggling with body anxieties, fears of fitting in, body shaming, body surveillance, eating disorders, medically transformed bodies, and colorism and weightism. Accordingly, this book—with the help of both fictional and factual narratives—addresses the pressures of beautification experienced by tomboys, aging women, queer women, trans women, regular as well as celebrity mothers, young girls, women with special abilities, and Dalit women, to name a few. And in doing so, this book channelizes empirical and quantitative conversations on female body image toward the realm of cultural and theoretical analysis. More important, if, like existing quantitative and empirical studies, this book views body image as a medical and psychological issue, it also substantiates body image as a socially constructed ideology that has profound personal, economic, and cultural repercussions on the lives of women and girls. While some of the bodily experiences discussed here are real and others fictionalized, all of them powerfully respond to and resist a culture that upholds normative beauty as a standard most Indian women are compelled to live up to. This book, then, interrogates the issue of female body image not simply as an empirical or medical construct but as a cultural discourse that both draws upon and undercuts many women's lived experiences with the politics of beauty.

Where theoretically nuanced discussions on female body image in neoliberal India are concerned, there exist very few but rather significant voices. For instance, Radhika E. Parameswaran has addressed the beauty imperative in essays such as "Global Beauty Queens in Post-Liberalization India" (2006), "Immortal Comics, Epidermal Politics: Representations of Gender and Colorism in India" (2009), and "Shaming the Nation on Public Affairs Television: Barkha Dutt Tackles Colorism on We the People" (2015) to point out how a market-driven agenda defines women's appearance in the present day. Shailendra Kumar Singh has published works such as "Destigmatization of the Fat Female Body" to discuss fat shaming and body positivity in Indian films and once again connect these to neoliberal conditions. Similarly, Jyotsna Vaid has a compelling take on skin lightness in "Fair Enough? Color and the Commodification of Self in Indian Matrimonials," which was published in Evelyn Nakano Genn's edited volume titled *Shades of Difference: Why Skin Color Matters* (2012), and Catriona Mitchell brought out an edited volume entitled *Walking Toward Ourselves: Indian Women Tell Their Stories* (2016) that discusses, among various other topics, the multifarious ways lookism impacts contemporary Indian women. Very recently, Nina Kullrich, in *Skin Colour Politics: Whiteness and Beauty in India* (2022), presented a powerful take on the preference of whiteness in India while connecting this problem to the nation's colonial past and its transnational present to finally claim that colorist biases in the country have deep-rooted indigenous and social significations. Finally, researcher Manisha Kalidas Kapadia's dissertation, "Body Image in Indian Women as Influenced by the Indian Media," is an example of research studies that focus on women's body image and the influence of visual cultures on them. Such studies, however, have been both sparse and sporadic. This is true despite the fact that since the early 1990s, globalized beauty discourses that augment concepts of an ideal body image have powerfully dominated India's aesthetic imagination. Parameswaran has investigated such cultural transformations by turning to Anita Anand's *The Beauty Game* to claim that "from 1996 to 2000 . . . there was a 25 percent growth in the cosmetics and personal care sectors, and the size of the 2000 cosmetics market was estimated to be about $160 million."[12] In the same essay, Parameswaran also adds that "Revlon, Maybelline, Oriflame, Avon, and L'Oreal have begun to compete for a share of the surplus income in middle-class Indian women's purses."[13] Even with such facts in place, not many South Asian scholars have attempted to connect the beauty conundrum with India's current socioeconomic status. Be that as it may, what cannot be denied is that the business of beauty and body image in neoliberal India has grown strong roots within both the nation's cultural consciousness as well as its women's psyches over the last three decades. Our collection therefore is a book-length intervention that not only augments academic discourses on female body image but also inaugurates a much-needed cultural debate on the injunctions of lookism, colorism, weightism, ableism, and ageism, among others, that in the present millennium beleaguer Indian women from various walks of life.

This volume, then, is cognizant of the fact that although normative ideals of beauty and femininity have always shaped (and shamed) women's bodies in India, it is in fact the liberalization of the 1990s that opened the floodgate of beauty expectations through the propagation of a consumer culture. Since the developed Western nations dominate economics and culture globally, and since many developing nations such as India have had a long history of colonial rule, such legacies, along with the contemporary forces of media and market, join hands to create an unshakable hegemony where beauty politics in India is concerned. Accordingly, a body ideal influenced by normative European and American constructs is upheld as the gold standard for Indian women as well. Since the 1990s, this image has been championed by international beauty, health, and fashion industries, which began to make inroads into India with globalization. Also since the 1990s, international beauty pageants won by Indian models (from Sushmita Sen to Manushi Chillar) altered the expectations of female beauty for large groups of indigenous people.[14] The bodies of "beauty queens" became not only desirable but also seemingly attainable through rigorous disciplining and beautification according to the propaganda from mass media and the Internet. Furthermore, since the 1990s, the film industry, which had always played a huge role in creating and perpetuating the nation's aesthetic ideals, started to uphold Eurocentric norms by casting female actors who were athletic, slim, and invariably fair and tall. With the coming of the new millennium, one increasingly encounters Bollywood film actresses who are tall, slim, and "Barbie doll" like while also being as close to the notorious "size zero" as possible. Over the years, then, Indian women, with their various shades of brown skin, genetically hardwired voluptuousness, and ethnically defined body heights, have been viewing this westernized body as an ideal one and often believe that in attaining it, they can find both acceptance and liberation.[15]

Since the genetic makeup of a vast majority of Indian women makes impossible the achievability of the ideal body that is constantly circulated and celebrated in various media, its scopophilic nature and impact makes more and more Indian women susceptible to self-scrutiny, body insecurity, and body anxiety today than ever before.[16] In addition, obtaining the so-called right weight, the ideal skin color, or an overall "attractive" appearance remains a chimera for most women. This is because the purportedly feminine and beautiful Indian body may suddenly be stigmatized as an ugly one if it simply puts on weight, gets tanned, undergoes childbirth, grows old, or is maimed or disfigured by accidents or illness, in addition to many other natural changes that can occur through one's lifetime. Parameters defining so-called attractive and unattractive bodies therefore do not function as a binary but work on an aesthetic continuum. And slight changes across the spectrum of acceptable and unacceptable appearance impact most women profoundly and can rob them of their confidence in a healthy self-image. It is this unsteady self-image—engendered by an omnipresent and ever-threatening beauty politics—among millions of Indian women that this book seeks to both reveal and reform.

While reading both literary narratives of the body, our volume is informed by the fact that twentieth-century literature ranging from Tagore's *The Home and the World* to Manto's "Bad-surati," from Premchand's "Sati" to Markandya's *Two Virgins*, and from Karnad's *Hayavadana* to Roys's *The God of Small Things* have variously explored the constructions of normative female beauty within the Indian context. It needs to be remembered here that within the Indian imagination, normative bodily appearance has traditionally been backed by powerful cultural myths and legacies, and the writers mentioned here have recursively critiqued these norms even as they are deeply informed by them. Hence, if corpulence—even while being viewed as a marker of prosperity—has been a symbol of greed and laziness,[17] dark skin tones have historically symbolized marginalized castes and classes and therefore are associated with moral/emotional flaws.[18] A differently abled body, likewise, while drawing people's pity, is seen as a karmic retribution for one's sins,[19] while an aging body, even as it is respected, is also rejected for its decay and infertility.[20] Notably, the highly acclaimed literary texts mentioned here insightfully underscore these values and the injustices of appearance bias in twentieth-century India while they speak of female embodiment. Adding to these voices, we note how a more contemporary group of popular Indian writers in English with their "chick lit" novels have taken to addressing beauty politics from a globalized and postmillennial vantage point. Names in this category include Vrushali Telang, Devapriya Roy, Suchi Singh Kalra, and Samah Visaria, whose *Can't Die for Size Zero* (2010), *The Weight Loss Club: The Curious Experiments of Nancy Housing Cooperative* (2013), *I Am Big. So What!?* (2016), and *Encounters of a Fat Bride* (2017), respectively, have vigorously questioned normative definitions of "perfect" female bodies and a culturally constructed discourse of "wellness" and self-actualization by giving the center stage to their fat or purportedly unattractive female protagonists. While these novels—sometimes doubling up as self-help manuals—foreground matters of choice and freedom for the modern Indian woman, they also implicitly portray how dietary and exercise regimes, along with dictates from the fashion and cosmetic industry, undercut female agency and autonomy. More important, such works of fiction endorse resistance to body shaming and encourage body positivity by demonstrating how their big or so-called ugly women protagonists fight deep-rooted body biases prevalent both in the outside world and within their own minds.

Like literature, Indian films, too, have responded variously to the normative ideals of femininity, including body image. We note how many mainstream Hindi films of the twentieth century, ranging from *Saudagar* of the 1970s to *Naseeb Apna Apna* in the 1980s to *Kuch Kuch Hota Hai* of the late 1990s along with *Vivah* in early 2000s, have depicted how beauty politics and women's body image issues are intertwined, where, if the purportedly ugly woman is shamed for her lack of aesthetic capital, the conventionally beautiful woman is often objectified and unduly sexualized for her so-called biopower. Ironically, then, these films depict women's conflicted relation with bodily appearance, which even now continues to be one of the most significant parameters for judging the worth of many Indian women. While it keeps such cinematic narratives in mind, our project is also informed by cultural transformations that have happened in the recent past when the hegemony of the "perfect" body has been challenged by Hindi films such as *Dum Laga Ke Haisha*, *Shaandaar*, *Ujda Chaman*, and *Bala* and regional Indian cinema such as *Shunyo e Bukey or Empty Canvas*, *Size Zero*, *Thamasha*, *Kakshi: Amminippilla*, and *Varane Avashyamund*, among others. Presenting a fresh and subversive take on dominant ideals of body image, these new age films have variously attempted to overthrow the tyranny of body shaming and hailed female embodiment in its various natural manifestations.

Significantly, like films that provide a visual medium for their audiences, discourses on beauty politics, body shaming, and body positivity are recursively published by many Indian fashion and fitness magazines that, in turn, boast largely of a female reader base. Examples of these include *Women's Health*, *Cosmopolitan*, *Women's Era*, *Women Fitness*, and *Health Care*, whose cover stories and headlines, while apparently addressing themes of wellness and body maintenance, also implicitly market technologized strategies of looking "good" and therefore feeling "good." The photoshopped and airbrushed images of men and women in these magazines uphold certain prescriptive norms of physical appearance and end up selling discourses on public health and consumption choices that convert many women (and men) into compliant consumers of products and services that promise them "good" looks and subsequently self-actualization. While this is true of many health and fashion magazines, it is also true that some publications, such as *Vogue* and *Femina*, have been variously promoting body positivity. These voices are interestingly being echoed by many Indian television serials, Internet series, advertisements, and social media posts that have both responded to and critiqued normative body image concepts by vigorously celebrating aging, non-normative gender identities, various shades of skin color, and different body weights and shapes, among others, and therefore added to globally growing instances of body positivity and body acceptance.

Despite growing voices that celebrate inclusivity, body image discourses in neoliberal and globalized India have taken a disturbingly complex form that affects many women in deeply personal ways. As mentioned previously, this problem is gradually but surely being opposed from various sensitized social segments within the nation. The beauty narrative, however, continues to control the nation's popular imagination, and an all-pervasive appearance bias impacts millions of women even today. The fact therefore remains that in India, there exists a beauty parlor and a gym in every nook and corner, and one constantly comes across billboards and advertisements for invasive/ medical procedures that can help one look "good." No doubt these avenues provide sustenance and employment to many, and yet they also end up bolstering the ever-elusive construct of an ideal body image. Predictably, many women—depending upon their socioeconomic capacities—are increasingly engaging in invasive and expensive beauty and fitness procedures in their real and virtual lives to live up to prescriptive body expectations. From finding acceptance within their own family and community to negotiating the marriage market, and very often while entering the job market, women hailing from diverse classes, castes, and communities are expected to check certain boxes where their height, weight, physical features, and skin color, among others, are concerned. Unfortunately, as existing research demonstrates, these problems have not been analyzed as grave cultural issues and the sporadically existing movements of resistance against them have not been clearly vocalized, especially within scholarly debates.

Informed by such cultural and economic paradigms, this edited volume focuses on globalized India by arguing that liberalization—which was a watershed moment of consumer culture—accentuated the nation's obsession with physical appearance. This collection identifies and investigates various cultural sites that have disseminated, perpetuated, and also undercut the discourse of an ideal female body image in India, such as literature, popular literature, print media, magazines, mainstream Bollywood, regional cinema, the Internet, advertisements, and social media, among others. Further, it locates the multiple jeopardies that variously marginalize women, especially with regard to embodiment, and appropriately engages with the beauty politics that is faced by Dalit women, women with alternate sexual identities, and women with differently abled bodies to demonstrate how these women are compelled to fight perceptions, discrimination, prejudice, and violence while navigating through the ideals of a normative heterosexual body image on a daily basis. While most of the chapters in this volume underscore how Indian women suffer under normative and prescriptive ideas of body and beauty, some hinge toward the discourse of body positivity in cultural texts and contexts as well.

This book is thematically divided into five sections, each of which address-es the problem of female body image through a specific critical lens. The first section of this book initiates a narrative analysis of bodies purportedly in-habiting societal margins and then moves on to examine representations of as well as resistances to the construction of the body beautiful by contem-porary Indian women authors. The next section dwells on how female bodies that have been variously disabled, disfigured, or maimed are treated within Indian culture and how media such as literature and films respond to the crisis-ridden embodiment of women with special abilities or alternate body types. The project then moves on to a section on cinematic discourses sur-rounding female body image, and by underscoring the popular appeal of cinema vis-à-vis depiction of female bodies, it demonstrates how the injus-tices of appearance discrimination define the hegemonic beauty norms for women, both on screen and in real life. Carrying forward the discussion on female body image and its ramifications within popular culture, the final sec-tion in this book examines both case studies and real-life narratives of wom-en's embodied experiences generated by advertisement, media, celebrity guidebooks, and even tomboys, who together represent the complex amal-gam of forces that at the same time reinstate and resist the celebratory rhet-oric surrounding an ideal female body image. In conclusion, this project both outlines and examines the various problems that impede the development of a body positive movement in India while also focusing on how such en-abling movements are gradually gaining strength and popularity in both real and virtual platforms across the nation.

The first section of this book, titled "Bodies on the Margins: 'Othering,' Hegemonic Beauty Norms, and Female Bodies," contains two chapters, one by Nishat Haider and one by Tanupriya and Aratrika Bose. If Haider's "Imag(in)ing the Dalit Woman: Body Image and Identity in Bama's *Sangati*" dwells upon the novel *Sangati* (2005) by Faustina Mary Fatima Rani, a.k.a. Bama, to foreground Tamil Dalit women's struggle with body image and their relationship with the "lived body" by drawing upon Merleau-Ponty's discus-sion on embodied consciousness, it also harnesses the sensual spirit and the oral and textual traditions that define issues such as beauty, sexuality, men-arche, and aging for Dalit women. Haider evaluates how body image can be a feminist project to highlight the troubled embodied experiences of Dalit women wherein physical appearance gets entwined with psychology, econom-ics, and issues of class and caste. With the help of body and gender studies experts, Haider examines how memory and experience are fused within the materiality of Dalit female bodies and how gender, bodily appearance, and skin color together relegate such bodies to societal margins. Likewise, Tanu-priya and Aratrika Bose, in "Bodies at Surveillance: Appearance, Social Control, and Female Body Image in India's Postmillennial Lesbian and Trans Narratives," focus on works such as Manju Kapoor's *A Married Woman* (2002), Abha Dawesar's *Babyji* (2005), A. Revathi's *The Truth about Me: A Hijra Life Story* (2010), and Manobi Bandyopadhyay's *A Gift of Goddess Laxmi* (2017) to address the problem of body image for women inhabiting societal margins, such as lesbians and those with transgender bodies. The authors of this chapter examine how women with nonnormative bodies negotiate survival within conditions obsessed with heteronormative female bodies and ideals of beauty. By drawing upon psychologists, queer theorists, and body studies scholars, Tanupriya and Bose argue that "not feminine enough" bodies of lesbian and trans women experience anxiety, in between-ness, and dissonance while also becoming traumatized sites of political control. Finally, if this chapter, with the help of both fiction and autobiography, explains how homophobia and transphobia govern the bodies and self-image of many Indian women with nonnormative sexual identities, it also presents a clarion call toward body positivity through a collective acceptance of lesbian and trans bodies with all their distinct attributes.

The second section of this book is titled "Reflections on Beauty Politics: Gender and Body Image in the Works of Contemporary Indian Women Writers." Developing on the fiction and nonfiction examined in the first section, this section offers a close reading of works by Indian women writers and intellectuals who, over the last few decades, have powerfully critiqued a pressing need among women to appear normatively beautiful. This section therefore begins with Swatie's "Writing Woman / Woman Writing: Shashi Deshpande and the Aesthetics of the Female Body," which engages with Shashi Deshpande's short stories, such as "Why a Robin?," "The First Lady," and "The Intrusion," with a specific focus on female body image. Delving deep into the complexities of mother-daughter relations, aging bodies, and domestic violence, this chapter connects women's appearance with their self-identity, social acceptability, sexual desirability, and marital relationships to ultimately uncover how a commodity culture creates and governs female embodiment. If Swatie, in this chapter, presents Deshpande as an intellectual responding to India's neoliberal experiences, she also presents the writer's feminist sentiments as precursors to the female body image discourse that globally gained momentum through the 1990s. The next chapter in this section is Shubhra Ray's "Manjula Padmanabhan and the Question of Problematizing Embodied Gender Identity: A Reading of *Getting There*." By arguing that the body is not just a biological reality but also a discursive construct, Ray deploys theories on body image to claim that in neoliberal and globalized India, women are expected to adhere to prescriptive norms of appearance, failing which they experience painful instances of body shaming. Ray connects these assertions with Padmanabhan's memoir, where the writer grapples with her own so-called physical inadequacies, her body weight, and her distaste for the institution of marriage, which, in turn, puts a heavy burden on women to look conventionally beautiful. Ray highlights the contemporaneity and relevance of *Getting There* for addressing how the embodied subjectivity of Indian women often inhibits them from unconditionally accepting their natural bodily selves. The final chapter in this section is Annika Taneja's "Future Forms: Female Body Image in Indian Dystopian Fiction," which examines three works of Indian science fiction, namely, *Harvest* (1997) by Manjula Padmanabhan, *The Lesson* (2015) by Sowmya Rajendran, and *Clone* (2019) by Priya S. Chabria. Taneja's chapter begins by outlining globally prevalent debates on female body image and how Indian women, too, are subject to dictates of prescriptive beauty. Taneja then proceeds to examine women's corporeality within fictional futures where she demonstrates how socioeconomic and transnational forces governing embodiment merge with technology to remodel women's bodily aesthetics. By delving into fictional dystopias that variously symbolize present-day India in the three novels, Taneja finally celebrates women who reclaim their bodies from the clutches of an overarching beauty myth to craft alternate and empowering forms of embodiment.

The third section of this volume, titled "Alternate Beauties? Disabled and Disfigured Female Bodies in Contemporary Indian Literature and Culture," borrows from feminist theory, body image scholarship, and disability studies to discuss how women with special abilities and alternate corporeal identities are often marginalized and stigmatized in India. It contains two chapters, one by Anurima Chanda and one by Samrita Sinha, that together problematize and conflate discourses of ableism and an ideal body image to underscore the vexed experiences of women with alternate abilities, body deformities, or bodies altered by disease and/or accident. Chanda's chapter is titled "Fitting In When Your Body Does Not: Young Girl Characters with Disabilities in Contemporary Indian English Fiction for Children" and examines two contemporary young adult Indian English novels—Leela Gour Broome's *Flute in the Forest* (2010) and Devika Rangachari's *Queen of Ice* (2014)—that portray girl characters with alternate physical abilities. Chanda's chapter argues that hegemonic discourses surrounding women's beauty and sexual desirability have serious and detrimental effects on differently abled girl children who inevitably grow up with a sense of shame toward their bodies, which, in turn, become the primary site of their identity formation. Chanda hails these novels for unapologetically celebrating impaired bodies, a strategy that, she argues, undercuts dominant beauty standards by generating an "oppositional gaze" that instead of focusing on the deformity highlights the functionality and appeal of differently abled bodies. Like Chanda, Sinha, in her chapter entitled "Pathologies of 'Body Fictions': A Comparative Study of *Margarita with a Straw* and *Kuch Bheege Alfaaz*," treats two cinematic narratives on alternately abled and nonnormative female bodies as counterdiscourses to dominant beauty norms. Informed by body image scholarship and psychoanalytic theories, Sinha discusses how women with disabilities or disfigurements are labeled abhorrent and dysfunctional and are systemically marginalized by society. Hence, Sinha examines how a queer young woman suffering from cerebral palsy in *Margarita with a Straw* and a young vivacious woman grappling with leukoderma in *Kuch Bheege Alfaaz* suffer body dysmorphic disorders and eventually subvert body ideals that celebrate ableist discourses of body aesthetics. In sum, if Sinha's chapter demonstrates how films as a visual media are powerful means to sensitize the larger culture about issues of aesthetics vis-à-vis disability, it also sets the stage for the next section, which powerfully captures the power of cinema in generating cultural messages on beauty politics.

The fourth section of this book, titled "Scopophilic Cultures: Female Body Image in Contemporary Indian Cinema," contains two chapters by Shailendra Kumar Singh that deal with Indian mainstream as well as regional cinema and its engagement with women's bodily aesthetics. A scholar of feminist body studies and media studies, Singh aptly challenges the various appearance-based injustices both practiced and propagated by commercial Indian cinema. In his chapter titled "Unjust Gradations of Fairness: Gender, Looks, and Colorism in Postmillennial Hindi Cinema," Singh examines India's fascination with and privileging of light skin tones by demonstrating how dark skin, which was earlier attributed to villains and vamps in Hindi cinema, has gradually come to be linked with the urban underclass and rural populace, symbolizing a lack of progress and opportunity. In this chapter, Singh examines two postmillennial Hindi films, namely, *Udta Punjab* (2016) and *Bala* (2019), where the dark-skinned female protagonist is either made to represent an impoverished rural India or within urban settings is made to fight a humiliating battle toward self-acceptance. In all, by proving how dark-skinned Indian women suffer enormous body shaming and social discrimination both on screen and in real life, this chapter highlights how contemporary Hindi cinema—even with its sporadic attempts at body positivity—is often guilty of failing to attribute cultural goodness and sexual desirability to dark skin. Singh's second chapter in this section, titled "Fetishism, Scopophilia, and the Fat Actresses of Bhojpuri Cinema," investigates regional Indian cinema to claim how representations of the fat female body engender an eroticized and disparaging ideology of embodiment while catering to certain types of audiences. Singh argues that in no way is the fat female body represented in Bhojpuri cinema a rebellion against the weightism that dominates Bollywood but instead is a vulgar fetish consumed voraciously by the voyeuristic male gaze of the regional audience. Bemoaning the misuse of the subversive potential of regional cinema in countering fat shaming, Singh claims that commercially successful Bhojpuri films, instead of creating enabling body discourses, end up pathologically eroticizing fat female corporeality.

Adding to debates on visual media surrounding womanhood and beauty politics as discussed in the fourth section, the fifth and final section of this book, entitled "Neoliberal Cultures and Female Body Image in Indian Advertisements and Popular Media," focuses on different kinds of visual cultures, such as advertisements and celebrity guidebooks as well as films and real-life case studies, to examine the problem of female body image in contemporary India. It begins with "Gender, Body Image, and the Aspirational Middle-Class Imaginary of Indian Advertising" by Kavita Daiya, Sukshma Vedere, and Turni Chakrabarti, who investigate female body image in contemporary Indian advertising produced between 2010 and 2020. Daiya et al. begin with a critically informed analysis of the advertising of skin-care products since the 1990s to argue that discourses on body normativity are propagated by the many Indian commercials that in turn are influenced by colorist and racist biases. The authors then turn their attention to jewelry commercials from the present millennium to demonstrate that while these ads no longer focus on conventions of familial prosperity and instead try to highlight the bride's individuality, they still remain trapped within heteronormative patriarchal values where issues of women's appearance and career choice/mobility are concerned. In the final section of this chapter, Daiya et al. examine matrimonial advertisements in Hindi digital media. By drawing upon the works of South Asian feminist scholars, the authors explore problems of body image and colorism in wedding advertisements to claim that while these ads superficially endorse women's empowerment and nuclear families, in truth they remain trapped within conventional paradigms of appearance and gender power politics. In the hope to augment feminist voices and activism, Daiya et al. conclude their chapter by stating that capital, technology, and gender oppressions come together in Indian commercials to bespeak the injustices propagated by the hegemony of an ideal body image that needs to be vocally countered. The next chapter in this section furthers the critique of normative embodiment by taking into account Indian women celebrities as well as other women who struggle hard to live up to the beauty imperative as they go through various phases of life, including motherhood. In "Unpacking Compliances and Resistances in the Indian Yummy Mummy," Sucharita Sarkar makes a compelling argument on the globally celebrated, media-generated, and disturbingly problematic construct of the "yummy mummy," with a focus on Indian mothers and their caregiving practices. Reading the construct of the yummy mummy as both a neoliberal extension of patriarchal motherhood as well as a globally hailed discourse on empowered mothering, Sarkar claims that this construct—endorsed by both celebrities and popular culture—compels many mothers to discipline and control their bodies to live up to normative beauty standards that have come to define motherhood. Deploying tropes of self-improvement, claims Sarkar, the yummy mummy concept in reality pushes many Indian women to suffer body dysmorphic disorders, anxiety, and fatphobia upon entering motherhood. As a result, adds Sarkar, such women undertake harmful body and beauty regimes and even surgical procedures hoping to achieve makeovers that apparently promise a more fulfilling and glamorous life. Simply put, Sarkar's chapter adds to the much-needed debate on mothering practices and maternal bodies that remain in thrall to an ideal body image in contemporary India. The third and final chapter in this section is "'Hey! She's a Bro!': Tomboys, Body Image, and Desire in India" by Ketaki Chowkhani. Delving into real-life case studies of women with nonnormative bodies, Chowkhani argues that for diverging from heteronormative female embodiment and its conventional aesthetics, tomboys in India make a marginalized category and suffer both discrimination and humiliation, especially with regard to social acceptance and romantic relationships. By drawing upon autoethnographies of tomboys, Bollywood cinema, and popular culture, Chowkhani argues that tomboys—or, more specifically, heterosexual tomboys—powerfully undercut contemporary hegemonic discourses on femininity, body image, sexual desire, and heteronormativity. In sum, Chowkhani's chapter adds to categories of women's nonnormative corporeality and their experiences of body anxieties and hence provides a fitting closure to this book's discussions on Indian women vis-à-vis beauty politics.

With the twelve chapters outlined so far, this book initiates a critical conversation on the politics of appearance that defines the lives of many Indian women in the present. More important, while this book attempts to address female embodiment across class, caste, communities, body types, age groups, and sexual identities, among others, it by no means claims to encompass Indian womanhood and its embodied experiences in all their various forms and guises. Instead, this book concludes with the hope that more debates and discussions will emerge to address women's embodiment from the point it leaves off and that these debates will go a long way with both academics and activists, who can together sensitize a larger culture toward body inclusivity. We also hope that these debates will grow in mass and momentum over the years so that it is not only the female body image that gains attention but also that the body image issues that plague men, adolescents, older adults, people with alternate sexual identities, and people with alternate physical abilities, among others, find the acknowledgment they rightfully deserve. That said, this book is also mindful of the body positive movement that is globally gaining recognition and hence concludes with a note on how body inclusivity is gradually taking shape in India. The fact that appearance discrimination and beauty politics are not going unquestioned but are being identified, examined, and challenged by certain quarters, however small and sporadic, is a welcome change, and this book aspires to add to such voices.

To sum up: given the significance of the body image discourse in contemporary India, and given the fact that it affects women at almost visceral levels, our edited collection brings together contributions from experts on literary analysis, film analysis, gender and sexuality studies, young adult literature, disability studies, caste scholarship, motherhood studies, gerontology, and body image studies with a focus on Indian literature and popular culture. Further, by viewing how fair skin, slimness, and tallness along with youthfulness, able-bodiedness, and agility are all viewed as desirable physical traits for Indian women, and how these traits affect the self-image of women across all age groups, castes, classes, and sexual and physical orientations, this volume seeks to initiate a debate on the appearance bias that is deeply entrenched in India's cultural consciousness. In addition, we hope that the book's intervention on popular culture depictions of technically advanced aesthetic procedures that many Indians are increasingly investing in—sometimes at the cost of their own physical and mental well-being—goes on to sensitize readers toward concepts of choice and autonomy as they think of body styling and alterations. All in all, this volume aspires to critique the hegemony of a "perfect" body that drives many women not just toward insecurity but also often toward self-harm. In conclusion, then, this book hopes to generate sensitivity and awareness toward body positivity that endorses healthy and happy bodies and minds while also rejecting the tyranny of a globally accepted prescriptive body image. As editors, we firmly believe that it is high time such a volume was published to not only add to body image scholarship but also to promote awareness and advocacy toward body positivity and body inclusivity in India.

NOTES

1. C. P. Chandrasekhar describes the advent of Indian neoliberalism in the following words: "India's tryst with neoliberalism—the economic framework that preaches market fundamentalism but uses the state to engineer a redistribution of income and assets in favour of finance capital and big business—is routinely traced to 1991." See Chandrasekhar, "Indian Neoliberalism."

2. For more details, see the introduction by Cash and Smolak in *Body Image*.

3. Lookism, beauty norms, and appearance-based discrimination when viewed as outcomes of Bourdieu's cultural and social capital (as discussed later in this introduction) provide deep and insightful paradigms of female embodiment. See also Chakravarty, "Reflections on the Body Beautiful"; Hakim, "Erotic Capital"; Anderson et al., "Aesthetic Capital"; and Hamermesh and Biddle, "Beauty and the Labor Market," for discussion on similar lines.

4. Parameswaran, "Global Queens, National Celebrities," 348.

5. See how effects of globally dominant discourses on embodiment affect women in Bartky, "Foucault, Femininity." Irene Diamond and Lee Quinby (Boston, MA: Northeastern University Press, 1997); and Liebelt, Böllinger, and Vierke, eds., *Beauty and the Norm*. In contrast with these arguments, Nancy Etcoff presents a persuasive hypothesis while defending the beauty ideal in *Survival of the Prettiest: The Science of Beauty* (2000) to claim that humans are biologically hardwired and culturally conditioned to be attracted to certain bodily attributes, which is why the beauty ideal continues to define human worth in profound and immutable ways. Positions such as Etcoff's have predictably been problematized and contested by feminists who want women's bodies to be accepted and cherished for their naturalness and not be subject to patriarchal and consumerist interventions.

6. This book draws the concept of appearance or beauty bias from Deborah L. Rhode, *The Beauty Bias*, where the writer demands that discrimination based on one's appearance be treated as a social as well as legal offence. Rhode points out that "most people believe that bias based on beauty is inconsequential, inevitable, or unobjectionable" (2). Existing across cultures in a globalized albeit unequal world, "prevailing beauty standards," explains Rhode, "privilege those with white-European features and the time and money to invest in their appearance," and she further argues that "women face greater pressures than men to look attractive and pay greater penalties for falling short" (7). We view appearance bias or beauty bias as a bias against women who do not befit prescriptive definitions of beauty and attractiveness, specifications of which have been discussed previously in this introduction.

7. This book is broadly informed by theoretical works of South Asian scholars, including Mankekar, *Screening Culture*; Chaudhuri, *Refashioning India*; Munshi, ed., *Images of the "Modern" Woman*; Majumdar, *Marriage and Modernity*; Menon, *Seeing Like a Feminist*; Thapan, *Living the Body*; Ghosh, *Impaired Bodies*; and Sangari and Vaid, eds., *Recasting Women*, among many others, to substantiate its claims on the intersectionality of oppressive and delimiting forces that beleaguer Indian women and their embodiment.

8. See studies like Wolf, *The Beauty Myth*; Bordo, *Unbearable Weight*; Brumberg, *The Body Project*; Peiss, *Hope in a Jar*; Huberman, *Through Thick & Thin*; and Jones, *Beauty Imagined*, for detailed and historicized discussions on how science, technology, and health care have, over time, merged with market forces to craft a powerful culture of body maintenance and enhancement, especially for women.

9. Bourdieu, "The Forms of Capital," 249.

10. Nguyen, "The Biopower of Beauty," 364.

11. See, for example, Shroff and Thompson, "Body Image and Eating Disturbance"; Gupta et al., "Weight-Related Body Image Concerns"; Rekha and Maran, "Advertisement Pressure"; Mendhekar et al., "Anorexia Nervosa"; Nagar and Virk, "The Struggle"; Vaidyanathan, Kuppili, and Menon, "Eating Disorders"; Garbett et al., "Cultural Adaptation"; and Lewis-Smith et al., "Evaluating a Body Image," as examples of psychological, medical, and empirical research on how real women are affected by the beauty ideal.

12. Parameswaran, "Global Beauty Queens," 420.

13. Parameswaran, "Global Beauty Queens," 420.

14. See Chatterjee and Rastogi, "The Changing Politics" and "Television Culture" for discussion on how beauty labor in neoliberal India has changed and how these changes are especially visible with the popular media of films and television.

15. See the general impact of globalization on women in neoliberal India in Chatterjee, "Feminism, the False Consciousness"; and Pathak, "Presentable," 314–329.

16. Body image discourses and appearance bias that have existed in India over centuries and have been examined by scholars are briefly touched upon in this introduction. Significantly, however, most other works on this subject mainly take into account an empirical and quantitative perspective with some inputs from philosophy and phenomenology while examining matters of embodiment. In addition, an important book on this matter is Dehejia and Paranjape, eds., *Saundarya*, but this book also focuses primarily on Indian aesthetics and the concept of beauty in art rather than the issue of body image as we understand it today.

17. See Praween Agrawal et al., "The Psychosocial Factors."

18. See Parameswaran and Cardoza, "Immortal Comics"; and Kullrich, "In This Country."

19. Gupta, "How Hindus Cope."

20. For stigma associated with the aging body, see Nussbaum's "Ageing, Stigma, and Disgust."

BIBLIOGRAPHY

Agrawal, Praween, Kamla Gupta, Vinod Mishra, and Sutapa Agrawal. "The Psychosocial Factors Related to Obesity: A Study among Overweight, Obese, and Morbidly Obese Women in India." *Women and Health* 55, no. 6 (2015): 623–645.

Anand, Anita. *The Beauty Game*. Delhi: Penguin, 2002.

Anderson, Tammy L., Catherine Grunert, Arielle Katz, and Samantha Lovascio. "Aesthetic Capital: A Research Review on Beauty Perks and Penalties." *Sociology Compass* 4 (2010): 564–575.

Ayyathan, Dinjith, dir. *Kakshi: Amminippilla*. Featuring Asif Ali, Ahamed Siddique, and Fara Shibla. Zarah Films, Kerala, 2019.

Bahl, Vikas, dir. *Shaandaar*. Featuring Shahid Kapoor, Alia Bhatt, and Pankaj Kapur. Phantom Films and Dharma Productions, Mumbai, 2015.

Barjatya, Sooraj R. dir. *Vivah*. Featuring Shahid Kapoor, Amrita Rao, and Anupam Kher. Rajshri Productions, Mumbai, 2006.

Bartky, Sandra Lee. "Foucault, Femininity, and the Modernization of Patriarchal Power." In *Feminism and Foucault, Reflections on Resistance*, edited by Irene Diamond and Lee Quinby, 29–44. Boston, MA: Northeastern University Press, 1988.

Bordo, Susan. *Unbearable Weight: Feminism, Western Culture, and the Body*. Berkeley: University of California Press, 1993.

Bourdieu, Pierre. "The Forms of Capital." In *Handbook of Theory and Research for the Sociology of Education*, edited by John Richardson, 241–258. New York: Greenwood Press, 1986.

Brumberg, Joan Jacob. *The Body Project: An Intimate History of American Girls*. New York: Vintage, 2010.

Cash, Thomas F., and Linda Smolak, eds. *Body Image: A Handbook of Science, Practice, and Prevention*. 2nd ed. New York: Guilford Press, 2012.

Chakravarty, Sumita S. "Reflections on the Body Beautiful in Indian Popular Culture." *Social Research* 78, no. 2 (2011): 395–416.

Chandrasekhar, C. P. "Indian Neoliberalism: A Toxic Gift from Global Finance." *Frontline*, September 24, 2021. Available at https://frontline.thehindu.com/cover-story/indian-neoliberalism-economic-reforms-at-30-a-toxic-gift-from-global-finance/article3629 0562.ece.

Chatterjee, Ipsita. "Feminism, the False Consciousness of Neoliberal Capitalism? Informalization, Fundamentalism, and Women in an Indian City." *Gender, Place, and Culture: A Journal of Feminist Geography* 19, no. 6 (2012): 790–809.

Chatterjee, Srirupa, and Shreya Rastogi. "The Changing Politics of Beauty Labour in Indian Cinema." *South Asian Popular Culture* 18, no. 3 (2020): 271–282.

———. "Television Culture and the Beauty Bias Problem: An Analysis of India's Postmillennial Television Serials." *Media Asia* 49, no. 3 (December 2021): 213–234.

Chaudhuri, Maitrayee. *Refashioning India: Gender, Media, and a Transformed Public Discourse*. Hyderabad: Orient Blackswan, 2017.

Dehejia, Harsha V., and Makarand Paranjape, eds. *Saundarya: The Perception and Practice of Beauty in India*. New Delhi: Samvad India Foundation, 2003.

Etcoff, Nancy. *Survival of the Prettiest: The Science of Beauty*. 2nd ed. New York: Anchor Books, 2000.

Friedan, Betty. *The Feminine Mystique*. 1957. Reprint, London: Penguin, 2010.

Ganguly, Kaushik, dir. *Shunyo E Buke or Empty Canvas*. Featuring Churni Ganguly, Kaushik Sen, and Kharaj Mukherjee. Forthright Media and Entertainment, Kolkata, 2005.

Garbett, Kirsty M., Helena Lewis-Smith, Anshula Chaudhry, Nora Uglik-Marucha, Silia Vitoratou, Hemal Shroff, Megha Dhillon, and Phillippa C. Diedrichs. "Cultural Adaptation and Validation of the Body Esteem Scale for Adults and Adolescents for Use in English among Adolescents in Urban India." *Body Image* 37 (June 2021): 246–254.

Ghosh, Nandini. *Impaired Bodies, Gendered Lives: Everyday Realities of Disabled Women*. New Delhi: Primus Books, 2016.

Gupta, Madhulika A., Santosh K. Chaturvedi, Praful C. Chandarana, and Andrew M. Johnson. "Weight-Related Body Image Concerns among 18–24-Year-Old Women in Canada and India: An Empirical Comparative Study." *Journal of Psychosomatic Research* 50, no. 4 (April 2001): 193–198. Available at https://doi.org/10.1016/S0022-3999(00)00221-X.

Gupta, Vidya Bhushan. "How Hindus Cope with Disability." *Journal of Religion, Disability, and Health* 15, no. 1 (2011): 72–78.

Hakim, Catherine. "Erotic Capital." *European Sociological Review* 26, no. 5 (2010): 499–518.

Hamermesh, Daniel S., and Jeff E. Biddle. "Beauty and the Labour Market." *American Economic Review* 84, no. 5 (1994): 1174–1194. Available at https://www.jstor.org/stable/2117767.

Hamza, Ashraf, dir. *Thamasha*. Featuring Vinay Forrt, Chinnu Chandni Nair, and Navas Vallikkunnu. Happy Hours Entertainment, Kerala, 2019.

Huberman, Warren L. *Through Thick & Thin: The Emotional Journey of Weight Loss Surgery*. New York: Graphite Press, 2012.

Johar, Karan, dir. *Kuch Kuch Hota Hai*. Featuring Shah Rukh Khan, Kajol Devgan, and Rani Mukherjee. Dharma Productions, Mumbai, 1998.

Jones, Geoffrey. *Beauty Imagined: A History of the Global Beauty Industry*. New York: Oxford University Press, 2010.

Kalra, Suchi Singh. *I Am Big. So What!?* New Delhi: Prakash Books, 2016.

Kapadia, Manisha Kalidas. *Body Image in Indian Women as Influenced by the Indian Media*. Ph.D. diss., Texas Women's University, 2009. ProQuest Dissertations and Theses.

Karnad, Girish. *Hayavadana*. New Delhi: Oxford University Press, 1975.

Katariya, Sharad, dir. *Dum Laga Ke Haisha*. Featuring Sanjay Mishra, Ayushmann Khurrana, and Bhumi Pednekar. Yash Raj Films, Mumbai, 2015.

Kaushik, Amar, dir. *Bala*. Featuring Ayushmann Khurrana, Bhumi Pednekar, and Yami Gautam. Maddock Films, Mumbai, 2019.

Kovelamudi, Prakash, dir. *Size Zero*. Featuring Arya, Anushka Shetty, and Sonal Chauhan. PVP Cinema, 2015.

Kullrich, Nina. "'In This Country Beauty Is Defined by Fairness of Skin': Skin Colour Politics and Social Stratification in India." In *Beauty and the Norm: Debating Standardization in Bodily Appearance*, edited by Claudia Liebelt, Sarah Böllinger, and Ulf Vierke, 245–297. New York: Palgrave Macmillan, 2019.

———. *Skin Colour Politics: Whiteness and Beauty in India*. Berlin: Springer, 2022.

Lewis-Smith, Helena, Kirsty May Garbett, Anshula Chaudhry, Megha Dhillon, Hemal Shroff, Paul White, and Phillippa Claire Diedrichs. "Evaluating a Body Image School-Based Intervention in India: A Randomized Controlled Trial." *Body Image* 44 (March 2023): 148–156.

Liebelt, Claudia, Sarah Böllinger, and Ulf Vierke, eds. *Beauty and the Norm: Debating Standardization in Bodily Appearance*. New York: Palgrave Macmillan, 2019.

Majumdar, Rochona. *Marriage and Modernity*. Durham, NC: Duke University Press, 2009.

Mankekar, Purnima. *Screening Culture, Viewing Politics: An Ethnography of Television, Womanhood, and Nation in Postcolonial India*. Durham, NC: Duke University Press, 1999.

Manto, Sadat Hasan. "Bad-surati." Rekhta. Accessed October 25, 2017. Available at https://www.rekhta.org/manto/bad-surati-saadat-hasan-manto-manto?lang=hi.

Markandaya, Kamala. *Two Virgins*. Delhi: Penguin, 1973.

Mendhekar, D. N., K. Arora, D. Lohia, A. Agarwal, and R. C. Jiloha. "Anorexia Nervosa: An Indian Perspective." *National Medical Journal of India* 22, no. 4 (2009): 181–182. Available at https://www.researchgate.net/publication/41396435.

Menon, Nivedita. *Seeing Like a Feminist*. Delhi: Penguin, 2012.

Mitchell, Catriona, ed. *Walking toward Ourselves: Indian Women Tell Their Stories*. Noida: Harper Collins, 2016.

Munshi, Shoma, ed. *Images of the "Modern" Woman in Asia: Global Media, Local Meanings*. Surrey: Curzon, 2001.

Nagar, Ishita, and Rukhsana Virk. "The Struggle between the Real and Ideal: Impact of Acute Media Exposure on Body Image of Young Indian Women." *Sage Open* 7, no. 1 (2017). Available at https://doi.org/10.1177/2158244017691327.

Nguyen, Mimi Thi. "The Biopower of Beauty: Humanitarian Imperialisms and Global Feminisms in an Age of Terror." *Signs* 36, no. 2 (Winter 2011): 359–383. Available at https://doi.org/10.1086/655914.

Nussbaum, Martha C. "Ageing, Stigma, and Disgust." In *The Empire of Disgust: Prejudice, Discrimination, and Policy in India and the US*, edited by Zoya Hasan, Aziz Z. Huq, Martha C. Nussbaum, and Vidhu Verma, 146–163. New Delhi: Oxford University Press, 2018.

Orbach, Susie. *Fat Is a Feminist Issue*. London: Arrow Books, 1978.

Parameswaran, Radhika E. "Global Beauty Queens in Post-Liberalization India." *Peace Review: A Journal of Social Justice* 17, no. 4 (2005): 419–426. Available at https://doi.org/10.1080/10402650500374702.

———. "Global Queens, National Celebrities: Tales of Feminine Triumph in Post-Liberalization India." *Critical Studies in Media Communication* 21, no. 4 (2004): 346–370. Available at https://doi.org/10.1080/0739318042000245363.

———. "Shaming the Nation on Public Affairs Television: Barkha Dutt Tackles Colorism on We the People." *Journalism Studies* 16, no. 5 (2015): 680–691. Available at https://doi.org/10.1080/1461670X.2015.1054175.

Parameswaran, Radhika E., and Kavitha Cardoza. "Immortal Comics, Epidermal Politics." *Journal of Children and Media* 3, no. 1 (2009): 19–34. Available at https://doi.org/10.1080/17482790802576956.

Pathak, Abhishek, dir. *Ujda Chaman.* Featuring Sunny Singh Nijjar, Maanvi Gagroo, and Saurabh Shukla. Panorama Studios, Mumbai, 2019.

Pathak, Gauri. "'Presentable': The Body and Neoliberal Subjecthood in Contemporary India." *Social Identities: Journal for the Study of Race, Nation, and Culture* 20, no. 4–5 (2014): 314–329.

Peiss, Kathy. *Hope in a Jar: The Making of America's Beauty Culture.* Philadelphia: University of Pennsylvania Press, 2011.

Premchand, Munshi. "Sati." Originally published 1927. Translated by Bharti Arora. In *Premchand: The Complete Short Stories*, edited by M. Asaduddin, 3:120–127. Delhi: Penguin Books, 2017.

Rao, T. Rama, dir. *Naseeb Apna Apna.* Featuring Farah Naaz, Radhika Sarathkumar, and Rishi Kapoor. Pen Studios: Mumbai, 1986.

Rekha V, Sasi, and K. Maran. "Advertisement Pressure and Its Impact on Body Dissatisfaction and Body Image Perception of Women in India." *Global Media Journal*, Indian edition 3, no. 1 (June 2012): 1–9. Available at https://www.researchgate.net/publication/255173411.

Rhode, Deborah L. *The Beauty Bias: The Injustice of Appearance in Life and Law.* New York: Oxford University Press, 2010.

Rothblum, Esther D., and Laura Brown. *Overcoming Fear of Fat.* New York: Routledge, 2019.

Rothblum, Esther D., and Sondra Solovay. *The Fat Studies Reader.* New York: New York University Press, 2009.

Roy, Arundhati. *The God of Small Things.* Delhi: Penguin, 1997.

Roy, Devapriya. *The Weight Loss Club: The Curious Experiments of Nancy Housing Cooperative.* Delhi: Rupa, 2013.

Roy, Sudhendu, dir. *Saudagar.* Featuring Amitabh Bachchan, Nutan Bhel, and Padma Khanna. Rajshri Productions, Mumbai, 1973.

Sangari, Kumkum, and Sudesh Vaid, eds. *Recasting Women: Essays in Colonial History.* New Delhi: Zubaan, 1984.

Sathyan, Anoop, dir. *Varane Avashyamund.* Featuring Shobana, Suresh Gopi, and Kalyani Priyadarshan. M Star Satellite Communications and Wayfarer Films, Kerela, 2020.

Shroff, Hemal, and J. Kevin Thompson. "Body Image and Eating Disturbance in India: Media and Interpersonal Influences." *International Journal of Eating Disorders* 35, no. 2 (March 2004): 198–203. Available at https://doi.org/10.1002/eat.10229.

Singh, Shailendra Kumar. "Destigmatization of the Fat Female Body in *Size Zero* and *Dum Laga ke Haisha.*" *Fat Studies: An Interdisciplinary Journal of Body Weight and Society* 7, no. 3 (2018): 247–263. Available at https://doi.org/10.1080/21604851.2018.1424411.

Tagore, Rabindranath. *The Home and the World.* 1919. Reprint, Delhi: Penguin, 2005.

Taylor, Sonya Renee. *The Body Is Not an Apology: The Power of Radical Self-Love.* Oakland: Berrett Koehler Publishers, 2018.

Telang, Vrushali. *Can't Die for Size Zero.* Delhi: Rupa, 2010.

Thapan, Meenakshi. *Living the Body: Embodiment, Womanhood and Identity in Contemporary India.* New Delhi: Sage, 2009.

Vaid, Jyotsna. "Fair Enough? Color and the Commodification of Self in Indian Matrimonials." *Shades of Difference: Why Skin Color Matters*, edited by Evelyn Nakano Genn, 148–165. Stanford, CA: Stanford University Press, 2012.

Vaidyanathan, Sivapriya, Pooja Patnaik Kuppili, and Vikas Menon. 2019. "Eating Disorders: An Overview of Indian Research." *Indian Journal of Psychological Medicine* 41, no. 4 (2019): 311–317.

Visaria, Samah. *Encounters of a Fat Bride*. Delhi: Random House, 2017.

Wolf, Naomi. *The Beauty Myth: How Images of Beauty Are Used against Women*. 1991. Reprint, New York: Harper Perennial, 2002.

I

Bodies on the Margins

"Othering," Hegemonic Beauty Norms,
and Female Bodies

1

Imag(in)ing the Dalit Woman

Body Image and Identity in Bama's Sangati

Nishat Haider

Introduction

Bama, the nom de plume of Faustina Mary Fatima Rani, is one of the first Tamil Dalit women writers to be translated into English.[1] Foregrounding Tamil Dalit women's everyday and lived experiences of their bodies in Bama's *Sangati* (2005), this chapter focuses on how Bama's narrative imagines, frames, and enunciates the notion of body image in the making of Dalit women subjects. The setting of Bama's narratives is Tamil Nadu, which is also the site of the first vigorous anticaste movement, known as the Self-Respect Movement (Suyamariyadai Iyakkam), led by E. V. Ramaswamy Periyar. Representing the Paraiyas, a subcaste within the Tamil Dalit community who converted to Christianity, Bama looks, among many other issues, at body image norms from caste and sociocultural perspectives in her feminist treatise, *Sangati*. Here Bama describes the plight of Dalit women who face the oppression by double patriarchies—*discreet* patriarchy of their own caste and an *overlapping* patriarchy of the upper caste. According to anthropologist Peggy Reeves Sanday, "Body and society are reciprocal mirrors, each reflecting the consequences of the other's conscious wishes and repressed desires. It is through the body image that human beings become not only self-aware but socially aware" (1994, xi). In this chapter, I provide an evaluation of the usefulness and relative merits of body image for a Dalit feminist project that seeks to understand and alleviate troubled embodied experiences. While looking at body image norms through the lens of a sociocultural framework, I then explore the alternative vocabularies of Dalit woman's embodiment in Bama's narratives to highlight the key elements of a potential new language for Dalit body image. The chapter consists of three parts: part one deconstructs the frame of body image as it intersects with the vectors of gender and caste while foregrounding *Sangati*; part two discusses the familial, social, psychological, and sexual aspects of Dalit body image; and part three addresses Bama's subversion of the upper-caste semiotic codes and notions of propriety in order to reclaim an appropriate language or vocabulary to represent the Dalit women's body image and embodied subjectivity. Throughout this chapter I refer to body image as a concept, as building blocks for discourse—not necessarily deterministic, but constitutive of discourse in complicated and potentially fluid ways. Here, body image is part of a broader sign of becoming a woman, a lexicon of the body that is usually used in association with examinations and arguments of beauty norms and ideals, body dissatisfaction or body shaming, sexual desirability, and femininity that emerge from psychology, language play, dialects, and linguistics.

Part I

Understanding Body Image: Historical and Contemporary Perspectives

While Dalit women's need to talk differently was framed as a response to "external factors (non-Dalit forces homogenizing the issue of Dalit women) and internal factors (the patriarchal domination within the Dalits)" (Guru 1995, 2548), Bama's *Sangati* establishes that Dalit women's spoken and written narratives tie in to represent the nuanced interplay between embodiment, body image, and the socio-historical context. As a point of departure from readings of Dalit narratives, I underscore some of the issues regarding the ways body image is framed and communicated, specifically its problematic relationship with gender and false universality. The general understanding of body image has been described as the "conscious perception of your body, how you see yourself and how you present yourself to the world" (Rathore 2019, 3–4). According to Cash and Smolak (2011), however, body image is complex and multidimensional and is made up of affective, behavioral, perceptual, and cognitive components of body experience. Rather than using the notion of body image as a reified, relatively fixed "schema-driven processing of information about, and self-evaluations of, one's physical appearance" (Jarry 2012, 339), I argue that it is more useful to consider body imaging as an interplay between embodied experience, identity, and display—that is, a process and an activity that "the individual engages in to modify, ameliorate and come to terms with their body in specific temporal and cultural locations" (Gleeson and Frith 2006, 88). Since the 1980s, we have seen a significant shift in focus in favor of expanding the notion of body image into a multifaceted construct that includes a "person's perceptions, thoughts, and feelings about his or her body" (Grogan [1999] 2008, 3). This includes the evolution in conceptualization of the female body in the sphere of psychoanalytical theory, which underscores the significance of ideas of "inner space," or the inner sexual organs of the female anatomy (Kestenberg 1968, 465; Erikson 1964, 266–267). The existence of women's inner space is "the matrix of femininity and motherhood," which is of great interest to understand and unpack the ways "it is manifested in childhood, in adolescence, and in the personality of the adult women" (Hägglund 1981, 4). In globalized neoliberal India, the increasingly complex issues regarding the attitudes of women toward their own bodies, as well as the relationship of the female body with the social environment, have revealed that body image often reinforces notions that light-skinned, tall, able, young, and thin Eurocentric bodies are ideal, which often becomes synonymous with the upper-caste and upper-class Hindu body, and both ultimately contribute to a problematic Brahminization of female corporeal aesthetics.

Historical, social, and collective memories to a large extent are constituted by and through institutionalized sites of memory like literature. And narrative is often implicated in the functioning of memory. Owing to "the androcentric bias of most modern national imaginings," specifically "the assumptions behind the masculinist, heterosexual economy hitherto governing the cultural matrix through which an Indian national identity has become intelligible" (Ray 2000, 3–4), there has been a silencing of the narratives of marginalized groups like the Dalit, which aids in the creation of a dominant Brahminical discourse. As Regina E. Spellers notes, "by studying personal stories, the tendency to naturalize one's experiences of reality as a universal experience of reality becomes minimized and we come to understand that there are different ways of knowing" (1998, 72) and understanding body image. While Dalit narrative accounts range from the detection of their exclusion from reform projects under British rule (Chatterjee 1993; Rao 2003; Sarkar and Sarkar 2008) to Dalit feminists' challenges to the Indian feminist movement's normative upper-caste matrix and Dalit patriarchy (Guru 1995; Rege 2006), there is much that still awaits to be unearthed regarding Dalit women's body image. Since there is incontrovertible evidence on the marginalization, exploitation, and powerlessness of Dalit women in the mainstream majoritarian history and in the present, it is imperative to explore the nexus among the making of women subjects, their body image, and the construction of their difference—largely through the analytics of caste—and resulting representations. Since women's bodies are significant sites for inscription and reading (Reischer and Koo 2004, 299–300), it is important to scrutinize the ways embodied experiences and representations of Dalit women's bodies are framed by a Dalit woman writer like Bama who breaks the *silence* imposed by upper-caste discourses and retrieves Dalit women's voices to counter upper-caste oppressive historical and literary constructions.

In *Sangati*, Bama reinscribes and reencrypts Dalit womanhood as "the voice of a defiant subalternity committed to writing its own history" (Guha 1996, 12). The word *Sangati* implies events, and thus the novel narrativizes the events that take place in the life of women in the Paraiya community through individual stories, anecdotes, and memories. Emphasizing that caste structures the everyday interactions, conversations, songs, personhood, and personal relationships of Dalit women, Bama draws our attention to issues of body image that are often disguised, stereotyped, or subsumed into other discourses by virtue of their everydayness. In *Sangati*, the following major factors influence, inform, and affect body image: cultural beauty norms, experiences of sexism and casteism, parental influences, peer influences, and identity-construction processes. Foregrounding Dalit women's consciousness and construction of body image, *Sangati* voices not only the Dalit and upper-caste or Christian divide but also intercaste contesting voices from different Dalit castes, including the Paraiyas, the Chaliyars, and the Pallars. While acknowledging the multilayered complexity of a rural Dalit community in India, this chapter offers a nuanced understanding of body image, stereotypes, and identity markers that highlights the question of the specificity and peculiarity of Tamil Dalit Paraiya women's body experiences as represented in Bama's *Sangati*.

Part II

Framing Sangati: (De)constructing Dalit Women's Body Image

Women's bodies are a locus of inscribed social meaning (Bourdieu 1977; Foucault 1977) that are marked by class, caste, gender, ethnicity, and culture. Addressing the aesthetic and discursive aporia regarding the complexity and multidimensionality of Dalit women's body image, Bama reconfigures and repositions the Tamil Dalit woman in *Sangati* as a subject whose life is rife with contradictions that result from a tension between the Brahminical and Dalit notions of body image and cultural values deeply embedded in the individual. If one reads the narrative text in tandem with Carolyn Steedman's opinion that "once a story is told, it ceases to be a story; it becomes a piece of history, an interpretative device" (1986, 143), Bama's present-day enunciations of alterity offer a hermeneutical tool not only to understand the degree of Dalit women's investment in their appearance and body image construction but also to unpack the socio-historical phenomenon of Brahminical aesthetics regarding body image as it applies to and complicates the life of Dalit woman in aspects such as hair, skin color, and physique that are some of the issues at the core of *Sangati*. Sometimes the adoption of Brahminical notions of beauty results in self-loathing that arises from the psychological effects of upper-caste hegemony.

Sangati, an autoethnography, weaves the narrative around several generations of Tamil Dalit women: the older women belonging to the narrator's Paatti [grandmother] Vellaiyamma Kizhavi's generation downward to the narrator's own, as well as the generation coming after her as she grows up. In fact, a genuine understanding of Dalit women's body image requires a deep appreciation for the diversity of their cultural and personal contexts of embodiment. The narrator is, in the earlier chapters at least, a young girl of about twelve years, and in the last three or four chapters, a young woman, but the thoughtful voice is that of an adult retrospectively meditating upon her lived experiences. The reflections that may seem instructive are a way of connecting experience and analysis, concluding with a practical call for action. The conversations among the generations map out the changing perspectives of women, their body image and experiences, their different needs, the different ways they are subject to oppression, and their coping strategies (Bama 2005, xix). These individual stories—anecdotes and memories of personal experience narrated in the first person—are then counterpointed by the generalizing comments of the grandmother and mother figures and later still by the author-narrator's reflections. Through these *alternate* Dalit women's narratives, Bama recuperates the silenced/occluded voices from the din of the monologic, authoritative, and hegemonic voice to highlight the question of the specificity and peculiarity of Dalit female body image and experiences, which include skin complexion, sex, sexuality, and reproduction; girls' bodies as political, economic, and sociocultural constructs; and girls' revolt against these constructs.

Body as Sites/Sights of Memory: Desire for the Fair and Lovely Body Image

Understanding Dalit women's body image requires insight into the lineage of the ideal Indian woman's body image construct. If one were to conceptualize and formulate the traditional Indian standards of women's beauty, one of the most helpful sources is ancient art embodied in images of the Hindu pantheon of goddesses. For instance, the Hindu goddess Parvati is "a slender bodied maiden of comely hips and moon-like face" (Dehejia 1999, 18). Other facial features of Parvati are also described adoringly by Shiva: her "eyes [are] like lotus petals," her eyebrows are like "the bows of Kama, her lower lip is like the bimba fruit," and her nose is like "the beak of a parrot" (Dehejia 1999, 19–20). Thus inspired by the religious imagery of Hindu goddesses, the ideal body image of Indian woman that has endured for centuries and been bolstered by legacies of British colonialism is that she should be fair or medium complexioned with a narrow waist but wider hips and breasts and should possess large eyes, full red lips, and long black hair. In addition, the caste system, believed to have been introduced by the nomadic Caucasian Aryan group when they arrived in India around 1500 B.C.E., is often blamed for first creating color-based divisions in Indian society. While the top of the caste pyramid was assumed by "the fair-skinned priestly Brahmins, . . . the Shudras or laborers fell to the bottom of the hierarchy and were comprised mainly of the darker-skinned menial workers, such as the Dravidians" (Shevde 2008, 5). The preference for light skin was further reinforced by the British colonizers. The brief history of gendered body image in India reveals not only that women were subjected to hegemonically defined standards of beauty but also that our knowledge of history, and of women in general, privileges upper-caste or Brahmin body image norms. Light-skinned, Sanskritic, endogamous, and unchanging Brahmans were a discrete, endogamous, and pan-Indian group that kept their "blood free from any inter-mixture" and positioned themselves as the guardians of "an institution closely akin to caste . . . described in the Sanskrit books" of Vedic times (Ghurye [1932] 1969, 117–118).

The caste of a woman's body thus had to make itself identifiable through "unambiguous visual markers—the style of clothing, the shape and position of the hair tuft, the differing styles and materials of ornaments permitted to be worn etc." (Poduval 2016, 29). Describing the upper-caste women in *Sangati*, the narrator's grandmother Paatti says, "When you look at them, each one of them is like a Mahalaksmi, a goddess" (Bama 2005, 12). Not surprisingly, the lightest-skinned women among the Paraiya women are praised and appreciated. Thaayi is one such very light-complexioned Dalit woman. When "women like that [Thaayi] smoothed their hair down, dressed well and made themselves up and all that, they looked like Nayakkar woman" (Bama 2005, 42), we are told. Naturally, Bama describes that how to pass off as an upper-caste Nayakkar woman is much aspired to by most Dalit women. Although appropriating the Nayakkar women's beauty standards boosts the confidence of Thaayi, one also learns that "never did a day go by without her being beaten up" (Bama 2005, 42) and thus is reminded of all that is terribly wrong with Dalit women's lives. Thaayi is forced into marrying a man who would "drag her along the street and flog her like an animal, with a stick or a belt" (Bama 2005, 42). The Brahmin women also add to the woes of the Dalit women, as the narrator in *Sangati* decries, "upper caste women show us no pity or kindness either, if only as women to women, but treat us with contempt, as if we are creatures of a different species, who have no sense of honour or self-respect" (Bama 2005, 66). Delineating the "intersectionality" of gender and class (Crenshaw 1991, 1245–1246) as it transects with caste, Bama shows that the bodies of Dalit women are palimpsests on which the upper-caste codes and edifications are coercively or discursively inscribed, which in turn devalue, degrade, and constrain the Dalit women's self and body image.

Sangati further demonstrates that Dalit women's body image is dependent not only on intrapersonal variables but also on oppressive cultural messages. Here, by alluding to Katherine McKittrick's contention that "the site of memory is also the *sight* of memory" (2006, 33), it can be emphasized that Bama's autoethnography as a locus of Dalit women's memories and lived experiences shows the premium placed on body image, gender, body appearance, and skin color / complexion in the landscape of the caste configuration in India. As Saltzberg and Chrisler note, "Beauty cannot be quantified or objectively measured; it is the result of the judgements of others" (1997, 135), Bama, too, proves how external messages regarding the acceptability of only *some* bodies and in *some* ways are either resisted or internalized—and often reconstituted interpersonally. In India, since upper-class and upper-caste standards of beauty continue to be stringent and marginalizing, many Dalit women develop a distorted body image and become frustrated with not being able to obtain the ideal body size and shape. In *Sangati*, when the narrator is born, her mother is "a little disappointed that [she is] so dark, and didn't have [her] sister's or brother's colour" (Bama 2005, 3). At this point, however, the Dalit woman Rendupalli philosophically proclaims, "Even if our children are dark-skinned, their features are good and there's a liveliness about them. Black is strongest and best, like a diamond" (Bama 2005, 114). Through this character, Bama reminds Paraiya women that power lies within them, and the stories that *Sangati* depict reinforce the existence of such a power. Finding strength in one's roots is a way of instilling self-respect and pride, and it is this pride that writers like Bama hope to invoke in Paraiya women. Bama also mentions how the Paraiyas (excluding other Dalit communities who remained Hindus) of her grandmother's generation converted to Christianity, influenced by the missionaries' promise of equality, free education, and a good life for their children. Much to the chagrin of Bama, the church itself is beset with the problem of biases of skin color, gender, and caste, which becomes evident during festivals when the church looks for "a fair-skinned boy to play Our Lady" and the most "light-coloured child" to play Baby Jesus (Bama 2005, 32–33).

Interpersonal and Familial Influences on Body Image

The development of a worldview always takes place in a context. In *Sangati*, Bama frames the interpersonal context as a significant factor in the development of the Dalit women's body image(ry). As humans are fundamentally social or relational beings who strive for attachments and acceptance by others, primarily through relationships with parents and peers, these relationships are considered the core social connections or contexts that influence body image. *Sangati* shows that the accumulated interpersonal experiences reflect and shape individual behaviors and attitudes about body image of self and others. For instance, the narrator's Paatti, Vellaiyamma Kizhavi, who attends every childbirth in the Perumaalpaatti village barring the upper castes, is loved and respected by all, and she has strong interpersonal relationships with most of the members of her community. Since she works as a *kothachi*, a person who organizes daily-wage Dalit women laborers for work and distributes them money on behalf of the upper-caste landowners, her suggestions and advice are very much heeded by the Paraiya community. When Paatti tells Sevathi, the narrator's mother, to tell her child to wear half a sari, for "it doesn't look good for her to be sitting in a class with boys when her breasts have grown as big as *kilaikkai* [fruit] pods," the narrator retorts, "I won't wear a *davani* [blouse with half-sari]," as the boys in her class would tease her terribly (Bama 2005, 9). At this Paatti is annoyed and says that even the schoolteacher, Lourdes Raj, looked at her from the corner of his eye instead of teaching the class. Later, Paatti reveals that Raj called her aside and asked her to send her granddaughter with a *davani*. The body policing and criticizing of girls embarrasses the narrator and makes her ashamed of her own body.

As the narrator along with her sister, Mariamma, and other Dalit girls of the Paraiya community grow and reach puberty, they begin not only to internalize the cultures objectification of women's bodies but also to monitor their own bodies. We know that while "clothing, jewellery, hairstyle, naming, food—all these constitute an elaborate sign system that had as its basis the system of caste differentiation," the movement of the Dalit woman's body in public spaces has been "regulated through a system of distance pollution—the sacredness of the space and the purity of the body being dependent on restrictions of access to other bodies in terms of visibility, touch, hearing, and clearly specified distances" (Kumar 2011, 215). Furthermore, since this body surveillance is based on unrealistic ideals, the Dalit women end up feeling ashamed of their bodies. While the body image (dis)satisfaction is an individual's evaluation of his or her physical size or shape, this subjective evaluation is an individual judgment based on internalized values and goals shaped by experiences with others in the social world. Thus, the behaviors, attitudes, and expectations of Paatti, Sevathi, and the other women—along with their families, siblings, peer group, and friends—play a formative role in teaching young girls that their bodies need to be hidden lest they catch the eyes of the boys and men who then get provoked to do shameful things. In other words, girls are instructed to make their decisions regarding clothing and appearance by adhering to the desires of the patriarchal community. The Dalit women therefore struggle to conform to these mainstream, upper-caste notions of aesthetics, which results in ambiguity as they contemplate the norms of femininity and beauty with which they have been raised and that are immanent to society. Predictably, this conflict or ambiguity leads to body dissatisfaction. While lack of conformity to upper-caste beauty aesthetics is viewed as unfeminine by self-doubting Dalit women themselves, Bama represents and celebrates those Dalit women who are in tune with their natural body-selves.

One of the most "vital aspects" of women's beauty, identity, and body image is hair, which can "impact on a person's psychosocial state, social interactions, and daily activities" (Hunt and McHale 2012, 482). Consequently, hair and its grooming in *Sangati* have an immense bearing on Dalit women's consciousness of their body image. For Dalit women, hair is personal because it is a part of their body, yet it is also public because it is on display for others to see. Hair also confers other advantages. Since taking care of the hair becomes almost ritualistic and involves peer groups, family, and friends in *Sangati*, it becomes an important component in Dalit women's acculturation and socialization, which also significantly influence the construct(ion) of femininity. The narrator's grandmother endearingly combs her hair with a fine-toothed wooden lice comb, and while "she was about it, she'd give me all the gossip of the village" (Bama 2005, 6), claims the narrator, while bringing to light the intimacies and female bonding linked with women's hair. The grooming of long black tresses is, then, intrinsic to the everyday life of Dalit women. Detailing the hair grooming of a *pushpavati*, or a girl who comes of age, Paatti sings:

> *Shake her hair dry and comb it with gold,*
> *Toss her hair dry and comb it with silver,*
> *Comb her hair dry with a golden comb,*
> *And women, all together, raise a kulavai [ululation].* (Bama 2005, 17)

In the text, Paatti always sings and chats about all sorts of things during such occasions.

The binary opposites of good and bad hair have for centuries been an epistemological tool used to juxtapose the so-called ideal beauty and the purportedly ugly unfeminine. This binary reinforces mainstream upper-caste aesthetics as *good* hair suggests an idea(l) of Indian upper-class and upper-caste woman's beauty, embodying pureness, sensuality, and feminine delicacy, while *bad* hair signifies low class and caste. Describing the upper-caste ladies from her village who go to the town every day, Paatti says, "Every time you look at them, their hair is sleek with oil and they are wearing fresh flowers. . . . It takes a whole hour to plait their hair, you know" (Bama 2005, 12). Here Paatti appears to be the voice of common sense where female beauty is concerned. Evidently, while grooming long black tresses is very much intrinsic to the identity of womanhood, Bama's text shows that poor Dalit women are often under greater pressure to conform to beauty ideals for a good life and better marital opportunities.

Body Image, Menarche, and Puberty

Speaking of female body image, scholars claim that women underscore "the multi-faceted psychological experience of embodiment, especially but not exclusively to one's physical appearance," which emphasizes the acceptability of only some bodies and in some ways (Cash 2004, 2). And, notably, an important related aspect of body image for women involves perceptions and feelings regarding menarche and menstruation. While *Sangati* represents issues that highlight the question of the specificity and peculiarity of Dalit female body experiences vis-à-vis the key body image concerns—which include sex, sexuality, and reproduction—it also underscores the wide caste and class cultural differences and their effect on a girl's first menstruation. As opposed to Brahmin girls, who are considered unclean and isolated during menstruation, the newly menstruating Dalit girls feel pride in their own bodies. Hence, while the Brahminic cultural messages facilitate shame and embarrassment about menstruation, Dalit ideals celebrate menarche, welcoming the girl into adult womanhood. Bama evocatively describes some of these events, which tell of rites of passage: a coming-of-age ceremony, a betrothal where gifts are offered by the groom to the bride, and a group wedding. On one such occasion, a song sung by Paatti at a girl's coming-of-age ceremony, with a chorus of *kulavai* (ululation) at the end of every four lines, begins thus:

> *On a Friday morning, at earliest dawn*
> *she became a pushpavati [the coming of age of a girl], so the elders said—*
> *her mother was delighted, her father too,*
> *the uncles arrived, all in a row—*
> *(chorus of kulavai, ululation)* (Bama 2005, 17)

Such empowering moments in Dalit women's lives are hailed by Bama. And throughout *Sangati* Bama teases out events, stories, and incidents that explore Dalit women's relationships to their own selves, their sexuality, and their sexual functioning and relate these to their body image.

Body Image, Self-Image, and Dalit Women's
Sexual Behavior/Functioning

As compared to general discourses on body image, appearance, and attractiveness, women's narratives rarely represent body image related specifically to menstruation and to women's anatomy and body parts, such as breasts. Owing to the obvious relevance of periods and breasts for sexual activities, it is important to map out the potential links between these specific aspects of body image and sexual functioning as one encounters in Bama's narrative. *Sangati* explores Dalit women's body image as a complex subjective construct that has a huge influence on their self-image through cognitive, affective, sexual, and behavioral means. Although sexual objectification is not confined solely to upper-caste and higher-class women who are closer to having socially constructed acceptable bodies, its impact on Dalit women has been underexplored. *Sangati* suggests that Tamil Dalit women are more likely to be dissatisfied with their bodies and identity regarding specific body parts. Breasts, for example, are an important part of female identity; and the attitude of Dalit women toward their body image vis-à-vis breasts is a psychosocial process starting in early childhood and taking shape through their perceptions of bodily stimuli, cognitive functions, and the messages they receive from the environment and their home. In *Sangati*, during a conversation with Sevathi, Vellaiyamma Kizhavi notes, "Just see whether she [the narrator] doesn't come of age in two, three months. Have you noticed the bloom on her face?" (Bama 2005, 9). She further suggests that as soon as the girl gets her periods, she should be dissuaded from studying further and handed over to a man to avoid any possible scandal. Paatti likewise appears worried that although Mariamma is old enough, "she hasn't developed breasts," and "people in the village gossiped about her and said that she would never menstruate" (Bama 2005, 9). Mariamma too is distressed about her marriage prospects and deeply dissatisfied with her body. Here, *Sangati* proves how in Indian society, where breasts are markers of femininity and sexuality, a so-called anomaly in this body part poses a massive threat to its bearer's body image.

Challenging the under- and/or misrepresentation of poor Dalit women's body image, *Sangati* represents the inenarrable oppression at the intersections of gender, class, and caste that, in turn, influences their body identities. In the popular imagination, Dalit women are ironically depicted as both hypersexual and submissive sexual objects, who become easy targets of caste-related teasing that marginalizes and denigrates caste-related bodily attributes (eye size or skin tone, for example). While women in general negotiate multiple contexts that shape how they are perceived and judged, in the case of Dalit women, as represented by Bama, it is the experiences of oppression that shape their body image beliefs. When the Dalit villager Arokkyam's young granddaughter Paralokam's breasts are squeezed by an upper-caste farm owner's son as he pretends to help her, she does not report the incident as she fears that the blame would be on the Dalit girl and that she would be labeled a whore and punished instead. Mariamma, too, is dissuaded and warned by her friends that she should not report the rape attempt on her when the upper-caste landlord, Kumarasami Ayya, tries to pull her into a shed to molest her. This physical violation has a significant impact on how Mariamma perceives and interprets her own embodiment. Even before Mariamma can think of lodging her complaint, the landlord approaches the village elders and fabricates a story that he caught Mariamma in a sexual act with another boy. The *naattaamai* (the village headman) then finishes the proceedings to claim, "It is you female chicks who ought to be humble and modest. A man may do a hundred things. . . . You girls should consider what you are left with, in your bellies" (Bama 2005, 26). Mariamma's father beats her up in public for being fined and bringing dishonor to the family. The compounding trauma of sexual violence and public humiliation breaks her down psychologically. Mariamma hereafter becomes a victim of body shame, depression, and body image dissatisfaction, and she loses interest in everything, including herself.

Part III

(Re)inscribing Dalit Women's Body Image

Bama uses a new corporeal vocabulary in *Sangati* to (re)inscribe Dalit women's body image. Body image and its constructions get reinforced time and again through the verbal interactions of individuals. Since an individual's identity constituted by body imaging is a social construction, and does not have significance in isolation from where it is practiced, such constructive processes create a new "negotiated" space of contested and negotiated individual identities via subversion and transgression (Bhabha 1990, 216), which Homi Bhabha calls "interpellative practices" (1994, 22–23). Dalit women in *Sangati* indulge in inventive wordplay embedded in body image that may be read as "interpellative practices." Describing Bama's female characters' instinctive ability to give appropriate nicknames to others as per their specific body image, K. A. Geetha notes that "Seyarani is called 'maikanni' because she has ensnaring eyes" and Gnanammaal is known as "'dammatta maaadu' because she goes round like a young bullock drugged and dazed without knowing what is going on" (2012, 423–24). Gnanammaal's nickname in Tamil, "damaatta maadu," signifies a young bullock that is garlanded, decorated, and taken around in villages by people who traditionally demand money. Akin to the poor bullock being dragged around unaware of what is happening, Gnanammaal unwittingly goes about her life without any perspective.

Alluding to the theoretical assumptions of critical discourse analysis (Fairclough 1992, 2003), it can be asserted that *Sangati* underscores not only the linguistic representation of body image norms but also the speakers' discursive positioning in view of these norms, which expose the societal power asymmetries and hierarchies in terms of caste.

In *Stories of Women*, Elleke Boehmer argues that "women's talk can be interpreted not only as a way of life but as a mode of self-making" (2005, 98). Some of the forms that Bama's Dalit women characters engage in for self-making in *Sangati* include oral and gendered forms of speech along with conversational storytelling (experiential narrative); gossip; oral gestures; laughter as a "corporeal event"; speech acts of swearing, wordplay, and jokes; lexical, syntactic, or grammatical deviation and innovation; code-switching; layered and cultural discourses; pragmatic and functional contextualization; local language importations; and songs and rhymes. Through such tropes, Bama explores Dalit women's dissatisfaction with their body image and embodied experiences that have not been articulated before. This is evident when Paatti questions, "Born as women, what good do we get? We only toil in the fields and in the home until our vaginas shrivel" (Bama 2005, 6–7). Further, the language of *Sangati* is full of expletives and profanities, quite often with obvious sexual references. Reading sexualized language as a specific language that is "a privileged area to study the culture" (Santaemilia 2008, 228), it can be argued that Bama uses dialectal Tamil full of profanities and invectives to undermine the sexist and caste-ridden body image vestiges present in traditional language. Hence, in *Sangati*, body image(ry) in bawdy vocabulary is used as a tool to fight physical violence and shame men. As the fight between Raakkamma, a poor Dalit woman from the Tamil village Kuppacchipatti, and her husband, Paakkiaraj, for instance, develops into a street fight, Raakkamma uses the following offensive words: "Disgusting man, only fit to drink a woman's farts! Instead of drinking toddy every day, why don't you drink your son's urine? Why don't you drink my monthly blood?" (Bama 2005, 61). After venting, Raakkamma lifts up her sari (lower garment) in front of the whole crowd. This scares her husband, and he moves away from her. Then Raakkamma retorts angrily, "If I hadn't shamed him like this, he would surely have split my skull in two, the horrible man" (Bama 2005, 61–62). In a sense, such body/bawdy language appears to be the only means of communication for the excessively oppressed Dalit woman. The expletives and abusive terms— like "donkey," "whore," "cunt," and *munde*—are often names of body parts, which evocatively suggest that "the body is the site of violence as well as the language of abuse" (Pai 2018, 95). Interestingly, Bama deploys the prism of body image vocabulary and turns it on its head to demonstrate what language can achieve while becoming more responsive to body violence and marginalization.

Conclusion

In *Sangati*, Bama frames Dalit women's body image as the combination of not only embodied and psychological experiences but also feelings and attitudes that relate to the form, function, appearance, and desirability of one's own body, which are, in turn, influenced by familial, interpersonal, class, and caste factors. Bama's account of Dalit women's embodied experiences, individual conversations, memories, and "speech as gossip, as private communication among women . . . works upon language anarchically, shattering everything" (Godard 1989, 44), including every assumption about body image, caste, and gender. The narrative addresses the making of women Dalit subjects and their body image in language(s) that can adequately describe not only embodied experience but also the existence of different, potentially competing vocabularies of the body that emerge from within and outside of body image discourses. Here, Bama accomplishes the rare creative feat of blending ethnography, autobiography, memory, fiction, polemics, and praxis and offers a new corporeal aesthetics that is fundamental to her ideological and identitarian politics. Bama's narrative creates a discourse of Dalit women's body image, of their body's situatedness in the world, and of the materialization of their bodies in the midst of intersecting and interacting axes of caste, class, gender, language, power, culture, and history.

NOTES

1. The word "Dalit" comes from Marathi (an Indian language) and means oppressed or ground down. It was first used by B. R. Ambedkar in preference to his own earlier term, "Scheduled Castes." The term began to be used by politically awakened ex-Untouchables in the early 1970s when the Dalit Panthers, a youthful group of activists and writers in Bombay, came on the scene to protest injustice (Michael 2007, 33). In Tamil Nadu, the term had been used intermittently along with *taazhtappattor* (those who have been put down) or *odukkappattor* (the oppressed) during the eighties, but it is only since the nineties that it has been used widely, not only by Tamil Dalit writers and ideologues in order to identify themselves but also by mainstream critics.

Although scholars like V. Geetha and S. V. Rajadurai point out that Tamil Dalit writing existed as early as the 1890s, the late twentieth century saw a resurgence of Dalit literature in Tamil that placed the Tamil Dalit woman's subjectivity at the center of its narrative. Although writers like Faustina Mary Fatima Rani (Bama), Palanimuthu Sivakami, Sukirtharani, and Azhagiya Periyavan share a common ground with Dalit men as marginalized groups, their experiences as Dalit women are unique. The setting of Bama's narratives is Tamil Nadu, also the site of the first vigorous anticaste movement, the Self-Respect Movement (Suyamariyadai Iyakkam), led by Erode Venkatappa Ramaswamy Periyar, Gail Omveldt (a historian of the Dalit movement), and Sivakami, a Tamil Dalit author and editor. The growing interest in Dalit writings is a result of the global alliances made by Dalits with other groups in the world who have suffered discrimination on the basis of work and heredity as addressed at the Durban World Conference against Racism in 2001.

REFERENCES

Bama [Faustina Mary Fatima Rani]. 2005. *Sangati*. Translated by Lakshmi Holmstrom. New Delhi: Oxford University Press.

Bhabha, Homi. K. 1990. "The Third Space." In *Identity: Community, Culture, Difference*, edited by Jonathan Rutherford, 207–221. London: Lawrence and Wishart.

———. 1994. *The Location of Culture*. London: Routledge.

Boehmer, Elleke. 2005. *Stories of Women: Gender and Narrative in the Postcolonial Nation*. Manchester, NY: Manchester University Press.

Bourdieu, Pierre. 1977. *Outline of a Theory of Practice*. Translated by Richard Nice. Cambridge: Cambridge University Press. Available at https://doi.org/10.1017/CBO97805 11812507.

Cash, Thomas F. 2004. "Body Image: Past, Present, and Future." *Body Image* 1 (1): 1–5.

Cash, Thomas F., and Linda Smolak, eds. 2011. *Body Image: A Handbook of Science, Practice, and Prevention*. 2nd ed. London: Guilford Press.

Chatterjee, Partha. 1993. *The Nation and Its Fragments: Colonial and Postcolonial Histories*. Princeton, NJ: Princeton University Press. Available at https://doi.org/10.2307/j.ctvzgb88s.

Crenshaw, Kimberlé. 1991. "Mapping the Margins: Intersectionality, Identity Politics, and Violence against Women of Color." *Stanford Law Review* 43 (6): 1241–1299.

Dehejia, Harsha V. 1999. *Parvati: Goddess of Love*. Ahmedabad: Mapin Publishing.

Erikson, Erik H. 1964. "Womanhood and the Inner Space." In *Identity Youth and Crisis*, edited by Erik H. Erikson, 261–294. New York: Norton.

Fairclough, Norman. 1992. *Discourse and Social Change*. Cambridge: Polity Press.

———. 2003. *Analyzing Discourse and Text: Textual Analysis for Social Research*. London: Routledge.

Foucault, Michel. 1977. *Discipline and Punish: The Birth of the Prison*. Translated by Alan Sheridan. London: Allen Lane, Penguin.

Geetha, Krishnamurthy Alamelu. 2012. "A Dalit among Dalits: The Angst of Tamil Dalit Women." In *Literature for Our Times: Postcolonial Studies in the Twenty-First Century*, edited by Bill Ashcroft, Ranjini Mendis, Julie McGonegal, and Arun Mukherjee, 411–432. Amsterdam: Rodopi.

Ghurye, Govind Sadashiv. (1932) 1969. *Caste and Race in India*. Bombay: Popular Prakashan.

Gleeson, Kate, and Hannah Frith. 2006. "(De)Constructing Body Image." *Journal of Health Psychology* 11 (1): 79–90. Available at https://doi.org/10.1177/1359105306058851.

Godard, Barbara. 1989. "Theorizing Feminist Discourse/Translation." *Tessera* 6 (Spring): 42–53.

Grogan, Sarah. (1999) 2008. *Body Image: Understanding Body Dissatisfaction in Men, Women and Children*. East Sussex, UK: Routledge.

Guha, Ranajit. 1996. "The Small Voice of History." In *Subaltern Studies IX: Writing on Southeast Asian History and Society*, edited by Shahid Amin and Dipesh Chakrabarty, 1–12. Delhi: Oxford University Press.

Guru, Gopal. 1995. "Dalit Women Talk Differently." *Economic and Political Weekly* 30, no. 41/42 (October): 2548–2550.

Hägglund, Vilja. 1981. "Feminine Sexuality and Its Development." *Scandinavian Psychoanalytic Review* 4 (2): 127–149. Available at https://doi.org/10.1080/01062301.1981.10 592399.

Hunt, Nigel, and Sue L. McHale. 2012. "Hair Loss Effects and Surgical/Drug Treatments for the Alopecias." In *Encyclopedia of Body Image and Human Appearance*, edited by Thomas F. Cash, 482–489. London: Academic Press.

Jarry, Josée L. 2012. "Cognitive-Behavioral Perspectives on Body Image." In *Encyclopedia of Body Image and Human Appearance*, edited by Thomas F. Cash, 334–342. London: Academic Press.

Kestenberg, Judith S. 1968. "Outside and Inside: Male and Female." *Journal of the American Psychoanalytic Association* 16 (3): 457–520.

Kumar, Udaya. 2011. "Self, Body and Inner Sense: Some Reflections on Sree Narayana Guru and Kumaran Asan." In *The Indian Postcolonial: A Critical Reader*, edited by Elleke Boehmer and Rosinka Chaudhuri, 214–237. London: Routledge.

McKittrick, Katherine. 2006. *Demonic Grounds: Black Women and the Cartographies of Struggle*. Minneapolis: University of Minnesota Press.

Michael, Sebastian Maria, ed. (1999) 2007. *Dalits in Modern India: Vision and Values*. New Delhi: Sage Publications.

Pai, Nalini. 2018. "Language and Translation in Dalit Literature." In *Dalit Literatures in India*, edited by Joshil K. Abraham and Judith Misrahi-Barak, 86–102. London: Routledge.

Poduval, Satish. 2016. "Not by Faith Alone: Religion, Gender and the Public Domain in India." In *Transcultural Negotiations of Gender: Studies in (Be)longing*, edited by Saugata Bhaduri and Indrani Mukherjee, 25–37. New Delhi: Springer. Available at https://doi.org/10.1007/978-81-322-2437-2_3.

Rao, Anupama, ed. 2003. *Gender and Caste*. New Delhi: Kali for Women.

Rathore, Aakash Singh. 2019. *A Philosophy of Autobiography*. London. Routledge.

Ray, Sangeeta. 2000. *En-Gendering India: Woman and Nation in Colonial and Postcolonial Narratives*. Durham, NC: Duke University Press.

Rege, Sharmila. 2006. *Writing Caste/Writing Gender: Narrating Dalit Women's Testimonios*. New Delhi: Zubaan.

Reischer, Erica, and Katherine S. Koo. 2004. "The Body Beautiful: Symbolism and Agency in the Social World." *Annual Review of Anthropology* 33 (1): 297–317.

Saltzberg, Elayne A., and Joan C. Chrisler. 1997. "Beauty Is the Beast: Psychological Effects of the Pursuit of the Perfect Female Body." In *Reconstructing Gender: A Multicultural Anthology*, edited by Estelle Disch, 134–145. Mountain View, CA: Mayfield Publishing.

Sanday, Peggy Reeves. 1994. Foreword to *Many Mirrors: Body Image and Social Relations*, edited by Nicole Sault, xi–xii. New Brunswick, NJ: Rutgers University Press.

Santaemilia, Jose. 2008. "The Translation of Sex-Related Language: The Danger(s) of Self-Censorship(s)." *TTR: Traduction, Terminologie, Redaction* 21 (2): 221–252.

Sarkar, Sumit, and Tanika Sarkar, eds. 2008. *Women and Social Reform in Modern India: A Reader*. Bloomington: Indiana University Press.

Shevde, Natasha. 2008. "All's Fair in Love and Cream: A Cultural Case Study of Fair & Lovely in India." *Advertising and Society Review* 9 (2): 1–10. Available at https://doi.org/10.1353/asr.0.0003.

Spellers, Regina E. 1998. "Happy to Be Nappy!: Embracing an Afrocentric Aesthetic for Beauty." In *Readings in Cultural Contexts*, edited by Judith N. Martin, Thomas K. Nakayama, and Lisa A. Flores, 70–78. Mountain View, CA: Mayfield Publishing.

Steedman, Carolyn. 1986. *Landscapes for a Good Woman: A Story of Two Lives*. London: Virago.

2

Bodies at Surveillance

Appearance, Social Control, and Female Body Image in India's Postmillennial Lesbian and Trans Narratives

Tanupriya and Aratrika Bose

Introduction

Lesbian and trans bodies are viewed as abject and hence become sites of political control. Narratives in the Indian context depicting the lesbian body's nonbinary desire and aesthetic spill over the gender cartography to destabilize the heterosexual imperative. Trans women negotiate their identities and bodies to fit in cultural contexts and find multiple ways to craft their identities. Not surprisingly, several Indian narratives by women with alternate sexual identities have touched upon the problem of body image. In this regard, one also notes how, within a commodity culture, heteronormative ideals pressure lesbians to look a certain way in order to be visible as lesbians. Sridevi Nair (2008, 408), in "Hey Good Lookin'!: Popular Culture, Femininity and Lesbian Representation in Transnational Regimes," for example, argues that this commodification of lesbian identity leads to an aestheticization of lesbian body image even though lesbian identity is constantly under threat from the state. Nair describes how films and movies present the lesbian body as an offshoot of the upper-middle-class heterosexual perspective on what bodies in public spaces should look like. Western gender critics like Caroline Huxley and Nikki Hayfield (2012, 3) have explored this problem and state that alternate sexualities become a regime; lesbian and gay appearances become policed to fit into an authentic sexuality. Critic Laura Kelly (2007) likewise informs that internalization of sociocultural norms is more influential to body image than a lesbian identity. Further, Kate Bornstein's (1994) seminal work,

Gender Outlaw, lists the dominant culture's perception of women based on appearance and contemporary lesbian anxiety about conforming to these ideals while retaining their sexuality. Evidently, the lack of appreciation of the lesbian body is linked to low self-esteem and resilience in everyday life (Chanana 2015). And all such disabling conditions form a part of the embodied experiences of the protagonists of the two main narratives selected for analysis in the present study, namely, Astha in Manju Kapur's *A Married Woman* (2002) and Anamika in Abha Dawesar's *Babyji* (2005).

The present chapter explores appearance vis-à-vis lesbian and trans body image with the central focus on intersections of experiences among sex, body image, gender behavior, and desire. It does so by taking into account how desire and gender are oppositional categories in nonheterosexuality (Butler 1990, 30; Chanana 2015, 26; Roy 2017, 176). Further, it explores how each protagonist's body image reflects her desire and gendered expressions and how gender expressions influence the meaning of desire. The politics of control in the lesbian sexualities of Astha and Anamika in *A Married Woman* and *Babyji*, respectively, are a representation of the internalization of hegemonic heterosexuality through their body image. Strikingly, both narratives are located within the fashion-conscious and appearance-obsessed capital city of India, New Delhi. Astha in *A Married Woman*, for instance, represents the essentialist practices of hegemonic femininity through a male voyeuristic lens. In *Babyji*, on the other hand, Anamika's deliberate rejection of the feminine self and her mimicking of masculinity are read as an attempt to appropriate her lesbian desire within oppressive heterosexuality. This chapter thus establishes two things. First, it examines how the writers of the two works, Manju Kapur and Abha Dawesar, focus on the critique of appearance as an ostensible gendered identity. Second, it reads how the authors address body image and appearance discrimination, which in turn problematizes and marginalizes lesbian and trans bodies. The two narratives, as this chapter proves, establish how body image problems hold true for women with nonnormative sexual identities. Further, Kapur's and Dawesar's narratives set the stage for examining trans women's body identities, issues that have been addressed in autobiographical works such as *I Am Vidya*, *The Truth about Me*, and *A Gift of Goddess Laxmi*. In sum, this chapter reads various postmillennial narratives of struggle that trans and lesbian women, with their so-called nonnormate or masculine bodies, face while attempting to fit into the hegemonic heteronormative female body image.

In addition to narratives by Kapur and Dawesar, a powerful discourse on the predicaments of trans bodies is found in Living Smile Vidya's autobiography, *I Am Vidya* (2007), where she mentions how she became a part of a cultural process, and where she, in a male body, tries to enact a femininity that opposes the dominant cultural ideals. Thus, Vidya, a trans woman from

Tamil Nadu in India, demonstrates how one experiences life with or through the body, which may or may not mirror the standards of an appropriate feminine body. Vidya states, "When I was in surroundings other than home or college, I generally felt quite free to be myself. On such occasions, I walked swaying my hips like a woman, sat with my legs crossed stylishly or rearranged my hair in a feminine way when the wind blew it across my forehead" (Vidya 2007, 44). The idea of femininity in a masculine body is considered inappropriate in a cultural milieu such as India since such a body subverts the social roles and norms linked to the female body. In truth, however, the body is in constant flux, altered by activities and technologies that are experienced through a gendered lens and judged by an oscillating set of standards. And this is what Vidya's narrative establishes. Similarly, autobiographical narratives such as *The Truth about Me* (2010) by A. Revathi and *A Gift of Goddess Laxmi* (2017) by Manobi Bandyopadhyay offer insights into the struggles of anxiety in a body that society calls anomalous for its in-betweenness and dissociation and highlights the politics of control that is effected through appearance norms, which in turn define cultural ideals of femininity. The examination of such narratives of struggle and resistance informs the core of this chapter.

Theories of Body Image and Nonnormative Female Sexual Identities

Female body image suffers largely from the politics of control and is constrained by the regimes and ideals that are directed against it. Early research also observed that body image assumes a heterosexual imperative, as "the phenomenon was limited to or most powerful when one of feminine beauty in the eyes of men" (Cash and Brown 1989, 362). Feminist critic Sandra Lee Bartky rightly questions the idea of docile bodies in the context of female bodies in "Foucault, Femininity, and Modernization of Patriarchal Power" and mentions:

> Where is the account of disciplinary practices that engender the "docile bodies" of women, bodies more docile than that of men? Women, like men, are subject to many of the same disciplinary practices Foucault describes. But he is blind to those disciplines that produce a modality of embodiment that is peculiarly feminine. (1997, 132)

The discipline of control and surveillance that is produced through a set of beauty standards is imposed on women because cultures associate certain ideals and modes of enactment as feminine, but what must be understood is that "we are born male and female, but not masculine and feminine" (Bartky 1997, 132). These sets of standards and ideals are imposed on female bodies and, in turn, engender female body image concerns. With regard to this standardization, Nancy Scheper-Hughes and Margaret Lock (1987) offer an explanation of body image and identify ways of viewing the body that can be useful for understanding and thinking about women and lesbian bodies. According to them, "body image refers to the collective and idiosyncratic representations an individual entertains about the body in its relationship to the environment, including internal and external perceptions, memories, affects, cognitions, and actions" (Scheper-Hughes and Lock 1987, 16). On similar lines, Sari H. Dworkin references fat politics to explain that lesbians suffer from body image problems because they "live and work within the heterosexual, patriarchal society" (1989, 33). It is thus evident that the female body is central to the analysis of many areas of social experience, self-presentation (Goffman 1956, 1963), and sexuality. And clearly, these are cultural dictates that associate mannerisms, behaviors, and attitudes as masculine or feminine. The body is a site in which cultural and social constructions come into being and are mapped onto individuals. Masculinity and femininity are culture-specific constructs that impart a set of instructions or prescriptions on being an ideal man or woman. Gender signifiers of femininity and masculinity are incorporated by individuals who mimic the heterosexual paradigm.

The gender hegemony in lesbian bodily identities is played out in demarcations such as "butch," "femme," "lipstick lesbians," "queen," "MSM," and so on (Halberstam 1998, 212). Such demarcations of butch/femme, as critic Lillian Faderman (1991) mentions, emerged in lesbian communities by the 1950s. Although butch/femme culture encompassed far more than just a dress code, appearance was nevertheless a significant feature. Butch/femme styles allowed lesbians to identify one another, while also affording lesbians a way of expressing themselves as distinct entities from the dominant culture. Appearance, in their case, therefore becomes the hegemonic gender performance for an individual. Judith Butler, in *Gender Trouble*, describes appearance as "a metaphor of the ontological material reality of the body" (1990, 60). It is through the surface of the body—that is, how a person looks, dresses up, or performs gender-specific behaviors—that a person's embodied identities are defined. Sociologist and gender critic Ahonaa Roy, in "Sexualising the Body: Passionate Aesthetics and Embodied Desire," defines appearance as one that "constitutes the cultural meanings imposed by the signifiers in the body that install certain social meanings through the materiality of their existence" (2017, 175). Body is thus socially and culturally shaped, and the politics of the body is different from the body politic, which in turn asserts that the body itself is politically inscribed and is shaped by practices of containment and control. Within this paradigm, the ordeal of not feminine enough affects the identities of trans women, who most of the time have to struggle with their masculine bodies to fit into the vexed ideal of femininity and often experience anxiety, in-betweenness, and dissonance. As they experience gender transition, which itself is born out of the hegemonic heteronormative female body image, they often have to grapple with established parameters of feminine embodiment. The standards of appropriate gendered appearance also dictate what it means to look like an ideal man or woman with corporeal ideals and hence are subject to cultural pressures. Body image concerns are associated with trans feminine identities, and trans women experience struggles with feminine characteristics and the primary and secondary markers of their feminine identity, and this results in conforming to the beauty ideas set by a hetero-patriarchal society. Butler explains femininity as an artifice, an achievement, "a mode of enacting and re-enacting received gender norms which surface as so many styles of flesh" (1985, 11) that shatters the hegemonic paradigm and opens discourses for male femininity and female masculinity. Such readings are crucial to the present discussion on the body image of women with alternate sexualities in India.

Patriarchal Control, Homoeroticism, and Body Image in Kapur's *A Married Woman*

The complex system of cultural production exercises a repetitiveness that comes to be understood as natural once it has been practiced for ages. The study of gender recognizes that in this deviously repetitive social order, all gender identities, including heterosexual male and female norms of embodiment, are produced and regulated through a repository of symbolic meanings. Specifically, in terms of women's bodies, such symbolic meanings are found in behavior, clothing, body shape, and appearance. Mimi Schippers terms this hegemonic femininity as "characteristics defined as womanly that establish and legitimate a hierarchical and complementary position to hegemonic masculinity and that by doing so guarantee the dominant position of men and the subordination of women" (2007, 94). These overt and idealized feminine traits in women, which are emphasized by the patriarchy and translated to compliance, nurture and ensure cis-male dominance over all femininities (Schippers 2007, 95). Therefore, any deviance from this hegemonic femininity—which is often read as lesbian desire, or nonfeminine appearance such as butch and other masculine femininities—is marginalized and regulated. This regulation of hegemonc femininity occurs through a systemic act of seeing, a panoptic power wherein the subject is controlled with a set of heterogeneous codes of conduct. This leads to self-censorship, a control that is often internalized by human subjects (Foucault 1982; Menon 2012). One encounters a powerful critique of this problem within the context of contemporary India in Manju Kapur's *A Married Woman*.

The surveillance of the body's appearance and its clothing assigns suitable behaviors and roles that the female body is worthy of performing. Delving deep into such politics, Manju Kapur, in *A Married Woman*, depicts how the protagonist, Astha, imbibes hegemonic notions of masculinity and femininity and how she is drawn to what she believes is safe—a physically strong man with masculine features. Kapur, through her tale of a broken marriage and a turbulent homosexual affair between her protagonist, Astha, and her lover, Pipeelika Khan, provokes her readers to examine how heteronormative bodies and images of femininity and female beauty plague modern Indian women. To begin with, Kapur depicts how Astha suffers from a deep sense of inadequacy in her body and its feminine features as she "marvels" at her so-called ugliness, wondering if she will ever find someone to love and marry (Kapur 2002, 8). Eventually, Astha marries Hemant, but she is caught in an unhappy marriage, only to find some respite in a homosexual relationship. It is worth recalling Foucault's "The Subject and the Power" (1982) at this juncture to examine how the panoptic seeing of the state/dominant culture via the hegemonic codes of femininity is a systemic act of controlling its lesbian subjects. The cultural panopticon arguably contests the sexual transgression of all women with alternate sexualities by essentializing the heterosexist and compulsory feminization of the body. Highlighting this, Kapur writes how Hemant, a flag bearer of said heterosexual hegemony but a liberal on the surface, likes Astha's legs perfectly waxed and how the smell of sweat and vaginal fluids makes him nauseous, so Astha powders herself constantly (Kapur 2002, 45). Obviously, her homosexual urges or her homoerotic body have become an anathema to her husband.

Astha's deep lack of self-worth based on her appearance and her lack of sexual confidence allow Hemant to occupy the entire space between them, and she is increasingly pushed to the margins. The only means by which she can reinforce her identity as a (desirable) woman is by her physical appearance, her gender role, and her behavior, all of which need to conform to the feminine. In a telling episode, Hemant coaxes Astha to wear a baby doll dress during sex, although she is hesitant. The baby doll highlights her perky breasts and effectively sexualizes her body to suit a male fantasy. Astha's helplessness here is redolent of gender critic Kuhu Sharma Chanana's essay entitled "Plurality of Lesbian Experience in Modern Indian Writers," where she writes how heterosexual pleasure is often about the satisfaction of the penis alone and leaves the woman wounded and dissatisfied both emotionally and physically (2015, 164). Clearly, in giving in to the fetishes of Hemant, Astha not only fulfills the culturally coded acts of a woman and wife, but her appearance and self-perception also reaffirm her own gender as a heterosexual wife and woman.

Initiating the contemporary debate on female body image in the West, Naomi Wolf, in *The Beauty Myth* (1991), asserted that a woman's self-perception of her beauty influences her sexuality and the actualization of her sexual desire. Wolf also argued that this notion of what constitutes beautiful creates a prescriptive parameter over women's body shape and appearance. Wolf also stressed that falsely interlocking the two makes it essential for a woman to be feminine in order to be sexual and that "the definition of beauty and sexuality constantly changes to serve the social order" (1991, 150). Since such body image dictates privilege heterosexual identity, they in turn adversely affect the self-image, confidence, and body image of lesbian and trans individuals. In Kapur's novel, Astha's body image is beleaguered by heterosexist definitions of femininity that make her feel ugly as she undergoes childbirth and then bears signs of aging. The bodily changes that alter her full breasts, narrow waist, and youthful skin make her feel less of a woman and reduce, in her mind, her feminine potential. In a telling episode, upon wearing a dress, Astha finds herself unattractive and hence also finds herself less appealing sexually.

Kapur, in *A Married Woman*, dethrones not only the discourse of a happy Indian marriage but also deeply problematizes the male gaze that often belittles the female body for not bearing an ideal body image. The narrative demonstrates how the female gaze in lesbian desire becomes a remedying experience for Astha, who suffers heavily under the male gaze of her husband, and society at large, while trying to uphold heterosexist femininity. More important, Pipeelika, Astha's lesbian lover, does not adhere to heteronormative standards of feminine beauty. She is shown to have "pale milky coffee" skin, as opposed to Astha's light skin tone, and strands of artificially colored hair (Kapur 2002, 62). Further, Astha observes how Pipeelika cares very little about her appearance whereas she herself worries constantly if she is well dressed or groomed enough (Kapur 2002). In one instance, Pipeelika takes off Astha's rings and bangles, at which Astha's insecurity is evident as she exclaims, "I look so pale without them," to which Pipeelika responds, "All the better" (Kapur 2002, 222). Through her nonchalance toward body image ideals, Pipeelika gradually and metaphorically unburdens Astha of the heteronormative pressure to constantly look beautiful and feminine. She takes Astha to the bathroom mirror and makes her look at her face and body in admiration, beyond her frail skin and aging face (Kapur 2002, 221). Hence, Pipeelika helps her find autonomy in body image and appearance beyond the conventional notions of beauty and sexual appeal. Therefore, it is only in her sexual awakening and her lesbian desire for Pipeelika that Astha is able to transgress the codes of hegemonic femininity. Toward the end, Astha's desires are no longer linked to her body's appearance and the incessant need to be physically attractive in the feminine way that Hemant desires. This enables Astha to redefine her body image and sexual appeal, opening up for her immense possibilities beyond the limitations of her corporeality.

Female Gaze, Lesbian Desire, and Body Image in Dawesar's *Babyji*

Appearance and the nonnormatively sexualized female body once again find a compelling rendition in Abha Dawesar's *Babyji*. It is common knowledge that clothes express the gender of a person, allowing categorization of the person into fixed identities in a geopolitical space. Clothing in India, for instance, helps to add taglines on sexuality such as "straight," "gay," or "lesbian," as well as labels on appearances such as "sexy," "slutty," or "aunty." Within lesbian identities, clothing and appearance styles can refer to the butch identity, where a woman is perceived as masculine, and the femme identity, which refers to a feminine lesbian. In *Babyji*, the protagonist, Anamika, observes how Indian society mandates that older women be called "aunty," hence taking away any sexual or female bonding between different age groups (Dawesar 2005, 2). In Anamika's numerous homoerotic affairs, it is this labeling of the female body and its appearance that she powerfully questions and often subverts. Significantly, Dawesar's narrative, when read in the light of Ahonna Roy's thesis on homosexuality, finds great relevance. Quoting Elizabeth Grosz, Roy argues that body inscription builds representational practices as "rendering to political economy of the body in terms of looks, sexual signifiers, gendered meanings, individual biography, cultural signifiers and so on" (2017, 182). This, claims Roy, establishes norms of attractiveness and ideas of beauty associated with femininity and often leads to the marginalization of women with nonnormative sexualities.

Strikingly, a posture Anamika adopts to counter hegemonic gender and appearance norms is to mimic the masculine ideal in order to appropriate her lesbian sexuality through her mannerism and way of dressing. The only way Anamika can normalize being sexually attracted to other women is by dressing up in a manner that makes her masculine—in her case, in checked shirts and jeans. On her first visit to her lover India's house, she decides to dress up as a young boy. Anamika reveals that a "lot of the clothes were still young and girlie" and that she "chose a red-striped boys shirt and jeans. I wore black boys' shoes, slapped some Old Spice on the neck from my father's toilette and rode my bicycle over" (Dawesar 2005, 7), all in the hope of attracting her newfound lover. One notes here how appearing male also impacts the concept of self-construction of a young lesbian individual like Dawesar's protagonist. In fact, Anamika's boyish clothing reaffirms her fantasy to be a boy or "prince." Discussing such forms of dressing, Grosz states that they "produce the meaning and intensity of the body's surface, underlining the psychic and bodily embodiments to its consciousness" owing to which "the body is . . . historically shaped and socially imagined, which fashions the perpetuation of identity semiotics" (qtd. in Roy 2017, 185). Understandably, in Anamika's case, such dressing to alter her appearance helps her affirm her own position as a budding homosexual woman.

These tendencies continue as Anamika embodies the gender roles and behaviors of men with her dream to study abroad and priorities career over relationships. One notes in her a constant need to rescue the women in her life and to play the hero, gestures that also reaffirm her nonnormative sexual self and her need to transcend her female limitations. Anamika is therefore flattered when Rani, her maidservant, mistakes her for a boy (Dawesar 2005, 14). Ironically, then, Anamika embodies the heterosexual imperative while being a lesbian woman. Her own appearance, way of dressing, and behaviors help her relate to a Brahmin, cis, upper-class, and therefore empowered man (27) while also validating her own homosexual urges. To her patriarchally inscribed female gaze, Anamika therefore considers herself unattractive and unappealing before the male gaze. At the bus stop, for example, when two men leer at her, she is surprised before she is disgusted at the prospect of men finding her sexually attractive. She exclaims, "I wore glasses and was relatively dark. I had short hair, I was average looking and flat chested. I wondered what on earth they were looking at" (84). Here Dawesar points out how Anamika disregards her own feminine appearance, considers beauty to be inconsequential to the mind, and wants to be an intellectual, all the while also showing a keen awareness of ideal female body image. Be that as it may, when it comes to her sexual choices and partners, Anamika views India and Rani as purely physical beings and is primarily attracted to their conventionally beautiful selves. "I saw them as women. I liked their flesh," she claims (130).

Anamika's female gaze and her understanding of female beauty therefore problematize the issue of heteronormative female body image. Most body studies scholars have challenged the ideals of beauty that Anamika likes in her partners as a means for lowering women's self-esteem and regulating their gendered performance. Further, Anamika considers herself ugly and as a result exercises her power in other ways or by imitating masculine strength and virility. In Anamika, therefore, one finds a convoluted extension of what Chanana calls the "narcissistic streak of the beauty" (2015, 191), which is expressed in the perverse power she feels for sleeping with normatively beautiful and sexy women like India and Rani. And, like a smug male after a sexual conquest, Anamika reduces her lovers to a trophy, an object, or "a doll, a toy" (Chanana 2015, 191). The complexity of Anamika's female gaze and the issue of female body image within homosexual paradigms therefore prove to be patriarchal, or what Laura Mulvey calls "scopophilic" (1975, 3). In Anamika's hetero-patriarchally defined albeit homosexual worldview, then, it is a heterosexual cis man who is not only intellectual but also powerful and attractive. It is not surprising that in a later episode where Anamika sits surrounded by India, Rani, and her mother, she calls herself the patriarch, feeling exhilarated for being surrounded by women she knew, by women who "belonged" to her (Chanana 2015, 162).

To examine Anamika's case, it is worth turning to Sridevi Nair's thesis in "'Hey Good Lookin'!," where she argues that the masculinization of the female gaze is a means by which women's subversive potential gets appropriated by a heteronormative and hetero-patriarchal culture. Nair argues that in media and in other discourses, women with nonnormative sexualities are

> comfortable to watch because they look like familiar everyday images of sameness. the butch disappears in light of the attention that the feminine (not femme) bodies command and there is literally no body/ nobody to disrupt the heteronormative and masculine gaze because even the butch is disciplined by commodity aesthetics. (2008, 417)

True to these assertions, Anamika views herself in the dominant and active role, especially when she is with Rani, whom she considers the submissive and passive partner given the latter's lower-class status. Not surprisingly, Anamika is brazen enough to force herself upon Rani against her comfort and for the sake of her own pleasure while disregarding Rani's individuality as a human. Anamika reveals:

> I threw her on the bed and started ripping open her blouse. She closed her eyes as if she didn't want to see me. The German guy from the porn magazine, but with Chakra Dev's face, the Brahmin from the movies with his servant, positions from the Kamasutra all mixed up in my head till I could no longer think. I felt rapacious and greedy for her. (Dawesar 2005, 95)

The violence here mimics the same sexual violence that Anamika and her last love interest in the novel, Sheela, experienced in an unfortunate bus ride. If Anamika here projects her humiliation and victimization onto Rani, who is the passive figure, she does the same with Sheela as well. In both cases the victims are marginalized in terms of class and gender. And also, in both cases, the two women, Rani and Sheela, are normatively beautiful while Anamika is not. In fact, Sheela is said to be light skinned and healthy; she keeps long polished nails, has perfectly waxed legs, and wears her school skirt higher than most girls, revealing her "shapely" legs (Dawesar 2005). Obviously, in Anamika's heteronormatively aligned thinking, her so-called beautiful partners are to be ravaged and consumed. This can be understood with the help of Chanana's argument that "women are culturally trained to love women only through masculine appropriation of power" (2015, 40). And in such discourses of power, body image, too, often follows heteronormative imperatives between trans and lesbian couples.

Anxieties of the *Wrong Body*: Female Body Image and Trans Narratives of Dissonance

Just as the lesbian women discussed in the two narratives earlier experience complex problems with regard to their body image, trans woman, too, are subject to much shame, ridicule, and even torture owing to their nonnormate bodies. Trans women and *hijras* (South Asian term for transgender people) call into question both the stability of sex and its relationship with the social and psychological categories of gender. And many times, as this section demonstrates, such individuals undergo gender transformation. Notably, the two primary aspects that are a part of this gender transformation include castration or emasculation and surgery, which ultimately leads to creating a female body along with other feminine markers of gender identity for trans women. Like in many other cultures, castration has cultural connotations related to *hijras* in India. Revathi, who was born a boy in rural Tamil Nadu, mentions her experience of the ritual in her autobiography, titled *The Truth about Me*. "Hijras who undergo this operation do not eat fruit or drink milk for forty days. On the fortieth day, they offer puja to Pothiraja Mata," claims Revathi (2010, 75). Surgery or emasculation here is the careful assessment of the body and then its transformation, which is executed medically. And such surgeries are performed to give trans women the body image that a larger heteronormative culture assigns to them.

In the context of surgeries, Nikki Sullivan (2006), a critical theorist of body, in "Transmogrification: (Un) Becoming Other(s)," examines similarities and differences between transsexual surgeries and other forms of bodily modifications such as piercing, tattooing, cosmetic surgery, and willful amputation, which are often carried out more out of choice than compulsion. Likewise, in her study entitled "Embodying Desire: Piercing and the Fashioning of Neo-Butch/Femme Identities," Lisa Walker (1998) critically examines dichotomous accounts of nonmainstream body modifications and cosmetic surgery in which the latter is understood as a form of compliance to normative gendered standards of beauty and the former is represented as a radical political practice and nonmainstream body modifications become a site of political control. In the light of such studies, it may be claimed that trans women, especially in India, mimic and accentuate feminine traits and mannerisms associated with heterosexual women—that is, name, attire, length of hair, and adoption of feminine pronouns and language. The use of nonverbal bodily presentations such as clothing, sartorial style, mannerisms, kinesthetic, and other factors influencing their presentation of the self are also geared toward a feminine identity. Such mimicking among trans Indian women brings to mind Foucault's panopticon where the threat of the cultural gaze is enough to ensure compliance with a rule. In fact, drawing upon Foucault, what Peter Conrad (1992) describes as medical surveillance is a form of social control in which bodily and mental conditions can be understood through a medical gaze such that authority is transferred from individuals to biomedicine, and this is once again true for many trans women.

Within the Indian context, such a heteronormative medicalized gaze becomes normalized and individuals continue to use techniques of medical surveillance to make sense of their own bodies. This invisible force of the gaze is naturally directed against trans women's bodies in order to accommodate the vexed notions of femininity despite the presence of their biologically nonnormative bodies. *Hijras* experience dissociation and anxiety in their masculine bodies and sometimes find themselves in between identities during gender transition. Revathi, we know, identified as a boy in the early years of her life, but by rejecting the notions of boyhood and claiming authority over her femaleness, she, over time, constructs her feminine identity. Her narrative depicts the essentialist heteronormative notion of femininity that can be enacted only in a female body, and *hijras* are ridiculed for their feminine appearance and mannerisms in masculine bodies, which in turn adversely affects their body image.

Like Revathi, Manobi Bandyopadhyay, in her autobiography titled *A Gift of Goddess Laxmi*, recounts a distaste with her body in the early years of her life. Bandyopadhyay reveals, "I was developing a distaste for my genitals. I just couldn't accept my balls and my penis. I wanted to have my sisters' genitals" (2017, 8). Clearly, such accounts display the body-dysphoria experiences that are often the lot of trans Indian women. The fetishization over the heteronormative female body ideal creates surveillance and regulates the body ordeal among trans women. Appearance therefore becomes an important axis for such entities as it connotes "the interplay between and appearing" (Roy 2017, 175), and, as Butler (1990) mentions, "body becomes a mark of institutionalised heterosexuality" (qtd. in Roy 2017, 175) and enables newer forms of feminine signification. Manobi accounts that "I craved to dress up as a girl and be taken as a girl" (Bandyopadhyay 2017, 13) and also mentions the effect of such signifiers of appearance on her body image. She discloses, "I would feel jealous of the girls. Why did no one look at me and tease me?

Was I not more desirable than those girls?" (11). Such disclosures foreground the dissonance in trans women who try to perform male roles while at the same time desire feminine bodies and male appreciation. The quest for visibility of a female body is communicated through the feminine signifiers and it is rendered invisible by the male body.

The narratives by Revathi and Manobi underscore how anxiety is a natural and common response among trans women for inhabiting so-called anomalous bodies, and hence body image concerns are an integral part of trans women's lived experiences. Critic Talia Bettcher's (2014) concept of the "wrong body" in transsexuality becomes relevant here because it involves a misalignment between one's gender identity and one's sexed body. The phrase "wrong body" describes the feeling that one's body is not a part of one's self. For a bearer of the wrong body, her inside does not recognize the outside of the body, and she suffers a deep disconnect. Manobi's account describes such dissociation of identity and in-betweenness among trans women:

> There were times in my life when I doubted myself and the path I took. In such instances, my mind would go into a state of flux and the turmoil would sear me from within. Am I really a woman trapped in a male body? Why is it the whole world think of me as a man who is nothing more than a sissy? (Bandyopadhyay 2017, 109)

Quite clearly, the existence and celebration of normative heterosexual female bodies are linked hegemonic cultural norms in every given society. Keeping this in mind, it is but natural to assume that Manobi yearns for dominant feminine signifiers and artifacts that accentuate femininity, as reflected in her autobiography. Manobi mentions, "I was desperate to come to terms with myself. . . . I thought of myself—a girl who did not have a vagina and whose breasts showed no signs of developing. I continued hating my penis and the very thought that I had one between my legs made me loathe myself more" (34). Here, ashamed of her natural trans or wrong body, Manobi wishes to associate herself with feminine markers of the body such as menstruation. Manobi bemoans, "I would yearn to menstruate. . . . In the privacy of my room, I would make similar sanitary napkins and tie them around my genitals to fake periods" (35). These attempts at feminine significations present the dominant cultural pressures and signifiers from a heteronormative gendered society on trans feminine bodies that make them anxious in their so-called wrongness.

Given their deep and insatiable need to appear feminine, trans women attempt to express their femininity through mannerisms, sartorial style, body language, and feminine gestures that are deemed as markers of femininity. In sum, they try to pass as women, an act that Susan Brownmiller (1984) in

Femininity describes as modified dress, manner, attitude, and voice adopted by someone who wants to be perceived as feminine (or weak) enough and hence be accepted. Befitting such discourses, Manobi narrates:

> I was not "male" in every sense of the word. They found me odd and made no effort to hide their surprise. My femininity was quite pronounced in my mannerisms and though I didn't wear women's make-up, my unisex attire, make-up, sunglasses and hairstyle make my sexual preference quite apparent. (Bandyopadhyay 2017, 91)

In the context of trans women's body identities, Arthur Frank's (1991) typology of body use in "For a Sociology of the Body: An Analytical Review" is suggestive of the social control trans identities experience in nonheteronormative bodies. Frank describes how the *disciplined* body becomes predictable through regimentation. Likewise, he argues that the *mirroring* body predictably reflects what is around it. It is also dissociated, assimilating only the objects made available for it to consume. The *dominating* body, claims Frank, is the male body characterized by the sense of lack, and it is contingent on its own fragile ability to dominate. Finally, the *communicative* body, in Frank's thesis, is in the process of creating itself. The body's desire is the reciprocal expression and the recognition of others rather than consumption, mirroring, and dominating. And this is entirely true for body identities of trans women like Revathi and Manobi.

Clearly, then, female bodies are not sufficiently female or feminine unless they assume social modifications. And they must be rebuilt by artificial means. Female bodies therefore often seem inadequate at best or ugly, disgusting, or threatening at worst, unless tamed or improved upon. Understandably, the likes of Manobi reject this construct; in her words, "I would not become a woman in the sense that nature or society understands a woman to be. I would neither menstruate nor would I bear children, but I would have a vagina and breasts to heighten my sexuality and that was of utmost importance to me because it would give me the identity that I had craved all my life" (Bandyopadhyay 2017, 134). It is apparent here that the female body is not naturally destined to be heterosexual, but it is made to fit the heterosexual gaze. And within this cultural paradigm, trans women's body anxieties are natural given that they are doubly marginalized under various intersectional body norms.

Conclusion

This study situates lesbian and trans narratives, both fiction and autobiographies, as cultural artifacts and reads how heteronormative female body image impacts trans and lesbian body identities. It does so not only because such an analysis is relatively absent from scholarship on LGBTQ identities in the Indian context but also because there is a need for a collective acceptance of lesbian and trans bodies that is contingent upon redefining and theorizing discourses privileging heteronormativity and patriarchy. Such narratives illustrate how lesbian and transgender bodies negotiate their ways through cultures obsessed with heteronormative feminine bodies and beauty ideals. The narratives under scrutiny represent how body image issues of lesbian and trans women condition them to conform to hegemonic femininity. Hence, if Anamika in *Babyji* chooses to appear tomboyish to appropriate lesbian desire and in turn ends up mimicking the pedantic cis-male gender standards of appearance and beauty, Revathi in *The Truth about Me*, through her sartorial style, attempts to mimic heterosexual femininity.

Arguably, then, within lesbian subcultures and communities of transgender women, dominant heterosexist beauty norms impose pressures on lesbians and trans women look attractive and conform to heterosexual standards of beauty. And while heterosexual women suffer from the patriarchal male gaze, lesbian and trans women experience body anxieties of being excluded from the category of "women" and therefore end up conforming to the appearance ideal. Astha in *A Married Woman* is therefore seen to validate several aspects of her identity—as a wife, a woman, and a lesbian—through forceful conformation to hegemonic beauty norms. Revathi likewise is also seen conforming to normative feminine beauty ideals. The pressure of such appearance norms is detrimental to her self-worth and confidence. And to defy these, Anamika actively denies her feminine self to authenticate her lesbian desire, yet chooses partners who appear beautiful according to heteronormative body image standards.

In the light of the narratives examined in this chapter, it may be concluded that lesbian and trans women's bodies are not reducible to organic processes or cultures of isolation. Embodiment is a dynamic discourse that produces the body and its capacities. Trans and lesbian bodies have the capability of articulating creative languages around the body, which in turn can produce varied gender discourses and experiences. It is therefore appropriate to conclude the present discussion with Diane G. Crowder's (1998, 50) argument where "she asserts that cultural gender definitions determine how the biological female is (re/de) constructed into a feminine woman," an imperative that lesbian and trans women must negotiate with every day.

REFERENCES

Bandyopadhyay, Manobi. 2017. *A Gift of Goddess Lakshmi*. Gurgaon: Penguin Books.
Bartky, Sandra Lee. 1997. "Foucault, Femininity and the Modernization of Patriarchal Power." In *Writing on the Body: Female Embodiment and Feminist Theory*, edited by

Katie Conboy, Nadia Medina, and Sarah Stanbury, 129–154. New York: Columbia University Press.

Bettcher, Talia Mae. 2014. "Trapped in the Wrong Theory: Re-Thinking Trans Oppression and Resistance." *Signs* 39 (2): 383–406.

Bornstein, Kate. 1994. *Gender Outlaw: On Men, Women and the Rest of Us.* New York: Routledge.

Brownmiller, Susan. 1984. *Femininity.* New York: Linden Press, Simon and Schuster.

Butler, Judith. 1985. "Embodied Identity in De Beauvoir's *The Second Sex.*" Paper presented at the American Philosophical Association, Pacific Division, March 22, 1985.

———. 1990. *Gender Trouble.* New York: Routledge.

Cash, Thomas F., and Timothy A. Brown. 1989. "Gender and Body Images: Stereotypes and Realities." *Sex Roles* 21 (5/6): 361–373.

Chanana, Kuhu Sharma. 2015. *LGBTQ in Select Modern Indian Literature.* New Delhi: Suryodaya Books.

Conrad, Peter. 1992. "Medicalization and Social Control." *Annual Review in Sociology* 18:209–232. Available at https://www.jstor.org/stable/2083452.

Crowder, Diane G. 1998. "Lesbian and the (Re/De) Construction of the Female Body." In *Looking Queer: Body Image and Identity in Lesbian, Bisexual, Gay and Transgender Communities*, edited by Dawn Etkins, 47–68. New York: Haworth Press.

Dawesar, Abha. 2005. *Babyji.* New York: Anchor Books.

Dworkin, Sari H. 1989. "Not in Man's Image: Lesbians and the Cultural Oppression of Body Image." *Women in Therapy* 8 (1–2): 27–39. Available at https://doi.org/10.1300/J015v08n01_03.

Faderman, Lillian. 1991. *Odd Girls and Twilight Lovers: A History of Lesbian Life in Twentieth-Century America.* New York: Columbia University Press.

Foucault, Michel. 1982. "The Subject and the Power." *Critical Inquiry* 8 (4): 777–795. Available at https://www.jstor.org/stable/1343197.

Frank, Arthur. 1991. "For a Sociology of the Body: An Analytical Review." In *The Body: Social Process and Cultural Theory*, edited by Mike Featherstone, Mike Hepworth, and Bryan S. Turner, 36–96. London: Sage Publications.

Goffman, Erving. 1956. *The Presentation of Self in Everyday Life.* Edinburgh: University of Edinburgh.

———. 1963. *Behavior in Public Places.* New York: Free Press of Glencoe.

Halberstam, Judith. 1998. *Female Masculinity.* New Delhi: Zubaan Books.

Huxley, Caroline, and Nikki Hayfield. 2012. "Lesbian, Gay and Bisexual Sexualities: Appearance and Body Image." In *Oxford Handbook of the Psychology of Appearance*, edited by Nichola Rumsey and Diana Harcourt, 190–202. Oxford: Oxford Academic. https://doi.org/10.1093/oxfordhb/9780199580521.013.0017

Kapur, Manju. 2002. *A Married Woman.* New Delhi: Roli Books.

Kelly, Laura. 2007. "Lesbian Body Image Perceptions: The Context of Body Silence." *Qualitative Health Research* 17 (7): 873–883.

Menon, Nivedita. 2012. *Seeing Like a Feminist.* Penguin India.

Mulvey, Laura. 1975. "Visual Pleasure and Narrative Cinema." *Screen* 16 (3): 6–18. Available at https://doi.org/10.1007/978-1-349-19798-9_3.

Nair, Sridevi. 2008. "Hey Good Lookin'!: Popular Culture, Femininity and Lesbian Representation in Transnational Regimes." *Journal of Lesbian Studies* 12 (4): 407–422. Available at https://doi.org/10.1080/10894160802278531.

Revathi, A. 2010. *The Truth about Me.* New Delhi: Penguin Books.

Roy, Ahonaa. 2017. "Sexualising the Body: Passionate Aesthetics and Embodied Desire." *Indian Journal of Gender Studies* 24 (2): 171–193. Available at https://doi.org/10.1177/0971521517697879.

Scheper-Hughes, Nancy, and Margaret M. Lock. 1987. "The Mindful Body: A Prolegomenon to Future Work in Medical Anthropology." *Medical Anthropology Quarterly* 1 (1): 1–14.

Schippers, Mimi. 2007. "Recovering the Feminine Other: Masculinity, Femininity and Gender Hegemony." *Theatre and Society* 36 (February): 85–102. Available at https://doi.org/10.1007/s11186-007-9022-4.

Sullivan, Nikki. 2006. "Transmogrification: (Un) Becoming Other(s)." In *The Transgender Studies Reader*, edited by Susan Stryker and Stephen Whittle, 552–564. New York: Routledge.

Vidya. 2007. *I Am Vidya*. Chennai: Oxygen Books.

Walker, Lisa. 1998. "Embodying Desire: Piercing and the Fashioning of Neo-Butch/Femme Identities." In *Butch/Femme: Inside Lesbian Gender*, edited by Sally R. Munt, 123–132. London: Cassell.

Wolf, Naomi. 1991. *Beauty Myth: How Images of Beauty Are Used against Women*. New York: Harper Collins.

II

Reflections on Beauty Politics

Gender and Body Image in the Works of
Contemporary Indian Women Writers

3

Writing Woman / Woman Writing

Shashi Deshpande and the Aesthetics of the Female Body

SWATIE

Introduction

Current scholarly discourses on female body image critique the notion of Woman, especially the beautiful Woman, as a construct and seek to highlight the everyday manifestations of body oppressions experienced by women.[1] The patriarchally constructed philosophical ideal of the former is often at loggerheads with the quotidian, feminist reality of the latter. Through dismantling the beauty ideals of Western patriarchy, such critical debates aim to uncover women as not an abstract category but rather an identity based on everyday practices and experiences of the body and its image. It is assumed within body image scholarship—and rightly so—that women's appearances are diverse and that the dictates of body image dissatisfaction are patriarchal constructs meant to place women at war with their own bodies. For instance, the terminology of "the fashion beauty complex"[2] is influenced by the coinage of the "military industrial complex"[3] and aims to subjugate women through a commercially defined beauty imperative. Within these discourses, however, the critique of patriarchy's dictates of women's appearance is centered largely on Western scholarly discourses.

One therefore notes how body image debates geared toward women of color, queer women, and women from the global South tend to place them in the same bracket since all such bodies are viewed by a globally dominant Eurocentric culture as a deviance from the norm of the body beautiful. In other words, it is assumed that beauty standards impact women in a homogenous manner and that studying the impact of body image compulsions on white Western women is enough because it appears as a universal, uniform issue. The assumption that women are uniformly impacted and attain similar kinds of body image dissatisfaction, for instance, squarely places white Western body image dissatisfaction as the norm and beauty standards or beauty oppressions faced by women of color as deviating from it in various capacities. In short, existing body image scholarship often misses out on the particularities of how patriarch*ies* construct beauty standards variously (with or without similarities to each other). Beauty norms governing a black woman in the United States, for example, have very different preoccupations than those regulating an Indian woman "coming out as Dalit." This is true even as the racism embedded in the lives of the former can be examined through similar instances of systemic violence as those faced by the latter category of women.[4]

It is clear that "appearance in general and body image in particular have become very important constructs in contemporary *Western* societies," as Marika Tiggeman, an Australian body image scholar, states.[5] Body image and beauty ideals, however, have not yet been examined with Indian culture in mind. There exists a gap in scholarship on how appearance and body image take shape within the Indian context, even as the incidence of eating disorders and complaints about body image dissatisfaction seems to be on the rise.[6] Existing scholarship, however scant, places the issue of unattainable beauty and body image dissatisfaction in a theoretical framework and critiques cultural discourses that ask Indian women to "replicate" Western standards of body image, leading, in turn, to body dissatisfaction.[7] Further, critical body image theorists studying the influence of media and infotainment on body image locate "television, magazines, video games, cinema, and the Internet" as channels that deeply impact body image formation,[8] and this is true for many Indian women. Significantly, however, examining body image issues in the Indian context in the absence of any previous research on the subject involves a broadening the horizon of what culture and media entail. In particular, there is a need to examine the literary sphere along with television, cinema, advertising, and the Internet, among others, as domains for both establishing and resisting coercions of the body beautiful. While the literary sphere as such is elitist in that it assumes literacy, it is also a popular avenue for the discussion of the body, which in turn is influenced by forces of both media and culture. Therefore, especially in the Indian context, literary narratives addressing issues of body image deserve special attention given their influence on young and impressionable readers.

The study of a writer like Shashi Deshpande provides fertile ground for themes and preoccupations with the constructed demands of patriarchy, especially the norms of beauty and body image for Indian women. Notably,

Deshpande's literary works have often been read as domestic fiction of the middle-class woman.[9] It has also been labeled by Western publishers as work of a Third World woman writing "under western eyes."[10] In this chapter I highlight how a bourgeois feminine subjectivity and body identity, one that is in the process of becoming, is textually produced in Deshpande's writing. I engage with her short stories and examine the trope of the female body in them to inquire about the textual production of body image. My chapter argues that a patriarchal norm of what constitutes womanly beauty informs a script by which the female body is read aesthetically in society. And I demonstrate how this script is unraveled ontologically in Deshpande's fiction. Further, I examine the relation between the aesthetics of the literary text—in this case, the short story—and the aesthetics of the body. In sum, the issues I problematize in this chapter are as follows: How is the body aestheticized and written in an already aesthetic literary space? What notions of beauty and desirability emerge in the process? And finally, what textual space is afforded to the (un)desirable body? In trying to answer these questions, I bring to the forefront the relationship among writing, female subjectivity, and body image in the short stories of Shashi Deshpande.

Discourses on Female Body Image in Neoliberal India

Female body image has been discussed within Western academia as a universal concern that transcends different sociocultural distinctions.[11] While the universality of the beauty norm is suspect—each cultural context has its specific codification of what counts as beautiful—the notion that women are oppressed by unattainable standards of beauty is a thread that is common in all discussions of female body image. In the Indian context, issues of beauty and body appearance have been considered a problem of the privileged while issues such as violence on women, for example, have been viewed as pressing concerns. Yet issues of beauty and appearance affect not just rich and middle-class women and their social image but can also be linked to violence on women across almost all classes and communities in India. And this is especially true in the context of neoliberal India, where body identities are hugely influenced by transnational ideals and images.

Rupal Oza notes how the economic changes in the early 1990s brought on by political will "began to materially and discursively construct a new India."[12] In fact, many scholars have noted how, with the advent of neoliberalism, there has been a move to "Macdonald-ize" and therefore globalize every aspect of Indian life.[13] This neoliberal agenda of westernization is not merely limited to commerce and industry but also affects the deeper cultural and psychological aspects of life. It has involved a thrust to privatization and a burgeoning media industry that, in turn, is governed by norms of bodily ap-

pearance and feeds into the beauty-fashion industry. This industrial/techni-
cally modulated creation of female body image of the normative and simultaneously perfect body has had a deep impact on India's cultural consciousness
over the last three decades. Such influences are particularly felt in media cov-
erage, in film and television, and in the fashion industry, all of which emphasize the visual frame. While the visual impact of an ideal body may have
been felt most strongly within the infotainment industry, this problematic
has been appropriated by the literary media as well. Hence, a scholarly analysis of female body image in contemporary Indian literature appears both
necessary and relevant. Significantly, this task has been carried out partially
through sociological and psychological analysis of India's neoliberal culture,
particularly through a gendered lens.[14] And such research reveals that wom-
en have been impacted and *recast* time and again given the demands of an
appearance-conscious culture.[15] Surprisingly, however, a scrutiny of how beauty norms impact body image through literary production remains under-
researched. Hence, as stated prior, my study examines at Shashi Deshpande
and her fiction for multiple reasons,[16] including those of female body image.

While critically reading Deshpande's works, in the present chapter I highlight how bourgeois feminine subjectivity, one that is in the process of *becoming* bourgeois given the nascent neoliberal economic context, is textually
produced. I specifically seek to understand how a distinctly bourgeois subjectivity is embedded in Deshpande's textual narratives and how these become narratives by and about women. In this context, I take into account
Rupal Oza's analysis of how economic discourses are themselves sexed.[17] Oza
claims that "as liberalization of the economy came to be realized as liberalization of sexual codes, debates by the state, women's organizations, and sec-
ular groups over the new 'liberal' Indian woman demarcated the boundaries
of her subjectivity."[18] Informed by such postulations, I highlight how the textual embeddedness of feminine subjectivity is not complete but one that is
in the process of being textually produced. I argue that this is a material practice, one encoded in the various literary as well as nonliterary media in neoliberal India. With this understanding, I engage with selected short stories
by Deshpande and examine them through the literary use of the body to inquire about the textual production of body image. My reading draws upon
the fact that body image—and, in particular, the emphasis on appearance—
is closely linked with the contestations of modernity and with increasingly
westernized models of economy and polity. Body image discourse therefore
needs to be highlighted as embedded in and through an aesthetics of gender,
and my chapter attempts this confluence. I deliberately chose the short-story
form for this analysis because of its ability to create a quick sketch of the narrating subject. This quickness in literary contouring becomes an act of chip-
ping away the unnecessary to produce a literary economy of the text. This

textual space is one that incorporates, in Deshpande's case, the body as a primary site of cultural and ideological markings. This is a notion of the body that is bourgeois and neoliberal, but female, and one caught in the process of coming into being.

Mother, Daughter, and the Beauty Conundrum in "Why a Robin?"

In Deshpande's short story titled "Why a Robin?," a textual moment of maternal envy is produced.[19] In this story, while endeavoring to develop a rapport with her child, the narrator-mother tries to help her daughter with homework. In parenting so, however, the narrator-mother finds herself enveloped in envy. This moment of maternal envy produces an interior emotional crisis in her since her own sense of lack of beauty is contrasted with that of her normatively beautiful daughter. This realization of the contrast between the mother and her offspring is also a somatic reaction. The mother states, "How did I, so plain, so common, get a daughter like her? Her beauty always gives me a physical wrench."[20] The mother appears envious of her daughter's physical beauty and is amazed at the connection between her own lack of conventional beauty and the overwhelming presence of beauty in her daughter. Further, her own sense of plainness is used to create a contrast as well as a *bodily* reaction to issues of *body* image.

This incident in the short story becomes a key moment to symbolize several aspects of interest. The narrator-mother creates a textual space for herself. Later in the story, she forges an emotional bond with her daughter. However, the story is rife with "the beauty myth"[21] and its repercussions on woman-to-woman bonds. Aspects of beauty and human appearance along with patriarchal dictates about what counts as beautiful are deployed to show an older generation of women who are affected by the diktats of "beauty and the norm."[22] Women of the younger generation, brought up with tools of beauty grooming, are shown as getting closer to ideals of normative beauty. Through this intergenerational disconnect, Deshpande's text produces an anxiety of aging that women from preliberalized India would have experienced when contrasted with the supposedly desirable postliberal concept of youth and beauty. In this short story, the narratorial voice is both sharing her feelings in confidence with the readers and creating the notion that conventional norms of beauty seem to *matter* even as they disempower.[23] The notion that beauty practices are not just abstract but are real and discursively constructed material practices is highlighted here. The space in the text, the voice of the narrator, and the feeling of inadequacy in terms of body image seem to go together.

The middle-class ethos that Deshpande creates in short stories like "Why a Robin?" has been commented upon several times. Rashmi Sahi, for instance, describes Deshpande's characterization as concerned with a "middle class Indian woman who is educated," which brings to mind that Deshpande herself is both educated and middle-class.[24] Sahi also comments on how the female protagonists in Deshpande's works are "fit to show the clash between idealism and pragmatism and tradition and modernity."[25] One may add to this that these clashes of modernity with tradition, manifest in the mother-daughter relation in "Why a Robin?," in turn are produced by the cultural forces emanating from a neoliberal state.[26] Further, Sahi also connects this middle-class existence of female characters to their submission to gender-defined roles and tradition, particularly through marriage. The mother's submission to motherhood in "Why a Robin?" becomes neoliberal India's way of making rigid previously loosely defined gender roles. It is as if the middle-class, in the moment of its emergence, is also creating the "new woman" (to use Oza's term) who is put under the diktat of patriarchy to counter cultural anxieties that the "new woman" brings. Deshpande's longer works also recount similar discourses; Rajeshwari Sunder Rajan, while examining *That Long Silence*, describes the character Jaya's writing "as an act of self-expression and liberation in so far as it leads to self-knowledge, truth-telling and catharsis, but it never becomes the communication, the entry into community, the contribution to a public discourse that its publication has resulted in its actually being."[27] For Rajan, forms of expression in the text and its relation to a community appear antithetical. My contention, however, lies elsewhere: the textual expression of isolation is also one that is born out of Deshpande's context in neoliberal India. The act of self-expression in the stories I examine is embedded in a profound experience of isolation. This isolation is both existential and social, and it engages with the mind and body of Deshpande's characters. Narratives like "Why a Robin?" highlight the crisis that a textual production of social isolation engenders.

I claim that the lack of community that is often stated as Deshpande's failure is actually an aesthetic. It is an aesthetic that writes the woman, that combines the existential despair of the modern Indian woman, particularly the beauty insecurities of this Indian woman that isolate her body. It can therefore be argued that the existential crisis in Deshpande's oeuvre is somatically produced through the body and its body image. The following discussions only cement this claim further.

Anxieties of the Aging Body in "The First Lady"

Deshpande's short stories render themselves to a material production of body image in several ways. Foremost, the familiar is presented as an existential moment of bodily crisis—for example, in the aging body. The First Lady in the story of the same name embodies this crisis perfectly. The First Lady is a nomenclature borrowed from American ideas of polity and carries with it ideas of the power, grace, and femininity the president's wife is supposed to symbolize. Within Deshpande's narrative, however, the eponymous character ironically bemoans this role instead. She thinks bitterly, "Why don't they tell me frankly that I am old and ugly and fat . . ." This is followed by the reader's comprehension that: "Ugly . . . the word gave her a pang even as she thought of it. But then, she consoled herself, what can you expect when you're nearly seventy?"[28] Predictably, in "The First Lady," notions of the desirable body, the ugly, and the beautiful prefigure as thematic concerns. This is presented along with the concepts of beauty and clothing, which in turn become womanly performances on display. That these beauty norms powerfully impact the seventy years of the First Lady's life is testament to their long-lasting and strong hegemonic roots—they have been internalized by many women, including Deshpande's protagonist. Ageist pejoratives with regard to feminine beauty are brought into the picture: perfect beauty is young, while the First Lady is not. Yet, her elegance is described in the language of the performative. And to her, liberty is the antithesis of such bodily performance. One learns this as the First Lady expresses her wish to be "sitting in my own room, with my feet tucked under me, and my bra, that is constricting me so, off, my petticoat strings loosened, my false teeth out."[29] Clearly, the narrator here is critiquing the beauty restrictions placed on her through her desire to cast them off. And later, the performance for normative beauty is played out in the language of a "pose" as she ruminates how "'the first lady' the magazines called her." She subsequently exclaims, "God! If only they knew what an effort it was to keep up the *pose* all the time!"[30]

At times in the narrative, this patriarchal diktat of performing prettified femininity is put forth as a cause of anxiety. Once such episode is when the protagonist examines her reflection in the mirror at the commencement of the short story. This *reflection*—thought and image—becomes a symbol of both a reflection of the self and a crisis of the community. The First Lady ruminates about not just her existential crisis but also the crises of the society at large. She laments, "It's not that I am old and fat; it's what I have become, what we have *all* become."[31] This moment coincides with her foray into politics and comments upon the condition of the country after independence. The husband politician and the difference in the political milieu are presented as a cause for crisis: the fiery speech he presents on the eve of the country's independence in an unnamed neighborhood resonates with Nehruvian trysts with destiny. This impromptu, passionate speech before a sparse crowd is juxtaposed with the subsequent parties and socializing and the fake performances encoded therein. These performances reek of patriarchal and conservative supremacy where the woman is reduced to an object of beauty, grace, and a particular brand of passive femininity. And she becomes entirely disposable if she lacks feminine charms, specifically beauty.

The rejection of the beauty norm in this short story is linked to the rejection of the socialite pose, where dictates of conventional beauty govern disposability. The protagonist's rejection of such a pose, linked to body image, also acts as a rejection of the socialite political imaginary that India appears to be in the story. The First Lady states outright:

> Gracious and dignified! No, I'm only a tired, old woman, whose feet swell up to grotesque proportions after an evening like this. . . . When they know, and I know, that the real trouble is I'm too fat. And I'm fat because I eat too much. And I eat too much because I'm bored. And I'm bored because there's no truth in anything we do or say.[32]

The protagonist's boredom here can also be read as a reflection of the political ennui surrounding her. It is one that tries to reject the patriarchal construction of the feminine through a foregrounding of the veneer behind the performance of the political. The feminine becomes another such performance.

Stories like "The First Lady" demonstrate that norms of beauty and propriety dictate body image by negating the visceral aspect of the body. In Deshpande's short stories, however, the visceral materiality of the body is written as a distinct marker of textual and literary spaces. Spaces, words, and narratives about the body become important. The body is, so to say, narrated into being. Aspects of childbirth, menstruation, and other literary encounters with the female body seem important to Deshpande and are described by her in detail. In fact, the impulse toward visceral femininity is also evident in Deshpande's own memoir. The episode of the game of dice in *The Mahabharata*, where a menstruating Draupadi is dragged by the hair and humiliated and then responds with a very logical argument, is put forth with provocative empathy in the writer's memoir. One finds in it the impact it has had on a young Deshpande. She writes:

> There was something about that passage that fired all of us, something about Draupadi's arguments filled us with excitement. We loved it. I remember one of the girls asking for the meaning of "rajasvala." In the passage, Draupadi says, "Aham rajasvala asmi." What did she mean? Our teacher, a man who did not even raise his eyes to look at us, hemmed and hawed, and finally said, using a euphemism, that it meant "I am menstruating." What an instant connection this made between us and that heroine of ancient times![33]

Here the beauty norm and the realm of the Derridean *propre* are rejected in favor of a more carnivalesque viscerality, one that has with it the subversive potential to craft a healthier body image. In the light of these debates, it may be claimed that Deshpande does not "astutely avoi[d] politics and its games,"[34] but by narrating the body, the female body, and body image in psychosocial terms, she profoundly engages with them.

Furthermore, the materiality of the body in Deshpande's oeuvre is presented in the aesthetic zone through the violence it is vulnerable to. The female body and the violent encounters it can possibly witness are a ritual of power that needs to be shown as significant. Women's bodies are otherwise understood as representable in clean, glamorous, and "proper" images—such as the images in beauty magazines—without underlining the pain and suffering they can possibly experience. The violence made possible on the female body is narrated in Deshpande through the figurative. This narrativization helps in creating a distinct literary space for female body image to emerge. Deshpande's writing, it is aptly claimed, uses a "language of silence" and carves a story out of the things communicated through silence or not communicated at all.[35] And it is this silence that speaks louder than words in her characters. In the subsequent analysis of marital rape in "The Intrusion," for instance, it is this aesthetic of silence—underlined with responses of the body—that plays a crucial role.

Dreams of Beauty and Realities of Violence in "The Intrusion"

"The Intrusion" is another short story by Deshpande where female frustrations involving a woman's bodily experiences owing to her husband's intrusions are addressed. "I was conscious of an unreasonable pang of irritation against him," the narrator discloses in the very beginning.[36] She follows this with a desire to protest but is unable to articulate her emotions. The narrator protagonist instead writes, "I wanted to protest, to release my arm from his constricting grip."[37] This silence (about the husband's grip in particular and husband in general) is figured in the novel as ominous and as a lack of agency on the part of the narrator. When the narrator describes how she felt revulsion, it is in the form of a visceral aesthetic as well. The narrator-wife writes, "and I felt suddenly, completely sickened."[38] Even later in the narrative, she describes a bodily response and reveals how she "was conscious of a slight headache, a faint nausea" in her husband's presence.[39] In "The Intrusion," therefore, the violence on the body and the literary aesthetic of violence are shown as merged through the representation of rape. Marital rape here is described in terms of the movement of the sea, with the observation that while the violence of which the sea is capable can be borne, the violence on the body cannot. The narrator describes how her husband's "movements had the same rhythm, the same violence as the movements of the sea" and later states that she "could have borne the battering of the sea better, for that would hurt but not humiliate like this."[40] In the plot of "The Intrusion," the sexual violation that the protagonist's body undergoes is linked to the imagery of violence in the literary space created. Yet the aspect that rape is not just violence on the body but also a form of torturous humiliation and a specific ritual of power gets highlighted.

In addition, "The Intrusion" appears to be narrating one's personal truth: the narrator survivor wishes to elaborate on the events as if to speak truth to power. More importantly, the linking of the text with the body prefigures, in this short story, the incident when the woman narrator of the story reads a book of erotica. The images of erotic beauty born out of male fantasies that the newly married narrator reads about are presented as the ideal she must emulate and thus feels tortured by. She confesses, "Quietly I went to my bed and lay down, trying to sleep, while countless erotic *images* came out of the pages of the book I had read and tortured my distracted mind."[41] The narrator internalizes norms of beauty through such patriarchal images of beauty, in this case through the book of erotica, and is traumatized by it.

The sexual violence encountered by Deshpande's woman narrator in "The Intrusion" may hereafter be read as a critique of the beauty myth, which as an ideal unleashes enormous violence on women across the world.[42] The images of beauty or sexual desirability that are used against women, according to Naomi Wolf, make them internalize body dissatisfaction. The erotic book Deshpande's narrator protagonist reads seems to portray patriarchal notions of sexuality, which she then internalizes. As a result, she labels herself frigid. One knows that representation of women in heteropatriarchy is posited as a binary, and since the narrator does not deem herself to be one of those sexually glamorized *other women*, she concludes that she must be frigid. The narrator-protagonist writes, "There was something furtive about the place, . . . which made me feel that the men who came here did so with 'other women'— girls, perhaps, bold-faced and experienced, who would laugh and chat with the men."[43] This ideological internalization of frigidity, and of body image dissatisfaction, acts as a powerful tool for patriarchy to justify men's domination over their wives and even marital rape.

Be that as it may, Deshpande's book of short stories becomes a different book, one where the aesthetics vary from the patriarchal erotica that the woman narrator of "The Intrusion" reads. Notably, the violence of the rape itself is not aestheticized to the point of sensationalism in Deshpande's story, however. Instead, bodily encounters with sexual violence are implicitly embodied in a textual space to articulate the truth hidden behind (patriarchal) power and women's internalized self-denigration. Significantly, Deshpande creates an aesthetic, understated yet strong textual space in which she narrates violence as a material reality, making it a compelling aspect of literary writing of the female body.

Shashi Deshpande and the Literary Aesthetic of the Female Body

Female body image in literary spaces as an *image* of the body and as the literary representation of the body is effectuated powerfully by Deshpande. Thus, her narratives contain a strong impulse to narrate the female body into being. This is a process of becoming whereby the body is narrated and therefore a space is carved out for the body. No doubt this space of the female body that gets written is distinctly bourgeois, domestic, and interiorized and responds to the sociocultural forces governing neoliberal India. Yet, in each of Deshpande's stories discussed here are narratives of middle-class Indian women and their domestic and private lives, as well as the psychic depths of the interior mind. Those outside these depths and spaces—the nonbourgeois, the nondomestic, the non-Savarna (those opposing caste hierarchies)—by implication are perhaps absent in this schema. Arguably, these social groups are conspicuously absent in order for the text to carve out a textual space for the middle-class woman. This, it is true, might have to do with the formulaic feminist writing carried out "under western eyes,"[44] as well as because of the politics of worldwide publishing, all of which apply to Deshpande's position as a neoliberal Indian writer.

Simran Chadha examines how, in Deshpande's oeuvre, the text introduces and carves out "a homogenised species called the Bharatiya Nari made popular by Indian cinema to a more nuanced and specific urban middle-class Indian educated woman."[45] Chadha here is correct that regional specificities, for instance, are not acknowledged. A universalization of bourgeois concerns also takes place in Deshpande's writing. However, it is my opinion that this aspect of homogenization also needs to be contextualized. The bourgeois feminism of Deshpande can be attributed to the neoliberalist impulse to privatize India during the 1990s. While neoliberalism has already been discussed, the notion that it brought with it a particular brand of neoliberal feminism remains unexplored. Here, literary history (through Deshpande's oeuvre) and economic history (the liberalization, privatization, and globalization regime of the 1990s) seem fused together. In this context, Maitreyi Chaudhuri remarks how gender and economics have always gone hand in hand. As a Marxist feminist, Chaudhuri explains how gendered images of modernity, through advertising, for instance, rely "on the argument that they can be fruitfully understood as the rhetoric of India's project of globalization."[46] For Chaudhuri, it is the economic realization of policy that impacts gender and affects notions of femininity, masculinity, and beyond. This argument, I insist, can be extended further to suggest that literary production is part of the economic discourse that impacts gender in a certain way that Chaudhuri insists. Implications of this dynamic appear powerfully in the literary narratives of Deshpande—and, as demonstrated here, in her crafting of the female body.

In fact, the impact of economics on gender identity and female body image is found in Deshpande's own memoir as well. In *Listen to Me*, Deshpande's own associations of modernity and sophistication with a commodity culture that creates particular notions of gender are clearly articulated. The author writes, "I can remember taking a step from this towards sophistication, when we made our first acquaintance with nail polish, which was then known as Cutex."[47] It is thus clear how the advent of neoliberalism and economics leaves its trace on literature and literary musings. Since literature is impacted by the politics of the publishing market, and since norms of beauty also follow the standards of this market, one finds its profound impact on a writer like Deshpande and her bourgeois female characters.

Much has been written on India's recast culture, tradition, and women in the colonial period and how the woman question became a site for redefining what constituted India's tradition and culture.[48] Following this, India's neoliberal culture is in a process of flux and has directly impacted its women, "real and imagined," actual as well as literary.[49] In addition, there has been a move to interiority and a *domestication* of the neoliberal project wherein its commercial forces have made a powerful entry within domestic spaces. Not surprisingly, then, neoliberalism becomes both privatized and domesticized in its literary avatar. However, instead of looking at this moment of interiority and privatization as failure, as Rajan does,[50] the effort in this chapter has been to recognize the intertwined existentialist crisis that such interiority exercises on the body. This intertwining creates a textual space for the body as a crisis of bourgeois subjectivity. It is as if this textual space, such as in Deshpande's case, is contesting the impact and the glamour of the neoliberal norms of body image and therefore the neoliberal production of femininity by incorporating it as a crisis. This complex admixture of forces greatly shaped the imaginative trajectories of Deshpande's literary corpus where the female body appears as a poignant site of cultural engraving.

Appropriately, the neoliberal recasting of femininity is substantiated in the textual space of Deshpande's works as a crisis. For example, in "The First Lady," this crisis is depicted as the female character gazes at the mirror. The female gaze (*mirrored* by the woman author) of the First Lady is shown to be caught up in a moment of anxiety. Deshpande recounts how the First Lady "moved heavily towards the dressing-table and sat before it, staring anxiously at her reflection."[51] Here not only is the woman looking at her reflection, she is *anxious* about her mirrored self. The trope of the woman gazing at her reflection, though old, is replete with symbolism that is both patriarchal and antipatriarchal. If one considers the line quoted previous, the woman is looking not only at the image of her body but also at her body image. In the given lines, she is also staring anxiously at what is reflected in the mirror. The anxiety that the woman's reflection creates gives truth to the feminist claim that women's bodies are policed and regulated in patriarchy through the beauty myth that causes negative body perceptions among women.[52] However, this line contours another concern as well. The image of the woman anxious about her reflection also figuratively creates a sense of anxiety about women's representation, both in life and in literature. The woman anxiously gazing at the mirror symbolizes the anxiety of what women as subjects under a neoliberal regime are in the process of *becoming*.

Conclusion

In conclusion, I argue that a patriarchal norm of beauty informs a script for reading the female body. Deshpande's short stories, especially the ones examined here, render themselves to a material production of body image in four ways. First, the familiar is presented as an existential moment of bodily crisis—for example, in the aging body. Notions of the desirable body, the ugly, and the beautiful prefigure here as thematic concerns. Second, the visceral materiality of the body is written as a distinct marker of textual and literary space. Spaces, words, and narratives about the body become important. The body is, so to speak, narrated into being. Third, violence on the body is narrated through the figurative, creating a distinct literary space for female body image to emerge. This is what occurs in the narration of the marital rape in "The Intrusion," for instance. Rape and its representation are shown to break away from a patriarchal display of sensationalism.[53] Fourth, this space of the feminine body within the literary imagination is distinctly bourgeois, domestic, and interiorized. Deshpande's bourgeois feminism here can be attributed to the neoliberal impulse to privatize that began with the 1990s in India. Yet, instead of looking at this moment of interiority and privatization entirely as a failure or an oppressive project, the effort in this chapter has been to recognize the intertwined existentialist crisis that neoliberal tendencies create on the female body. This intertwining creates a textual space for the body as a crisis of bourgeois subjectivity that Shashi Deshpande's fiction provocatively captures.

NOTES

1. Body image issues among women have been recurrently highlighted by many contemporary scholars. See Cash, *Encyclopaedia of Body Image*; Cash and Smolak, *Body Image*; and Grogan, *Body Image*.

2. See Bartky, *Femininity and Domination*, 39.

3. See Eisenhower, "Farewell Address."

4. See more about caste and gendered violence in India in Dutt, *Coming Out as Dalit*.

5. See Tiggeman, "Sociocultural Perspectives," 12–20, emphasis added.

6. See the take of psychologists on this issue in Shroff and Thompson, "Body Image."

7. Shroff and Thompson, 198.

8. What Western theorists have established on this issue is also largely true for the Indian context. See Levine and Chapman, "Media Influences on Body Image," 101.

9. See discussions by Gopal, *The Indian English Novel*, and Mehrotra, *A History of Indian Literature*.

10. This is Mohanty's central argument and also Sunder Rajan's take on Deshpande. See Mohanty, "Under Western Eyes"; Mohanty, "Under Western Eyes' Revisited"; and Rajan, "The Heroine's Progress."

11. Cash and Smolak, *Body Image*; Bartky, *Femininity and Domination*; Bordo, *Unbearable Weight*; Grogan, *Body Image*; Orbach, *Hunger Strike*; and Brownmiller, *Femininity*.

12. Oza, *The Making*, 11.

13. Dutta, "MacDonaldization of Gender."

14. See Chaudhuri, "Gender and Advertisements."

15. See Sangari and Vaid, *Recasting Women*.

16. These include, but are not limited to, the writer's thematic preoccupations with ideal femininity and its challenges, the textual production of writing in a global language like English, and her contextual placement in nascent neoliberal India.

17. Oza, *The Making*.

18. Oza, 18.

19. Deshpande, *The Intrusion and Other Stories*, "Why a Robin."

20. Deshpande.

21. Here I refer to Wolf's famous and in many ways universal take on the cruel injunctions of the body beautiful on women's lives and minds. Wolf, *The Beauty Myth*.

22. Recent theorists have added to the debate on female beauty and body image started by third-wave feminists like Naomi Wolf and Susan Bordo. See Liebelt, Böllinger, and Vierke, *Beauty and the Norm*.

23. To understand how appearance and identity are intertwined for social acceptability, see Butler, *Bodies That Matter*.

24. Sahi, "Human Relationship," 167.

25. Sahi, 186.

26. It must be remembered that the publication of these stories was in 1993, and the neoliberalization of India in the 1990s was not a mere coincidence.

27. Rajan, "The Heroine's Progress," 227.

28. Deshpande, *The Intrusion*, "The First Lady."

29. Deshpande.

30. Deshpande, emphasis added.

31. Deshpande, emphasis added.

32. Deshpande.

33. Deshpande, *Listen to Me*, 37–38.

34. Some of the charges leveled against Deshpande include these. See Bande, "A Woman's Dilemmas."

35. Chakravarty, *Indian Literature*, 188.

36. Deshpande, *The Intrusion*, "The Intrusion."

37. Deshpande.

38. Deshpande.

39. Deshpande.

40. Deshpande.

41. Deshpande, emphasis added.

42. Wolf, *The Beauty Myth*.

43. Deshpande, *The Intrusion*, "The Intrusion."

44. Mohanty, "Under Western Eyes," 61.

45. Chadha, "IE Fiction," 241.

46. Chaudhuri, "Gender and Advertisements," 373.

47. Deshpande, *Listen to Me*, 16.

48. Sangari and Vaid, "Recasting Women"; Chaudhuri, "Gender and Advertisements."

49. Rajan, *Real and Imagined Women*, 123.

50. Rajan.

51. Deshpande, *The Intrusion*, "The First Lady."

52. Wolf, *The Beauty Myth*.

53. Higgins and Silver, *Rape and Representation*. Higgins and Silver present a feminist analysis of the patriarchal uses of the aestheticization of rape and the erasure of the feminine voice within artistic representation.

BIBLIOGRAPHY

Bande, Usha. "A Woman's Dilemmas." *Indian Literature* 53, no. 5 (2009): 244–246. Available at https://www.jstor.org/stable/23340249.

Bartky, Sandra Lee. *Femininity and Domination: Studies in the Phenomenology of Oppression*. New York: Routledge, 1990.

Bordo, Susan. *Unbearable Weight: Feminism, Western Culture, and the Body*. Berkeley, CA: University of California Press, 1993.

Brownmiller, Susan. *Femininity*. Newburyport, MA: Open Road Media, 1984.

Butler, Judith. *Bodies That Matter: On the Discursive Limits of "Sex."* London: Routledge, 1993.

Cash, Thomas S., ed. *Encyclopaedia of Body Image and Human Appearance*. London: Academic Press, 2012.

Cash, Thomas F., and Linda Smolak, eds. *Body Image: A Handbook of Science, Practice and Prevention*. 2nd ed. New York: Guilford Press, 2011.

Chadha, Simran. "IE Fiction and the Urban, Middle-Class English-Educated Woman." *Indian Literature* 56, no. 4 (2012): 241–243. Available at https://www.jstor.org/stable/23345943.

Chakravarty, Radha. *Indian Literature* 49, no. 6 (2005): 188–191. Available at http://www.jstor.org/stable/23346313.

Chaudhuri, Maitreyi. 2001. "Gender and Advertisements: The Rhetoric of Globalisation." *Women's Studies International Forum* 24, no. 3 and 4 (2001): 373–385. Available at https://doi.org/10.1016/S0277-5395(01)00174-1.

Deshpande, Shashi. *The Intrusion and Other Stories*. Kindle ed. New Delhi: Penguin Random House India Private Limited, 2018.

———. *Listen to Me*. Chennai: Context, 2018.

Dutt, Yashica. *Coming Out as Dalit*. New Delhi: Aleph Book, 2019.

Dutta, Anindita. "MacDonaldization of Gender in Urban India: A Tentative Exploration." *Gender, Technology and Development* 9, no. 1 (2005): 125–135. Available at https://doi.org/10.1177/097185240500900107.

Eisenhower, Dwight D. "Farewell Address." Speech, 1961. The Avalon Project. Lillian Goldman Law Library, Yale Law School. Available at https://avalon.law.yale.edu/20th_century/eisenhower001.asp.

Gopal, Priyamvada. *The Indian English Novel: Nation, History, and Narration*. Oxford: Oxford University Press, 2010.

Grogan, Sarah. *Body Image: Understanding Body Dissatisfaction in Men, Women and Children*. 3rd ed. Abingdon, UK: Routledge, 2017.

Higgins, Lynn A., and Brenda R. Silver. *Rape and Representation*. New York: Columbia University Press, 1991.

Levine, Michael P., and Kelsey Chapman. "Media Influences on Body Image." In *Body Image: A Handbook of Science, Practice and Prevention*, edited by Thomas F. Cash and Linda Smolak, 2nd ed., 101–109. New York: Guilford Press, 2011.

Liebelt, Claudia, Sarah Böllinger, and Ulf Vierke. 2019. *Beauty and the Norm: Debating Standardization in Bodily Appearance*. Cham, Switzerland: Palgrave Macmillan, 2019.

McKinley, Nita Mary. "Feminist Perspectives on Body Image." In *Body Image: A Handbook of Science, Practice and Prevention*, edited by Thomas F. Cash and Linda Smolak, 2nd ed., 48–55. New York: Guilford Press, 2011.

Mehrotra, Arvind Krishna. *A History of Indian Literature in English*. New York: Columbia University Press, 2003.

Mohanty, Chandra Talpade. "Under Western Eyes: Feminist Scholarship and Colonial Discourses." *Feminist Review* 30 (1988): 61–88. Available at https://doi.org/10.1057/fr.1988.42.

———. "'Under Western Eyes' Revisited: Feminist Solidarity through Anticapitalist Struggles." *Signs* 28, no. 2 (2003): 499–535. Available at https://doi.org/doi:10.1086/342914.

Murnen, Sarah K. "Gender and Body Images." In *Body Image: A Handbook of Science, Practice and Prevention*, edited by Thomas F. Cash and Linda Smolak, 2nd ed., 173–179. New York: Guilford Press, 2011.

Orbach, Susie. *Hunger Strike: The Anorectic's Struggle as a Metaphor for Our Age*. London: Penguin, 1993.

Oza, Rupal. *The Making of Neoliberal India*. New York: Routledge, 2006.

Rajan, Rajeshwari Sunder. "The Heroine's Progress in Recent Women's Fiction." *India International Center Quarterly* 23, no. 3/4 (1996): 222–238. Available at https://www.jstor.org/stable/23004621.

———. *Real and Imagined Women: Gender, Culture and Postcolonialism*. London: Routledge, 1993.

Sahi, Rashmi. "Human Relationship in the Novels of Shashi Deshpande." *Indian Literature* 42, no. 4 (1998): 167–170. Available at https://www.jstor.org/stable/23341922.

Sangari, Kumkum, and Sudesh Vaid. *Recasting Women: Essays in Colonial History*. New Delhi: Zubaan, 1984.

Shroff, Hemal, and J. Kevin Thompson. "Body Image and Eating Disturbance in India: Media and Interpersonal Influences." *International Journal of Eating Disorders* 35, no. 2 (2004): 198–203. Available at https://doi.org/10.1002/eat.10229.

Tiggeman, Marika. "Sociocultural Perspectives on Human Appearance and Body Image." In *Body Image: A Handbook of Science, Practice and Prevention*, edited by Thomas F. Cash and Linda Smolak, 2nd ed., 12–20. New York: Guilford Press, 2011.

Wolf, Naomi. *The Beauty Myth: How Images of Beauty Are Used against Women*. London: Vintage Books, 2015.

4

Manjula Padmanabhan and the Question of Problematizing Embodied Gender Identity

A Reading of Getting There

SHUBHRA RAY

Introduction

Getting There—Manjula Padmanabhan's memoir—is about a transitional phase in her life and chronicles a literal as well as a metaphorical journey, in the course of which she mentally traverses a considerable distance from being a woman with zero self-image who goes on a diet to become somebody else, the failure of it, and finally moving on to being a person who is comfortable in her own skin, all in the face of the complete breakdown of her social networks of safety, which had been the hallmark of her existence until then.[1] Padmanabhan's reaction to what it means to be a woman is one of the themes of *Getting There*, which, in concentrating on her life between 1977 and 1978, offers insight into the struggles of being her twenty-something self. She is biologically a woman and is heterosexually oriented but refuses to accept the cultural connotations of her gender identity—be it the primacy accorded to reproduction or the devaluation or celebration of womanhood. In this chapter, keeping in mind the unique trajectory that Padmanabhan's self-expression takes and her process of accepting her body and her self-image, I read *Getting There* to explore the complicated relation the author has with her embodied identity and the individualistic manner in which she comes to terms with it, sometimes going against hegemonic body perceptions and at other times incorporating divergent feminist insights into the matter.

It is pertinent to note here that Padmanabhan's struggles of adhering to perceived norms of beauty and gendered social acceptance in the 1970s resonate profoundly with the current Indian cultural milieu, where the emphasis on the normativity of a certain kind of feminine appearance—nonadherence with which often leads to body shaming—has aggravated the anxiety and insecurity of Indian women regarding their bodies in a manner that was hitherto unprecedented. Forces of liberalization and globalization after the 1990s and the Internet revolution leading to ubiquitous social media influence have left women vulnerable to greater surveillance and subject to prescribed injunctions regarding (un)desirable components of their embodied subjectivity. It has been argued that following the institution of neoliberal politics of reform and India's encounter with global capital, there has been a reification of national and gender identities to establish "India's independence and cultural difference from the West," following the perceived loss of sovereignty of the state, in the face of the onslaught of transnational market forces (Oza 2006, 2). The displacement of public anxiety "associated with a globalizing nation-state" onto "women's bodies" has had far-reaching consequences, where, in legal arbitrations to determine what constitutes the global and the local, "women's sexual autonomy [is often] designated as foreign to 'Indian culture'" (24, 3).

This has led to a paradoxical situation over the past few decades where, on the one hand, the Indian woman has been portrayed as an informed consumer with the power of choice (Oza 2006, 18; Kullrich 2019, 270–271; Chakravarty 2011, 407), and on the other, she has been subjected to greater scrutiny and surveillance, in the name of protection of national interests. Globalization has led not only to a burgeoning beauty and fitness industry but also to a proliferation of prejudice associated with overweight bodies. "Slim-body ideals" and "fat-stigmatizing beliefs" have led to pejorative moral connotations associated with obesity, in addition to its medical and economic concerns, even in societies where earlier "fat bodies were reported to be valued or viewed neutrally" (Brewis et al. 2011, 269). The ideal of skeletal thinness—epitomized in skinny models and through "digital modification" of body size—underscores the impossibility of it being attained and leads to dissatisfaction with the body, in perpetuity (Tiggemann 2011, 13).

The situation is even more complicated in India not only on account of the prevalence of similar cultural discourses on embodiment but also because of the excessive importance associated with fair skin, especially by the indices of the matrimonial market. Even though colonization is generally held as culpable for the national obsession with fairness, it has been shown that this preoccupation and the "cultural capital" associated with it have both "precolonial and transnational" antecedents (Vaid 2009, 148, 151). This, in turn, has been built upon by market forces following liberalization, evident in skyrocketing sales of fairness creams and bleaches (Kullrich 2019, 254–255, 269; Chakravarty 2011, 407). In the case of fair-skin preference, as well, there has been a documented rise in its mention in matrimonial advertisements after the 1980s for the Indian diaspora in the United States. As Jyotsna Vaid establishes, it "is currently close to 25 percent for second generation Indian-American women" (2009, 165). Despite the presence of movements like Dark Is Beautiful since 2009 in India—with its tagline, "Celebrating 1.3 billion shades of Indian"—the idea of inclusivity, as far as beauty is concerned, remains an unrealized project. Rather, as matrimonial columns make clear, "the ideology that fair is beautiful continues to exert a pernicious effect on the self-esteem of women who have been repeatedly reminded that if they are not the former, they cannot be the latter" (165). Padmanabhan's struggles with her supposed inadequacies based on her appearance, her association of her excess weight with a lack of moral fiber, and her vehement opposition to the idea of marriage because of what it entails for the woman—all point to the relevance that her memoir continues to have for contemporary Indian women as they struggle with prescriptive indictments from various quarters regarding their embodied subjectivity.

Between Struggles and Resistances: The Body Beautiful in *Getting There*

Right at the outset of *Getting There*, Padmanabhan talks about her intention of going on a diet. While her family and her boyfriend, Prashant, are skeptical about the need for it, she is adamant about it even while not sharing with them the immediate impetus behind her decision. With the progression of the narrative, it becomes clear that while there is no sudden thrust behind her desire to change her appearance, it is a culmination of the social narratives she had internalized regarding the fate of a woman and the part that perceived beauty plays in the entire process. She discloses that she had felt inadequate all her life—ugly and a misfit—and had grown up believing that romantic love was not her due because of her looks:

> I believed that love was a condition too fine and rare to be within my reach. I had come to this conclusion because of my appearance. All the stories I had read as a child stressed the importance of beauty in a heroine's life. A girl might make her entrance in a story looking deformed or wretched but by the end of it, if she was a heroine, she would miraculously become beautiful. . . .
>
> Yet when I, as the main character in my own life's story, stared into mirrors, I did not see a heroine's face. Quite obviously, then, I would not enjoy a heroine's fate. (61)

One learns that Padmanabhan had been "pudgy and cross-eyed" as a child and "grew frontally" at fifteen and sixteen, all the while struggling with pimples and frizzy hair, and grew to look like an "inverted pear" (2000, 61). As the narrator-protagonist, she had a curious relationship with her body and was shocked to see herself naked for the first time at the age of seventeen—a conscious acknowledgment of the fact that her body had not been a part of her psyche. As she states, it was a surprise for her to see that she "looked remarkably similar" to the other figures that she had seen growing up, even though she did not have the "ideal statistics" (149). She then goes on to analyze that "On the one hand it could mean that I didn't see myself objectified in the way of nude models in photographs. On the other hand, it could mean that I had been wandering around for years in a body that I inhabited as if it were a fancy dress belonging to someone else" (149). While a keen awareness of not possessing an ideal female body marks much of her growing-up years, the unrequited love that she feels for her teacher when she is sixteen further reinforces her negative self-image. Following the mortification of this one-sided affair—with teenage emotions compounding her angst—she made up her mind to die at thirty to avoid the humiliations that awaited her. By the time Padmanabhan was in her twenties and had met her boyfriend, Prashant, she still held on to these views rather than outgrowing them. She had also created a self-professed artist's persona, with her hallmark sartorial code being bright clingy clothes, lots of jewelry, and loud makeup.

What is interesting, however, is that despite her low self-esteem, the narrator-protagonist remains adamant about not conforming to the expected norms of her well-heeled, conservative family. Padmanabhan's close relations are well settled in their respective professions—her father is a retired bureaucrat of the Indian Foreign Service; her brother, Raghu, is a successful corporate lawyer; and her sister, Radha, is a doctor based in the United States. Both her siblings are married and have children—or in other words, are decent, "respectable" people by the standards of middle-class Indian society (50). Within such a class, marriage remains the high watermark in women's lives despite their professional qualifications and achievements. For Padmanabhan, marriage is an anathema because she believes that one of its main purposes is ensuring the survival of the human species. And, as she makes it clear to the psychiatrist at the diet clinic, she has had a deep-seated antipathy toward children ever since her own childhood. Cooking, housekeeping, nurturing—activities that are integrally connected with the conception of the female/feminine role—do not find favor with her. Ironic and scathing comments about marriage and the supposed fulfillment that women derive from domesticity abound in *Getting There*. Notable among them is the incisive remark that she makes about the projection of women in the context of domesticity and marriage, by the late 1970s American media, and her inability to belong to such a milieu:

> Soap operas like *All My Children* and *General Hospital* were a revelation, commerce and monotheism in passionate embrace. The one true god was represented by the loyal, omniscient, omnipotent and dandruff-free husband. Heaven was a place of static-free carpets and gleaming glassware . . . [and women were] priestesses in the church of good housekeeping. . . . Where in this dish-washer-friendly universe in which a woman's worth was assessed by the sparkle on her cutlery, did I fit? Nowhere. (191–192)

Against this background of sanctification of a certain construct of marriage as *natural* law, Padmanabhan, with her profession as a freelance illustrator/cartoonist and her boyfriend whom she does not want to marry, stands out as an aberration. There is immense pressure on her to get married, not only from her family—especially her brother, Raghu—but also from strangers like Kamala, who consider her behavior "un-Indian" through a nonresident Indian's gaze in America (166). In fact, Raghu views her as a weed—he is unhappy with their parents for having allowed her to grow up "unruly and unchecked"—but would have preferred if she had not been allowed "to sprout" at all (47). He terms her behavior and lifestyle as akin to "roaming the streets like a bitch on heat" (50).

While Padmanabhan does not respond verbally to the insults and accusations coming her way, preferring to remain silent rather than getting into a conflict, she continues to live life on her own terms. It gives her immense pleasure to "flaunt" Prashant as a boyfriend, "not a spouse," as that confirms her view of herself as a "counter-culture revolutionary, living outside the confines of social acceptance" (41). It is against this complicated context of a woman who chooses to live on the margins of social respectability, who reacts to the injunctions placed on her impetuously and yet struggles with an abysmally low self-worth, that Padmanabhan's desire to diet needs to be placed. As the narrator-protagonist, she is aware that these disciplinary regimes of feminine embodiment have far-reaching implications because they keep women preoccupied with their looks, and yet she embarks on one of her own accord, because of the associations of despair and despondency with obesity in her mind.

For instance, after being berated by her roommate, Sujaya, for not being responsible and considerate, her immediate reaction is not a denial of these accusations but to engage in an extensive act of self-criticism, where her behavioral and mental traits become linked with her physical characteristics. Obesity becomes not only a repugnant bodily trait but also the explanation of several other undesirable qualities in her, including her inability to succeed in her professional life. As Padmanabhan states wryly:

> Yes, I was inconsiderate, incompetent and self-indulgent. I was fat after all. I was a person whose intake of fuel exceeded her body's needs. Fat stored as unsightly wads of flesh was the physical expression of greed, black money in the body's fuel-efficient economy. Time is also a kind of fuel except that it can't be stored. Nevertheless, I could feel the rolls of unused hours lying in unsightly heaps across the sagging belly of my days. (45–46)

The yearning to slim down, by inversion, becomes an aspiration for a different life altogether:

> The desire to lose weight, I now saw, with my teaspoon poised above the plain white dome of the egg, was really about becoming someone else. Someone efficient and industrious who could fight minotaurs before breakfast, someone who would succeed in her quest to be financially independent and ideologically pure, someone whose illustrations would soon be the talk of the town, be sought after and valued. Someone of consequence, taste and wit. (31)

It is true that becoming attractive is one of the reasons behind Padmanabhan's decision to diet, and yet due to the complications that were a part of her mental makeup, it would be rather simplistic to reduce her aspiration to merely that. Before going on to discuss how the body or the act of dieting assume an individualistic signification for Padmanabhan, this chapter examines the cultural connotations of female embodiment and femininity in India and their variegated and loaded usage.

At one level, all human beings are embodied creatures—the body is a biological reality and therefore biological differences between men and women lead to differences in female and male embodiment. The body, however, is also a discursive and cultural construct, being situated in and articulated through various sociological, anthropological, historical, medical, and religious discourses. This kind of approach depicts the fallacy of the position that male superiority and female inferiority are based on *essential* attributes. Biological differences become the basis of a cultural devaluation and stigmatization of the female body. The very fact that women are able, in general, to menstruate and give birth is enough to suggest a potentially dangerous volatility that marks the female body as out of control. In contrast to the apparent self-containment of the male body, the female body demands attention and invites regulation. In short, women are just their bodies in ways that men are not, biologically destined to an inferior status in all spheres that privilege rationality. At the same time, however, that women are seen as more wholly embodied, the boundaries of their embodiment are never fixed and secure. As the devalued process of reproduction makes clear, women themselves are, in the conventional masculinist imagination, not simply inferior beings whose civil and social subordination are both inevitable and justified but objects of fear and repulsion.

The expression of this kind of anxiety about women's bodies has taken different forms in different cultures—ranging from the celebration of certain bodily aspects to severe repression— and almost all of them are inextricably connected with the idea of the need for regulating female sexuality. In the Indian context, especially within the Hindu religious tradition, the worship of women as the embodiment of Shakti, the strictures associated with the lives of widows, and the stigma associated with menstruation are all manifestations of the aforementioned idea in various forms.[2]

Such ideas have been widely pervasive and have negatively affected the way women think about their bodies and subsequently their selves. The social constructionist position—a critique of biological essentialism—"emphasizes the view that a woman experiences her body, sexuality and feminine identity as a social being located in a particular cultural setting with its dominant values and norms" (Thapan 1997, 5). Power is exercised in such a manner by dominant cultural tropes and structures that the ideas propagated become internalized, a case in point being the pervasiveness of the idea of the negative status of the feminine body among women themselves. Michel Foucault's influence has been pivotal in the development of this theoretical perspective, especially his exposition of the workings of power in social processes. Foucault's (1977, 1990) analysis of the discursive body examines its capacity to be manipulated, molded, constructed, and changed and explains the manner in which the body is invested with different and changing forms of power.

The female body is manipulated and control is exercised over it not only through the discourses of history, religion, or medicine but also through the discourse of ideal feminine beauty, an attainment of which results in the objectification of female bodies. Sandra Lee Bartky and Susan Bordo have critiqued the setting up of normatives that expect social conformity, foremost among them being diet and exercise regimes that are designed to attain the ideal female body size and configuration. With the proliferation of images of women with beautiful faces and figures in print as well as electronic media, "the homogenizing, elusive ideal of femininity" (Bordo 1993, 166) has become pervasive. The sheer number of articles in women's magazines describing how to dress, apply makeup, and present an appropriate image attest to the fact that there are codes of behavior to which women must subscribe (Greer 1999, 19–32). Moreover, Bordo maintains that through the disciplines of diet, makeup, and dress, women are rendered less socially "oriented" and more focused on "self-modification" (1993, 166). The disciplinary regimes of femininity have political implications because they keep women attending to their appearance, looks, bodily comportment, and image rather than to the material and political circumstances of their lives. What is more dangerous is that these kind of attainments, such as perfect skin, body, or hair, have increasingly come to be projected as integrally connected with the liberation or freedom of women—a matter of choice and not a constriction. The internalization of representations of the female body by women thus becomes fundamental to the formation of the feminine identity. Women not only internalize the *overarching gaze* of the patriarchal/male connoisseur but also learn to consider their bodies from a position of alterity. As Bartky puts it, "women live their bodies as seen by another, by an anonymous patriarchal other" (1988, 72).

The obese woman attracts greater opprobrium even within the gender-skewed universe of adherence to normative body ideals (Levine and Chapman 2011, 102) because of the association of the "'fat' female body as a site of disease and failure" (Murray 2008, 7). Given that obesity has acquired the status of a medical epidemic, the overweight woman is subjected to immense social discrimination, with control being exercised through various disciplinary discourses. Hence, what Murray claims of Western culture is true for many urbanized Indian settings as well:

> Living "fat" and female in contemporary Western culture is difficult: we are socialised to be ashamed of our bodies, and to engage in endless processes to alter them, to improve them, to normalise them. "Fat" women are regarded as sexually unattractive, unclean, unhealthy, unintelligent, and unwilling to change. In light of this, "fat" women are treated with suspicion, and often with unabashed hatred and disgust. (5)

Critiques of this marginalization in the West have taken the route of "philosophical analysis" in search of a more "productive, enabling, embodied politics" (181), as well as fat activism—which, in contradistinction to the body positivity movement, aims to foreground the lived experiences of fat bodies—as a way of engaging with the widespread dehumanization that marks their reception (Cooper 2016).

While the negative role of media-propagated images in engendering body image dissatisfaction cannot but be underlined, it has been recognized that "the relation between sociocultural influences and body image" can only be "complex, multiply determined, and bidirectional" with the extent to which an individual internalizes these injunctions, being "moderated by levels of self-esteem (or autonomy), such that women with high self-esteem will be less influenced by societal ideals and pressures" (Tiggemann 2011, 18, 14). Further, the protests against biological reductionism and discursive control have assumed various forms. What is significant is that in consonance with the emphasis on heterogeneity, plurality, and the celebration of differences that has been a hallmark of feminist movements in recent decades, the theorization regarding feminine embodiment has intensified not with the hope of "recovering an authentic female body unburdened of patriarchal assumptions, but in the full acknowledgement of the multiple and fluid possibilities of differential embodiment" (Price and Shildrick 1999, 12).

Ahead of Her Times: Padmanabhan and the Discourse of Female Embodiment

Padmanabhan's memoir precedes these theoretical concerns and activism(s), but it demonstrates acute sensitivity to these issues and movements. This becomes evident at her discomfort on realizing the extent of the unconscious conditioning regarding women's bodies that dominates our thoughts: it hits the narrator-protagonist particularly hard when she is shown nude slides of women who had successfully lost weight at the doctor's clinic where she enrolls. Padmanabhan bemoans, "We are so used to seeing pictures of female nudes who look like articulated dolls that when we see the more typical sort of woman without her clothes on, she looks diseased" (10). This also makes her ruminate on how a debilitating exercise like dieting had been normalized by the multibillion-dollar weight-loss industry and what the business was promising to sell:

> Being thin was only one element in a complex mutation. Being sexually available was another. Being obviously wealthy was a third. Poor people, for instance, are thin but that doesn't make them beautiful. It is the slenderness of those who choose not to be fat that is admired. . . . The glamour is essential. Without it a thin person merely looks poor. (22–23)

Naturally, the practice of photographing patients naked, chronicling the various stages of their weight loss, leaves the narrator-protagonist feeling unsettled:

> The prize patient, whose success had seemed so spectacular when she was clothed, looked like a sack of loose brown skin standing to attention when she was naked. . . . Her appearance suggested that she came

from a deeply conservative, traditional background, yet here she was, posing naked for a doctor's unsympathetic camera. . . . Had she agreed out of her own volition or had her husband forced her? Was he in the room with her when these pictures were taken? Had she agreed because she imagined she was making a valuable contribution to a study of weight loss amongst obese Third World women? Had she been convinced on the grounds that she represented that rarest of breeds, a Third World woman who was yet rich enough to have weight to lose? (10–11)

When Padmanabhan is asked to do the same, she refuses. For her, it was akin to relinquishing control over her body, which she was not comfortable doing, despite its so-called unattractiveness and undesirability.

The process of dieting has intended consequences—she loses five kilos in a matter of weeks—as well as unintended ones. During the diet, and especially during her psychological evaluation with Mrs. Prasad, she is hard-pressed to examine her purported ideologies and belief systems. While she had looked down upon her fellow patients at the clinic initially—using epithets like the "latest little dumpling in human form," among others, to describe them—she soon realizes that it was sheer hypocrisy on her part:

I wanted to sneer at this apparition in female form sitting across the room from me, but Mrs. Prasad's probing enquiry had shown me that my so-called ideology was thinner than a coat of nail varnish. . . . Would I, too, be weighed down with gold, my face obscured under a mask of rouge and mascara? *No!* I thought, *Never!* But I had told Mrs. Prasad that I was fond of jewellery and make-up, and here I was, sitting in the same diet clinic as that other woman, seeking the same goal. How different were we really? It humbled me to realize, not much. (23)

Further, on account of the conflicts that this process engenders with her close relations, especially her brother and her boyfriend, and her chance encounter with Piet—a Dutch man who had come on a spiritual quest to India and was staying at the same paying-guest accommodation as she was—Padmanabhan is forced to reevaluate her life in a way she had never done before.

Padmanabhan had been in a comfortable relationship with Prashant for over two years but had desisted from calling it love, as she did not believe that romantic love was her due. The term was further problematic for Padmanabhan because of its inevitable culmination in marriage, an institution she was not ready to engage with. As she puts it, "The price of romance for heterosexuals is the enormous expenditure of energy and resources which goes into getting married and raising children. If I wasn't willing to pay the price, then in a real sense, I couldn't afford to be 'in love'" (235). Her relationship with Prashant had been sustained as he had been accommodative of her quirks of not wanting to get married and her plan to die at thirty, which the other romantic interests in her life had not been supportive of. Prashant is described as an "exceptionally good natured" person and one who comes close to being as "perfect [a] boyfriend as anyone could hope to find" (60). And yet, after meeting Piet, the narrator-protagonist decides to sleep with him, even while being in a relationship with Prashant.

This emotional transgression becomes a deliberate move on Padmanabhan's part in her quest for supreme confidence and control over life, which she found projected by Piet. In attempting to emulate Piet, she realized that her notions of sexual fidelity—and, for that matter, everything else—were based on shaky foundations. Padmanabhan hereafter tours America with Prashant but feels guilty all the while for going to bed with Piet in a calculated way—and, in order to stop discussing uncomfortable issues, she continues to eat compulsively, leading to a complete failure of her diet. No doubt it had given her pleasure to flaunt Prashant in the face of familial and social disapproval, but the fact remained that their relationship was based on a reaction. And Padmanabhan soon realizes that Prashant, especially after he wants to be married, is very much a part of the entire setup that she feels suffocated by and wants to escape.

The showdown with her brother, on the other hand, makes it clear to her that the luxuries she had taken for granted—her sister paying for her trip to America, her relatives being there to bail her out from tricky situations, and the social spaces of South Bombay that she has access to—are beyond her capability to create for herself. The price for these safety nets was, of course, the expected pursuit of preconceived notions of her class-based gender normativity, escaping which would require more than mere impetuous reactions:

> I had grown up wearing the jewelled harnesses that kept me and others like me in our place within our social class. The only time we ever felt our bondage was when we strained against it in the direction of some forbidden pleasure. But eating frugally had apparently caused a change to take place. I had shed weight, literally as well metaphorically. I was now loose within the harness . . . [and] planned to slip it off altogether. (115–116)

Obviously, such transformations are easier said than done since they entail "reversing the habits of self-indulgence and passivity" (116) that she had grown up with and getting out of her comfort zone. Nevertheless, Padmanabhan's acquaintance with Piet leads her to yearn for the kind of control and complete responsibility he enjoys—that is, his ability to unmake and remake his life in ways she had never experienced before. After her encounter with Piet, she imagines that she can explore the unexplored if she can be on a sojourn, free of all known faces:

> If I had never seen it, I may not have permitted myself to feel the dissatisfactions of my life as keenly as I did. But a door had opened and the confines of my life had been flooded with the light of other possibilities. . . .
>
> The basic idea involved taking a vacation from my life. It couldn't be just a change from the city I was living in or the people I knew. What I needed was to step outside the skin of known associations that the people I knew had of me and to walk around a bit like that, skinless, waiting to see who I became and what would happen when there were no constraints upon me. (79)

The rest of the narrative of *Getting There* is about the various adventures she has in America, Germany, and Holland and the insights she gains. Padmanabhan's transitional state of being, where she feels "like a yolk sac of ideas, not yet solidified into the substance of a living being" (118), makes her look at her dieting from a different perspective altogether, in contradistinction to the gender-defined codes associated with it earlier. She eventually realizes that her attempt at dieting was not the outcome of a desire to match a fictitious ideal. Rather, it had been an attempt to flee her corporeality, in keeping with her death wish: she had felt trapped in her body, and the diet became her way of being liberated. She explains, "I began to feel the way a caged animal might, when it sees that the door to its prison has been left ajar: a soaring sense of my ability to flee the Dungeon of my Body" (27). It is in this light that her provocative statement, "Maybe the desire to diet was actually a yearning to step out of the suit of soft, fat filled female clothes that I had been given to wear at birth" (236), needs to be viewed. Her wish for a different body therefore is not the aspiration for a "superior" masculine identity, since for her the masculine role is equally if not more debilitating, and she claims, "I could easily imagine how violently unhappy I would have been if I had been a man" (236). For the author, her physicality needs to be understood without subscribing to accepted notions of gender, even if she deliberately leaves nebulous the articulation of her gender aspiration.

Conclusion: Body Acceptance in *Getting There*

Padmanabhan has been categorical in stating—in later interviews as well as her personal correspondence—that she rarely thinks of herself as a "woman"[3] and also that she does not like writing from the perspective of the typical victim because she does not believe that chains are a natural condition of womanhood.[4] But, as opposed to her confident assertions later, in *Getting There*, her autobiographical persona is at a crossroads. Here Padmanabhan is caught at an intersection of various fragmented identities: the tension arises out of a conflict between the pressure to accept the cultural connotations of gender and an attempt to go beyond it, with her conception of what it normatively means to be a woman and her aversion to it playing a vital part in the rejection of her gendered identity. As she puts it:

> I had considered feminism a peg on which to hang my resistance to romance, but Mrs. Prasad, the psychiatrist, with her droopy eyelids and her laser vision, had cut through my flabby rhetoric: she had shown me that much of what I did and said was an expression of non-acceptance of a woman's destiny. . . . I did not rejoice in any but the most superficial aspects of being female. (235)

The complications and ethical dilemmas also arise because of the peculiar traits of her personality. As Padmanabhan states, "So much of what I had considered problems were instead a kind of frenzy brought by my ignorance about reality. A more robust person would not have encountered even a tenth of my difficulties, or having encountered them would not have interpreted them as difficulties at all" (329).

To conclude, the diet in *Getting There* becomes a catalyst in engendering certain necessary changes in the writer's self-perception. The initial success and eventual failure of it compelled her to come to terms with certain unpalatable truths about herself and the abominable way she had treated people in her life because of her impulsiveness. It also becomes clear to her that her diet was not an attempt to attain a preordained body ideal; rather, it was a reiteration and extension of her death wish. Padmanabhan also realizes that she had attached extraordinary importance to other people's thoughts and had sought approval unconsciously, even when defying accepted norms. In reacting to certain gender-based strictures impetuously, she had not really thought them through, and when confronted with difficulties, she had taken an escape route rather than facing them. However, in Amsterdam, bereft of all physical and social security, especially after surviving an asthma attack in a dark, cold, dilapidated building, while inhabiting a fat and lonely body, "unbathed, penniless, ticketless and visa-free in a foreign country," (330) the narrator-protagonist realizes that she can be mentally self-sufficient and does not need the crutches of social approval to lead her life. This proves to be a moment of both self-realization and liberation for Padmanabhan as she declares:

But I was no longer concerned about what he or anyone else thought.

I felt like a ship whose decks had finally been cleared of all its extra passengers. Not just the more recent ones like Piet or Japp but all the earlier ones as well, including many people whom I loved and many others whom I didn't . . . there were so many people trying to wrest control of my ship, telling me which ports I should visit and what cargo I should load, when to speed up and how to drop anchor. Some did it gently and others were rough, but in the end, they were all just passengers. Whereas I was the captain, I was the ship and I was all my crew. (329)

For Padmanabhan, then, *getting there* becomes less about a geographical location and more about a metaphorical journey of reaching an elevated mental state: of intense self-realization, equanimity, and unconditional acceptance of her mind and her body.

NOTES

1. In this chapter, my reading of *Getting There* is based on the edition that came out in 2000 (London: Picador). In a personal interview conducted in 2004, Padmanabhan had shared that she had intended her work as a memoir but her editor at Picador was apprehensive marketing it as such, because the autobiography of a relatively unknown woman writer would be hard to sell. It was much safer for Picador to bracket *Getting There* within the categories of travel writing or novel. This kind of a forced categorization as well as the "lowbrow" way in which it was marketed affected the reception of the book (Manjula Padmanabhan, interview with author, April 29, 2004). *Getting There* was also excised of a large portion of the Holland section of the text by Mary Mount, her editor at Picador, which, if retained, would have rendered the work "solemn and philosophical" (Padmanabhan, interview). Indeed, as a look at the manuscript of the unedited Holland section of the text revealed—*Getting There* is divided into four such sections: Bombay, New York, Munich, and Holland—it was marked by philosophical musings and greater self-reflexivity (Padmanabhan, *Getting There*, manuscript, 159–204). A new edition of *Getting There* (Gurugram: Hachette India, 2020) addresses these concerns: a note by the author mentions that it is indeed a memoir, and the Holland section has additional chapters. However, for the purposes of this chapter, which focuses on her engagement with issues of diet and body image, these revisions do not influence the reading—which is why I have continued to use the 2000 edition.

2. Padmanabhan (1996, 205–229) has a poignant story, "Stains," on the issue of menstruation and the negativity associated with it. "Stains" can be read as the story of a young African American woman, Sarah, coming to terms with her body. She grows up believing that she is perfectly comfortable with it, but it takes an act of rudeness from her boyfriend's mother, Mrs. Kumar, to make her realize how far from the truth that is. When she is "made to feel small" for "staining" the sheets, and treated like an "invalid," she realizes that somewhere in her mind she has internalized the guilt and negativity associated with menstruation. But Mrs. Kumar's behavior and her own subsequent sense of alien-

ation make her question her conditioning and attempt to come to terms with it as something natural. She begins by paying conscious attention to it and refuses to accept the silence around it. Menstruation stops being dark, dirty, or something to be guilty about for Sarah when she learns to accept her bodily process for what it is—a bodily process.

3. In an interview with Sheela Reddy (2002), Padmanabhan says, "I rarely think of myself as a woman . . . my struggle in the early days was a straightforward essential one: how to be a human being who writes/draws and how to support myself financially." The statement was made in response to Reddy's query regarding how the epithet "woman writer" is viewed by women who write.

4. Manjula Padmanabhan, "Re: On Reading *Getting There*," e-mail to author, April 18, 2004.

REFERENCES

Bartky, Sandra L. 1988. "Foucault, Femininity, and the Modernization of Patriarchal Power." In *Feminism and Foucault: Reflections on Resistance*, edited by Irene Diamond and Lee Quinby, 61–86. Boston, MA: Northeastern University Press.

Bordo, Susan. 1993. "The Body and the Reproduction of Femininity." In *Unbearable Weight: Feminism, Western Culture and the Body*, 165–184. Berkeley: University of California Press.

Brewis, Alexandra A., Amber Wutich, Ashlan Falletta-Cowden, and Isa Rodriguez-Soto. 2011. *Current Anthropology* 52, no. 2 (April): 269–276. Available at http://www.jstor.org/stable/10.1086/659309.

Chakravarty, Sumita S. 2011. "Reflections on the Body Beautiful in Indian Popular Culture." *Social Research: An International Quarterly* 78, no. 2 (Summer): 395–416.

Cooper, Charlotte. 2016. *Fat Activism: A Radical Social Movement*. Bristol, UK: HammerOn Press.

Foucault, Michel. 1977. *Discipline and Punish: Birth of the Prison*. Translated by Alan Sheridan. New York: Pantheon.

———. 1990. *The History of Sexuality*. Vol. 1, *An Introduction*. Translated by Robert Hurley. New York: Vintage.

Greer, Germaine. 1999. *The Whole Woman*. New York: Alfred Knopf.

Kullrich, Nina. 2019. "'In This Country, Beauty Is Defined by Fairness of Skin.' Skin Colour Politics and Social Stratification in India." In *Beauty and the Norm: Debating Standardization in Bodily Appearance*, edited by Claudia Liebelt, Sarah Böllinger, and Ulf Vierke, 245–281. Cham, Switzerland: Palgrave Macmillan.

Levine, Michael P., and Kelsey Chapman. 2011. "Media Influences on Body Image." In *Body Image: A Handbook of Science, Practice, and Prevention*, edited by Thomas F. Cash and Linda Smolak, 2nd ed., 101–109. New York: Guilford Press.

Murray, Samantha. 2008. *The "Fat" Female Body*. Basingstoke, UK: Palgrave Macmillan.

Oza, Rupal. 2006. *The Making of Neoliberal India: Nationalism, Gender, and the Paradoxes of Globalization*. New York: Routledge.

Padmanabhan, Manjula. 1996. "Stains." In *Hot Death, Cold Soup*, 205–229. New Delhi: Kali for Women.

———. 2000. *Getting There*. London: Picador.

Price, Janet, and Margrit Shildrick. 1999. "Openings on the Body: A Critical Introduction." In *Feminist Theory and the Body: A Reader*, edited by Janet Price and Margrit Shildrick, 1–14. Edinburgh: Edinburgh University Press.

Reddy, Sheela. 2002. "Rooms, Views." *Outlook*, October 28.

Thapan, Meenakshi, ed. 1997. *Embodiment: Essays on Gender and Identity.* New Delhi: Oxford University Press.

Tiggemann, Marika. 2011. "Sociocultural Perspectives on Human Appearance and Body Image." In *Body Image: A Handbook of Science, Practice, and Prevention*, edited by Thomas F. Cash and Linda Smolak, 2nd ed., 12–19. New York: Guilford Press.

Vaid, Jyotsna. 2009. "Fair Enough? Color and the Commodification of Self in Indian Matrimonials." In *Shades of Difference: Why Skin Color Matters*, edited by Evelyn Nakano Glenn, 148–165. Stanford, CA: Stanford University Press.

5

Future Forms

Female Body Image in Indian Dystopian Fiction

Annika Taneja

Introduction

The female body in contemporary India is a site of myriad discourses, debates, and negotiations. Since the nation first gained independence in 1947, the watchful eyes protecting Bharat Mata ("Mother India") have expected women and girls across the country to conform to a series of external forces that have attempted to shape their bodies and identities in more ways than one. In their article entitled "Body, Gender and Sexuality: Politics of Being and Belonging," Sabala and Meena Gopal trace the history of the complex and often conflicting ways the female body has been socially constructed in modern India:

> Women have always received contradictory messages about their bodies. When expedient, it is glorified by ideal images of goddesses; honour of the nation/family/community and sometimes the same body is projected as shameful, embarrassing, vexatious, fearful and disgusting. . . . Through this comes the distorted picture of how we view our bodies. (Sabala and Gopal 2010, 44)

This "distorted picture," in turn, affects women's relationships with their own bodies. It does not simply impact their aesthetic choices but may also impact what they do, how they speak, where they go, and so forth. As Sabala and Gopal further explain, both the female body and female body image have become subservient to the anxieties of a patriarchal worldview that situates its culture and its morality in its women. From school uniforms and religious diktats to popular culture and mass media, there is a constant stream of information delivered to women on how they should appear. In other words, "the public gaze whether male or female is always speculating on women's bodies, how next she will clothe her body or adorn it or maintain it or manipulate it or shape it to perfection" (Sabala and Gopal, 47–48). But what impact does such speculation have on women in India today, and how will it affect the generations of women to follow?

This chapter seeks an answer to this question in three works of science fiction (SF) by three Indian women writers: *Harvest* (1997) by Manjula Padmanabhan, *The Lesson* (2015) by Sowmya Rajendran, and *Clone* (2019) by Priya Sarukkai Chabria. It begins with a discussion on body image, both within academia and within India specifically; it then critically analyses female body image in the fictional futures of the three texts in order to unearth the social, cultural, and technological roots of women's body aesthetics in present-day India. Finally, it examines the plotline of the three texts together to establish the significance of Indian women who dare to imagine and author alternative forms of embodiment while questioning and subverting the discourses that dominate female body image today.

Female Corporeality and the Body Image Discourse

The term "body image" has been notoriously nebulous since it first appeared in Paul Schilder's seminal volume *The Image and Appearance of the Human Body* (1935). In 1988, building upon Schilder's definition, Peter David Slade defined body image as "the picture we have in our minds of the size, shape and form of our bodies; and to our feelings concerning these characteristics and our constituent body parts" (Slade 1988, 20). By the 1990s, the definition of the term expanded to include both body image as well its affective attributes—that is, an individual's relationship with her body image—and the focus of body image research markedly shifted toward those with "disturbed" or faulty models of self-perception, such as women with eating disorders or body dysmorphia.

In this manner, the body came to be considered a blank canvas upon which external forces exerted influence in order to make it adhere to certain aesthetic ideals. However, in the process, the several identities that mark the human body prior to its encounter with the external world were erased, with all bodies being considered equally susceptible to all influences. It was not until feminist theorists such as Judith Butler, Susan Bordo, and Elizabeth Grosz intervened that such a "neutral"—but, in fact, white, capitalistic, and patriarchal—conception of body image was challenged and corrected, shifting "the body from a purely biological form to an historical construction and medium of social control" (Bordo, 182). Sylvia K. Blood's *Body Work: The Social Construction of Women's Body Image* traces the history of these feminist discourses, which challenged psychology's reduction of "women's distressing experiences of their bodies" to simply "a concern about physical appearance" (2005, 3). Blood uses the social constructionist approach to question the assumption that "'truths' about individuals and their behavior can be obtained through the correct use of scientific methods," advocating instead for an approach that allows space for investigating not simply disturbed body images but the norms and ideals that create them in the first place (29). The work of these feminist theorists thus shifted women's dissatisfaction with their bodies from an individual experience to a broader systemic issue.

Body Image Scholarship in India

Though Eurocentric ideas of female beauty might dominate the Indian imagination today, it is safe to assume that the Indian subcontinent's long and complex history would have given rise to multiple ideals and manifestations of the female body over time. There is, however, scarce documentation of such ideals, and most can only be gleaned retrospectively by examining the representation of "desirable" women in the art, literature, and culture of the past.[1]

The formal study of body image in India is a relatively recent phenomenon. For a while it was believed that body image issues were a "Western" problem, and few studies were conducted around the subject in the subcontinent. But with the entry of a global visual and media culture into the Indian consciousness—first as a result of economic liberalization and then as a result of the Internet boom—there has been an increase in research that examines prevailing beauty standards and their impact on women in different parts of India. There are now many emerging studies on body image "disturbances," such as eating disorders, colorism, and diet culture, especially among young women and college students. Some examples include research conducted by Chakraborty and De (2014), Rajagopalan and Shejwal (2014), and Kapadia (2009). However, there remains a relative paucity of research on the larger forces and discourses that construct such body image ideals in contemporary India in the first place.[2]

Informed by such debates and concerns, this chapter—by examining female characters from works of Indian SF—aims to move beyond perceptual models of body image to speculate how the sociocultural ideals that render Indian women uncomfortable in their own skin today may operate in the future. It seeks to interrogate how—and, indeed, if—these long-held embodiment ideals might impact Indian women's attitudes toward their bodies and how they present themselves in the years to come. Finally, it asks if it is indeed possible to unplug the Indian female body from dominant ideals of gender and sexuality and imagine it afresh. The three works of Indian feminist SF under consideration—written by women and featuring female protagonists—use the genre of dystopia to introduce precisely such fresh female forms into the consciousness of their readers.[3] In *The Lesson*, Sowmya Rajendran extrapolates the patriarchal ideologies of contemporary Indian society into a living nightmare. Manjula Padmanabhan's award-winning play, *Harvest*, written in 1997 and set in a then-unknown 2010, examines the idea of bodily autonomy in a world where the sale of organs is legalized. Finally, Priya Sarukkai Chabria's *Clone*, set in an autocratic, posthuman world, locates the seeds of revolution in one clone's act of self-determination. In each of the texts, it is a woman whose disobedient and divergent body becomes the site of a power struggle between societal norms and individual desires and irrevocably alters how she perceives and ultimately uses her body. Read together, the three texts offer their readers a continuum of resistance to both patriarchal and techno-industrial constructions of women's bodies and body image(s), embodying the uniquely transformative potential of feminist SF, which scholars of the genre have long championed.[4]

Object of Beauty/Object of Consumption: Female Bodies and Body Image in *The Lesson*

The first text under consideration, Sowmya Rajendran's *The Lesson*, is a dystopian satire that foregrounds the structural and systemic violence Indian women face every day. The central narrative device—in which the names of all characters and institutions are their social or institutional roles—spotlights this violence by literalizing it. The Capital City of Rajendran's undated future is ruled over by the President of an organization known as the Adjustment Bureau. The "adjustment" in question is the transition of human subjects into an orderly, "normal" existence as hetero-patriarchal families, and all legal and political institutions of this regime are dedicated to ensuring that the fabric of society remains unsullied. There is literally a Moral Police Force that patrols the city, keeping a sharp eye out for any occurrences of premarital sex, revealing clothing, or other "deviant" behaviors. At the lowest rung of this force are people like the Dupatta Inspector, whose job is to monitor the attire of college-going girls and ensure no cleavage is visible. At the top of the order is a man simply known as the Rapist, whose job is to teach disobedient women the proverbial and titular lesson. His victims, we are told, have committed a range of offences—"They wore short clothes. They went to pubs. They smoked. They were not virgins. They had several boyfriends" (Rajendran 2015, 2)—all of which are unpardonable.

On the one hand, then, the women of this world are expected to follow a strict set of rules and become—as well as raise—obedient wives, mothers, and daughters. They must not display cleavage, wear too much makeup, or be seen with a man who is not their husband. But on the other hand, these women must also live up to the prevailing standards of beauty, attractiveness, and desirability and in doing so remain enslaved to certain oppressive codes of thought and behavior. For example, Rajendran's protagonist—a woman known simply as the Second Daughter—is pressured to fix her looks and join the heterosexual institution of marriage as soon as she comes of age, as the narrative reveals:

> They started off by sending them [the girl's family] reminders in the form of well-meaning uncles and aunts who patted her head kindly and asked her when she was getting married and if she knew how to make sabudana vada. She could lose some weight, straighten her hair, go to a good photo studio and take some portrait pictures—had she done any of that? (23)

The Second Daughter is constantly reminded that she must fashion her body and her body image well within the sanctions of society—she must be shapely but not too skinny or overweight, she must be attractive and confident but not sexy or obscene, she must have long tresses but no body hair, and so forth. Throughout the course of the novel, the metric of beauty and morality keeps shifting arbitrarily, moving along a sliding scale of what is acceptable and what is punishable. The Dupatta Inspector, for example, makes up many of his rules as he goes along. Across each page, however, the underlying belief remains the same—that any unbridled expression of female freedom and sexuality is antithetical to the larger interest of society.

Rajendran's language echoes the familiar lexicons of body shaming, moral policing, and gender-based violence that continue to shape women's relationships with their bodies in contemporary India, where morality and sexuality (or, indeed, any kind of uninhibited self-expression) are often seen as mutually exclusive domains. These politics of perception define and redefine what sociologist Smitha Radhakrishnan terms as "respectable femininity," under which an Indian woman is conditioned to locate herself "within the terms of a larger Indian cultural landscape that she feels unable to escape" (2009, 206). This larger landscape is dictated by the tenuous and constantly shifting middle ground between traditional Indian mores and morals and modern, transnational neoliberalism, with its emphasis on beauty and material success. The female body becomes the site of such negotiation, and a woman's body image becomes inextricably implicated in this double bind. Radhakrishnan elaborates:

The important thread running through all the narratives women articulate is the idea of the "right" amount of freedom—not as much as abroad, where your sexual and leisure behaviors might indicate a rejection of family, and thus, a loss of culture, but not so little freedom as in either an earlier Indian generation, or, implicitly, those less educated and less well-off Indians who cannot exercise these freedoms. (207)

For most of the novel, the unnamed protagonist is struggling to toe this fine line. She tries to be educated, but not too educated. She tries to be attractive, but not too attractive. When she first goes to the Bureau to file a divorce, she makes sure to don the uniform of the good Indian woman: a "blue starched sari she'd carefully picked out" (Rajendran 2015, 152). But after her plea for divorce from her abusive husband is rejected, she rebels, and the President assigns her to the Rapist. To buy herself time, she feigns a pregnancy, hoping that if the President believes that she is a mother-to-be, he will no longer consider her a threat. We are told the following:

The Rapist did not know if he should proceed with the President's request in the altered circumstances. It could be the problem had resolved itself. The woman would go back to being a dutiful wife for the sake of the child. (94)

But her plan backfires, and once her ruse is discovered, the Council decides to televise her rape as a lesson to society at large. Because it is still illegal to publicly disclose the identity of a rape victim, the Council instructs the Second Daughter to wear a mask during her rape. On the day of the broadcast, however, she decides to remove her mask on live TV, revealing her face to millions of viewers. Through this simple act, she reclaims her individual body from the state yet also opens herself up to an extremely unjust and unprecedented judgment. The President had hoped to punish her by equating her body with who she is and using the sexually violent act of rape to break her spirit. But instead of allowing such a conflation of her vagina and her will, the Second Daughter embraces her "deviant" body and mind, demanding her right to exist outside the holy trinity of daughter, wife, and mother, despite the many risks.

Rajendran chooses to end her novel at this point, denying both the audience within and the audience without (her readers) the comfort of closure. This refusal leaves the reader in a lurch, as once the Second Daughter successfully strips herself of the lexicon of the world Rajendran has built, her future literally becomes a blank page. Her new, "monstrous" body exists outside the language of Capital City, its Moral Police, and its judgmental gaze.

This "filling in" of the blank, however, becomes a crucial, material intervention in deliberating what constitutes a "desirable" versus an "undesirable" female body in contemporary India. The women reading the novel are forced to reckon with the difficult questions the narrative raises: Is the female body desirable and beautiful only as long as it is also pliable and palatable to a patriarchal and capitalistic agenda? Can the forces that control how Indian women look be divorced from the forces that control how they live? In her landmark work on female body image, *The Beauty Myth*, Naomi Wolf asserts that beauty is "always actually prescribing behavior and not appearance" (Wolf [1991] 2002, 43). By exposing the many misogynistic ideas that circulate through Indian society in the guise of aesthetic ideals, Rajendran compels her reader to reexamine her own environment and how its yet-unwritten rules impact her own relationship with her body.

Poverty, Technology, and Female Body Image in *Harvest*

In Manjula Padmanabhan's play, *Harvest*, the forces that control the protagonist's life are both traditional and technological. Written in 1997 and set in 2010, it tells the story of Jaya, a woman who lives in a slum in Mumbai with her husband, Om, and his family. After being laid off from his job, Om decides to sell his body to InterPlanta Services, a corporation that connects Third World organ donors with First World patients. From the beginning, the narrative makes a malignant connection between the bodies of the developed world and those of the "developing" world, intensifying this nightmarish scenario as its Indian protagonists increasingly suffer under the Eurocentric dictates of an ideal body image. As the play progresses, InterPlanta's technology drives itself deeper and deeper into the family's lives until the border between the human and the machine are completely dissolved.

Padmanabhan has described her play as an exploration of "what it means to have agency over one's personal container" (2017, xiii), or one's body. But for most of the play, Jaya appears to lack precisely that. From the moment we meet her, her relationship with her body is controlled by the punishingly patriarchal setup of her marital home. Her husband, Om, rejects her sexually by never expressing any desire to be intimate, leading her to seek comfort in the arms of her brother-in-law, Jeetu. But while it is evident that Jeetu does care for Jaya, he cannot offer her more than a few stolen moments of pleasure. Her mother-in-law, meanwhile, is unwilling to acknowledge any flaws in her son and blames Jaya for the absence of a grandchild. For most of the play, she verbally abuses and body shames Jaya, comparing her to various animals and declaring her to be inferior.

Living in crippling poverty, Jaya is left to languish both physically and emotionally, with any instance of being liked and desired reduced to a distant dream. The breaking point is when her husband signs his body over to InterPlanta, taking away her only chance at having a child and curbing her desire to experience motherhood. Once InterPlanta enters the picture, Jaya, her husband, and her mother-in-law lose the right to their bodies: they must now live under the corporation's surveillance, eat its food, and follow its schedule. At the center of this trade is Virginia, or Ginni, the ailing, American organ receiver for whose sake Om must maintain his health. To ensure that her rules are being followed, Ginni video calls the family daily, using a device called the Contact Module, and interrogates them about their day.

The body politics of *Harvest* lies in the visual contrast between Jaya, an impoverished, brown woman from the developing world, and Ginni, who only appears on stage in the form of a hologram via the Contact Module. The latter is presented to us as the epitome of a beautiful white woman—she has fair and radiant skin, blue eyes, blonde hair, and a sweet voice. She even floats above the family like an angelic apparition, leaving them with no choice but to look up to her. On the other end of the scale is Jaya, whose beauty and youth, we are told, have faded under the hardships of her daily life:

> Thin and haggard, she looks older than her nineteen years. Her bright cotton sari has faded with repeated washing, to a meek pink. . . . She wears glass bangles, a tiny nose-ring, ear studs, a slender chain around her neck. No make-up aside from the kohl around her eyes and the red bindi on her forehead (the colour indicates she is married). (1)

Evidently, Jaya's is a world where her brown body is destined to be at the service of its white counterpart, in addition to being exploited by her own patriarchal environment. This politics of this intersection of economy, colorism, and technology run throughout Padmanabhan's play. As the scholar Radhika Parameswaran writes in her thesis on the color divide that also divides the developed and developing parts of the globe, "fairness" acts as an "[agent] of remedy, salvation, and upward mobility" in an "India that is caught up in the neoliberal rhetoric of its own transformation, from occupying marginal 'third world' status to becoming a lucrative 'emerging market' and 'rising global power'" (2015, 681). Thus, in every way, Jaya's life is in sharp contrast to Ginni's, with the former occupying an impoverished world within which poverty, colorism, body image, and gender come together to oppress her.

In the future Padmanabhan imagines, skin tones continue to color how people perceive each other and themselves, continuing South Asia's long history of color bias. Despite the fact that Ginni intends to harvest Om's organs, his mother still perceives her as a benevolent and angelic presence simply because of her fair skin and First World breeding. Significantly, this association of outer beauty with inner beauty is not limited to the world Padmanabhan creates on stage. Even before the Indian subcontinent was colonized and racial discourses came into play, colorism was a part of the vocabulary of South Asian society. Under the caste system, fairer skin tones were typically believed to be an embodiment of the "purity" and "superiority" of the Brahmins, while dark skin was believed to be a mark of the "inferiority" of lower or laboring castes.[5] This colorist social hierarchy carried over to independent India, where it was adapted to speak the language of institutions such as popular culture, the beauty industry, and the matrimonial market, to name a few, with the correlation between fair skin and a better life continuing to have a stronghold on the Indian imagination. A result of this are the many fairness creams and skin-lightening products that are sold and used in the subcontinent. The advertisements for these products often depict a darker-skinned woman struggling to get a job or a romantic match until she uses the product in question, after which all attention lands on her and she achieves everything she wants. Thus, it is not simply a question of skin tone and beauty, as the success of this colorist ideal hinges on the idea that fair skin grants access to a set of experiences and relationships that dark skin cannot. As Natasha Shevde argues in her paper "All's Fair in Love and Cream: A Cultural Case Study of Fair & Lovely in India":

> In truth, the power of [fairness creams] transcends the mere desire to look beautiful and instead embodies an Indian woman's dreams, hopes, and aspirations. While "normal" cosmetics, such as foundation creams, could provide similar results in terms of making one appear fair, the prolonged outcome of fairness derived from creams such as Fair & Lovely is the strength of the product's promise in societies like India. In sum, given that "fairness equals godliness" is ingrained in the female Indian population and that most girls are brought up believing that fair skin is their key to success (whether in their careers or personal lives), the overwhelming demand for Fair & Lovely comes as no surprise. (2008, 10)

Alongside the strong color biases that exist within the world of *Harvest*, beauty, health, and particularly hygiene also become commodities that are sold to residents of the developing world, by a white woman, in exchange for access to their bodies. In many ways, this invasive demand parallels the civilizing projects that were often undertaken to justify acts of colonization. As Srirupa Prasad writes in her book, *Cultural Politics of Hygiene in India, 1890–1940*, "The phrase 'sanitary awakening' not only referred to a state of governance within which the cause of sanitation was given a fresh lease of colonial urgency, but also to a new form of 'consciousness,' a new moral-political realization, which could bring about a very different order of social transformation and become another element of the civilizing mission" (2015, 4). Here, too, the larger end goal—harvesting the body parts of these same residents—is eclipsed by the fairness of Ginni's skin, which is read as a direct reflection of the fairness of her actions. While the specter of repayment literally hangs over Om and his family in the form of Ginni and her watchful gaze, it is off-set by the fact that she grants them access not simply to necessities such as water and shoes but to luxuries such as television and makeup. The bodies on the stage, enveloped by Ginni's world, transform into healthier and wealthier bodies, while Jeetu—who has spurned the InterPlanta way of life and con-tinues to work as a prostitute—is covered in sores, bruises, and lice. The large-ly cosmetic changes to the characters' lives (they have more material comfort but continue to live in a slum and occupy a low rung of the socioeconomic ladder) are perceived to be fundamental changes thanks to the redemptive promise of beauty Ginni symbolizes. In her 1997 edition of the play, Padma-nabhan emphasizes these transformative effects through Jaya's body, describ-ing her as a changed woman in the opening of the second act: "JAYA is sit-ting on the sofa and doing her nails. She looks overdressed, her face is heavily made-up, jewelry winking from her ears, wrists, ankles and throat" (1997, 37). The means of this transformation, of course, is the white and First World woman, Ginni, who epitomizes both an ideal body and an ideal life.

At the end of the play, however, the family are in for a rude shock: the angelic Ginni is in fact an elderly American man named Virgil, who created a female avatar in order to grow closer to Om and his family. Virgil, it is sug-gested, possesses an understanding of the colorism at work in the world of the play and uses it to his advantage. One way he gains access to these bi-ases is by listening in on all the family's conversations, which includes Om's and his mother's—and, ultimately even Jeetu's—many exaltations of Ginni. These exaltations are inextricably tied to her whiteness and her appearance. As a result, throughout the play, any critique of their benefactor put forth by Jaya is ignored and misinterpreted as an expression of her insecurity now that a more "beautiful" woman is a part of Om's life:

MA: Oh she's jealous of our Ginni-angel! Look at her face? Pinched with envy!

OM: (*contemptuously*) How little you understand of Westerners! They are not small, petty people.

JEETU: I'd never seen her, till just now! I thought she was an old wom-an! You never told me she was so—so *young*! And beautiful. Why didn't you tell me, Jaya? (Padmanabhan 2017, 66)

For Virgil/Ginni, however, the bodies of Om and his family exist only to be exploited. In the third act of the play, Virgil also reveals that his intention has not been to simply secure either Om's or Jeetu's body for himself but also to impregnate Jaya and further his bloodline—an ability the residents of the First World, we are told, have lost forever. Jaya's own opinion is of little concern to Virgil, as he believes that the material and financial wealth he can offer her in return will suffice. Her reproductive capabilities become a commodity that can be bought for a sum through the machinery of InterPlanta. To seduce her into agreeing, in the final scene Virgil appears in front of her not as a white man, but in Jeetu's body. However, by this time the stage has been emptied of Om and his mother—two powerful influences on Jaya's body and her body image. Furthermore, her suspicions about Virgil/Ginni's intentions have been confirmed, and she no longer trusts her holographic benefactor. Thus, despite Virgil's appeals and manipulations—which include a claim that he has fallen in love with her and wants to raise a child with her—Jaya is able to wrestle her body from the clutches of both Western technology and Indian patriarchy for the first time since we met her.

Read within such a framework, *Harvest* offers a strong critique of the long-standing colorism that affects Indians' assessments of their own bodies and the bodies of those around them. By the end, the illusion of the superiority of fair skin stands shattered by the material evidence of Virgil's exploitative agenda and the implosion of the traditional Indian family unit. For the first time, the audience hears Jaya's thoughts, uninterrupted by her mother-in-law. Once she destroys the Contact Module, severing Virgil's line of contact as well, Jaya sets the stage to assess her own body on her own terms—not as a brown body in contrast to a white body, but as an autonomous being with a mind of her own, free to forge her own relationship with her body.

Of Corporeal Manipulations: The Body (Un)natural and Body Image in *Clone*

While *Harvest* contrasts two versions and visions of femininity, Priya Sarukkai Chabria's *Clone* problematizes the female body in an entirely different manner: not through extreme difference, but through extreme similarity. *Clone* is a dystopian novel set in the twenty-fourth century, a time when the Indian nation-state is replaced by a geographically and demographically smaller territory known simply as the Global Community. This Community functions on a hierarchy that in turn lies at an intersection of biological and technological determinism. At the very top are the Originals, a small group of human beings who provide the genetic blueprints for the other three species—the Firehearts, the Zombies, and the Clones. Each of these artificially created species has been genetically enhanced or weakened in order to fulfill specific socioeconomic roles.

In this bleak future, the human body has been homogenized into a pop-ulation of standardized subjects in order to achieve social and economic sta-bility. Furthermore, these un-Original species are interchangeable and de-void of individuality by design. Our protagonist, Clone 14, is herself just one of a larger batch of fifty-four, all of whom are identical to their unnamed Orig-inal. Our narrator, Clone 14, describes it as follows:

> All of us wore brown size 6 ankle boots, our voices were of the same pitch, our eyes brown-black, our hair cut in pageboy style, the wid-ow's peak on our foreheads dipping exactly. (Chabria 2019, 25)

In Chabria's dystopia, the bodily standards enforced by modern humanity reach their nightmarish zenith. Clones must not simply aspire to look like their Originals, they must resemble them down to the last gene. The process of creation is artificial and technological, expunged from the bodies of wom-en and the biological process of reproduction, except when fresh Originals need to be produced. In such cases, we are told, "The colony of Originals is kept segregated for the purpose so that fresh Originals and their blueprints are available for societal betterment. Their Matings are brief and pre-select-ed to give optimum results" (6).

At its core, however, Chabria's novel is not simply a cautionary tale about technologies of cloning, it is a rejection of all technologies of similarity that attempt at crafting a homogenized body for all. The fictional erasure of bodi-ly difference and diversity in the Global Community can be read as a critique of the real and rigid standards of beauty that have circulated across cultural and national barriers as a result of neoliberal globalization as well as tech-nologies such as the Internet.[6] The latter, particularly in the form of social media, has driven the mass production and dissemination of standardized images of beauty as well as desirability for women in the twenty-first century to the point that identical ideals of beauty have formed across national and cultural barriers. For instance, American journalist Jia Tolentino (2019) coined the phrase "Instagram Face" to describe the "single, cyborgian face" that has been birthed by social media's "algorithmic tendency to flatten everything into a composite of greatest hits." The mass dissemination of photo modifi-cation technologies such as FaceTune and filters has only served to encour-age women across different ages, races, cultures, and nationalities to reimage themselves to fit the norm.[7]

Trapped in a world dictated by sameness, our protagonist, Clone 14, whose body and its image are mirrored back to her manifold in the form of the other Clones of her Original, spends the majority of the narrative trying to find a sense of self in a society that denies her any marker of individual identity, including gender. Though her Original was a female, and she possesses the same physiology, Clone 14's body itself has been regulated to a point of absolute neutrality through a pill known as The Drug, a type of hormone blocker that halts the menstrual cycle and the growth of body hair. The biological tailoring of her body, in turn, corrects Clone 14's body image—or, rather, her lack of one. She has no conception of herself beyond her Original, an "ideal form" she must not simply aspire to but faithfully and unerringly duplicate. The turning point in the novel arrives once Clone 14 starts questioning the life she has led thus far and, encouraged by other rebel Clones, ceases taking The Drug, prompting her body to mutate. She grows moles and body hair and eventually starts her period. Her nonconformist physical form, however, is a liability in the world she occupies. Desperate to hide these changes from the Community, she begins to shave to maintain the neutral, nonbinary appearance required from each Clone. The labor of conforming to the regularized norms of the Community, and the effort and maintenance it takes to be an acceptable (let alone beautiful) body, echo the myriad activities that have been normalized in our own world. In the twenty-first century, multiple industries—makeup, fitness, and fashion, to name a few—covertly or overtly body-shame women into conforming to both local and global conceptions of beauty. The anxieties created by these cultural institutions ensure that the labor of beauty and conformity becomes an essential part of women's everyday lives, as bodies that are different, deviant, or disabled carry the risk of being met with judgment, ridicule, or even violence. Naomi Wolf notes the consequences of this:

> Because "beauty" lives so deep in the psyche, where sexuality mingles with self-esteem, and since it has been usefully defined as something that is continually bestowed from the outside and can always be taken away, to tell a woman she is ugly can make her feel ugly, act ugly, and, as far as her experience is concerned, *be* ugly, in the place where feeling beautiful keeps her whole. ([1991] 2002, 36)

Within the Global Community, the consequences for nonconformity are far more dire—Clones who disobey the rules are disposed of altogether. As disobedient and, more unacceptably, different bodies, they carry the threat of destroying the tenuous social fabric of the Community altogether. A group of rebels with precisely this goal takes Clone 14 under its wing. However, her cover gets blown, and the Community leaders soon realize that she is undergoing a transformation. She is transported to the city of the Originals, where they can keep a closer eye on her. Unlike the city of the Clones, this is a world where identity is embodied through hair, makeup, and clothing—in other words, through self-presentation. Clone 14 is given a makeover and a full-length mirror, in which she sees the complete, unfragmented image of her body and, consequently, herself for the first time.

But even then, Clone 14 remains an aberration, not simply because her body is different but because she is *aware* of its differences. Over time, her perception of her body—its capabilities, its functions, its strength—has mutated and expanded as well. This transformative, and almost dangerous, potential of body image is a thread that runs throughout her journey from a laboring body to a body in labor (at the end of the novel, she is able to get pregnant). Aided by her fellow rebels, Clone 14 is finally able to escape from the watchdogs of the Community and begin asking the forbidden questions regarding what lies beneath one's flesh and form:

> What are we made of? Are we only what is seen, and known? What of the spaces of thought and emotion, and that something else that makes us human, that something else that makes us grieve with others? (Chabria 2019, 278)

This ability to reimagine and reimage one's body, differently from how society has constructed it, is a turning point that occurs in *Clone*, as well as the two other works under consideration. The climactic moment when each of the three protagonists cast off society's reading of their body as unnatural, undesirable, and untenable precipitates a resurgence and a reclamation of their physical self, as well as their identity. It is a paradox that such a moment of reckoning comes at the cusp of an uncertain future, one all three may or may not live to see. However, the incompleteness of these narratives serves a far greater purpose: making the reader try and answer what lies ahead for Indian women who dare to demand self-determination.

Conclusion

In *Metamorphoses of Science Fiction* (1979), the theorist Darko Suvin coins the term "feedback oscillation" to describe one of the central narrative devices employed by dystopian fiction—the manner in which it draws its inspiration from contemporary circumstances and exaggerates and extrapolates upon these to deliver a warning about the future. He argues that as the reader uncovers the tensions, contradictions, and failings of such dystopian worlds, she stands to discover critical strategies that apply just as seamlessly to her own (Suvin 1979, 71). When this connection comes full circle, it forms what he calls a feedback loop, allowing the reader to see her context through the lens of the text and begin recognizing the systemic issues of her own world. Thus, as literary critic Tom Moylan stresses in his discussion of Suvin's theories, it is not simply the work of dystopia, but the way that it is read, that lends the literary form its historic transformative potential. Moylan asserts:

> A refusal of an engaged, cognitive reading process risks committing discursive violence to the text and further risks the perpetuation, or at least acceptance, of that ignorance and violence, injustice and domination, that rages in the world outside the text, in that everyday life to which we all return upon turning the last page and closing the book. (2000, 25)

The three works under consideration in this chapter employ precisely such feedback loops to challenge the prevailing bodily norms of the worlds occupied by both their characters and their readers. This metatextuality manifests in the slow breakdown of the protagonists' illusions about their own bodies and the manner in which they have been trained to view themselves. The tools that these fictional women employ to deconstruct and challenge their environments offer the reader a way to decode and dismantle dominant constructions of the female body in the world she occupies. As SF theorist Marleen Barr puts it:

> SF writers who create feminist metafiction magnify institutionalized—and therefore difficult to view—examples of sexism. These writers seem to peer into metaphorical microscopes while playing at being scientists—artful practitioners of soft sciences who expand women's psyche and unearth an archaeology of new feminist knowledge. They refresh embattled feminists by using language artistically to create power fantasies and to play (sometimes vengefully) with patriarchy. (188)

By embracing newer, often unprecedented versions of their bodies, the Second Daughter, Jaya, and Clone 14 destabilize the cultural norms that form the bedrock of beauty in their respective contexts. These experiments with form transcend the boundaries of these texts and spill into the reader's reality by equipping and encouraging her to interrogate what constitutes an acceptable body in her own world. What begins as a mode of questioning carries within it the power to transform into a mode of resistance and, ultimately, a way of rewriting one's relationship with one's body. Such a transformation, according to Naomi Wolf, is at its core a form of empowerment:

> A consequence of female self-love is that the woman grows convinced of social worth. Her love for her body will be unqualified, which is the basis of female identification. If a woman loves her own body, she

doesn't grudge what other women do with theirs; if she loves female-ness, she champions its rights. ([1991] 2002, 145)

At a time when body image discourse in India remains preoccupied with conversations around weight, color, and clothing, *The Lesson*, *Harvest*, and *Clone* serve to disrobe the complex historical and social discourses that form the foundation of these aesthetic ideals and the sexism that lies at their heart. By forcing their readers to confront the consequences of a rampant culture of body policing and body shaming rooted in misogyny, they precipitate a critical reading of contemporary constructions of female body image in India, particularly the tenuous link drawn between a woman's anatomy and her autonomy. Instead of replicating patriarchal femininity rooted in deep-seated cultural ideals, the authors of the three novels deploy the trope of futuristic dystopia to envision how an Indian woman might look if she had the freedom to determine her own image—a year, a decade, or even centuries from now.

NOTES

1. For a detailed discussion, see Wujastyk (2009).

2. A notable exception is Meenakshi Thapan's (1997) article titled, "Femininity and Its Discontents: The Woman's Body in Intimate Relationships." However, it focuses on body image and shame as a tool of oppression within the domestic sphere, rather than within society as a whole. For a more detailed discussion of the same, see Thapan (2009).

3. Here, I use Lyman Tower Sargent's definition of dystopia as "a non-existent society described in considerable detail and normally located in time and space that the author intended a contemporaneous reader to view as considerably worse than the society in which that reader lived" (Sargent 1994, 9).

4. For a detailed discussion of science fiction by Indian women authors, see Kuhad (2021).

5. The precise history of colorism remains disputed, with some scholars tracing its root to the varna within the caste system, while others argue for a more diverse set of causes, including regional diversities and class divisions. For a detailed discussion, see Mishra (2015).

6. For a detailed discussion, see Liebelt, Böllinger, and Vierke (2019).

7. For a detailed discussion, see Mills et al. (2018).

REFERENCES

Barr, Marleen S. 1987. "Feminist Fabulation; or, Playing with Patriarchy vs. the Masculin-ization of Metafiction." *Women's Studies: An Interdisciplinary Journal* 14 (2): 187–191.

Blood, Sylvia K. 2005. *Body Work: The Social Construction of Women's Body Image*. East Sussex, UK: Routledge.

Bordo, Susan. 1999. "Feminism, Foucault and the Politics of the Body." In *Feminist Theory and the Body*, edited by Janet Price and Margrit Shildrick, 179–202. London: Routledge.

Chabria, Priya Sarukkai. 2019. *Clone*. New Delhi: Zubaan Books.

Chakraborty, Rituparna, and Sonali De. 2014. "Body Image and Its Relation with the Concept of Physical Self among Adolescents and Young Adults." *Psychological Studies* 59 (4): 419–426.

Kapadia, Manisha Kalidas. 2009. "Body Image in Indian Women as Influenced by the Indian Media." PhD diss., Texas Woman's University.

Kuhad, Urvashi. 2021. *Science Fiction and Indian Women Writers*. London: Routledge.

Liebelt, Claudia, Sarah Böllinger and Ulf Vierke, eds. 2019. *Beauty and the Norm: Debating Standardisation in Bodily Appearance*. London: Palgrave Macmillan.

Mills, Jennifer, Sarah Musto, Lindsay Williams, and Marika Tiggemann. 2018. "'Selfie' Harm: Effects on Mood and Body Image in Young Women." *Body Image* 27 (December): 86–92.

Mishra, Neha. 2015. "India and Colorism: The Finer Nuances." *Washington University Global Studies Law Review* 14 (4): 725–750.

Moylan, Tom. 2000. *Scraps of the Untainted Sky: Science Fiction, Utopia, Dystopia*. Boulder, CO: Westview Press.

Padmanabhan, Manjula. 1997. *Harvest*. New Delhi: Kali for Women.

———. 2017. *Harvest*. Gurugram: Hachette.

Parameswaran, Radhika. 2015. "Shaming the Nation on Public Affairs Television." *Journalism Studies* 16 (5): 680–691.

Prasad, Srirupa. 2015. *Cultural Politics of Hygiene in India, 1890–1940*. London: Palgrave Macmillan.

Radhakrishnan, Smitha. 2009. "Professional Women, Good Families: Respectable Femininity and the Cultural Politics of a 'New' India." *Qualitative Sociology* 32 (2): 195–212.

Rajagopalan, Jaya, and Bhaskar Shejwal. 2014. "Influence of Sociocultural Pressures on Body Image Dissatisfaction." *Psychological Studies* 59 (4): 357–364.

Rajendran, Sowmya. 2015. *The Lesson*. New Delhi: Harper Collins India.

Sabala and Meena Gopal. 2010. "Body, Gender and Sexuality: Politics of Being and Belonging." *Economic and Political Weekly* 45 (17): 43–51.

Sargent, Lyman Tower. 1994. "The Three Faces of Utopianism Revisited." *Utopian Studies* 5 (1): 27–28.

Schilder, Paul. 1935/1950. *The Image and Appearance of The Human Body*. New York: International Universities Press.

Shevde, Natasha. 2008. "All's Fair in Love and Cream: A Cultural Case Study of Fair & Lovely in India." *Advertising and Society Review* 9 (2): 1–9. Available at https://doi.org/10.1353/asr.0.0003.

Slade, Peter. D. 1988. "Body Image in Anorexia Nervosa." *British Journal of Psychiatry* 153 (2): 20–22.

Suvin, Darko. 1979. *Metamorphoses of Science Fiction: On the Poetics and History of a Literary Genre*. New Haven, CT: Yale University Press.

Thapan, Meenakshi. 1997. "Femininity and Its Discontents: The Woman's Body in Intimate Relationships." In *Embodiment: Essays on Gender and Identity*, edited by Meenakshi Thapan, 172–193. New Delhi: Oxford University Press.

Tolentino, Jia. 2019. "The Age of Instagram Face: How Social Media, FaceTune, and Plastic Surgery Created a Single, Cyborgian Look." *New Yorker*, December 12, 2019. Available at https://www.newyorker.com/culture/decade-in-review/the-age-of-instagram-face.

Wolf, Naomi. (1991) 2002. *The Beauty Myth: How Images of Beauty Are Used against Women*. New York: Harper Collins.

Wujastyk, Dominic. 2009. "Interpreting the Image of the Human Body in Premodern India." *International Journal of Hindu Studies* 13 (2): 189–228.

III

Alternate Beauties?

*Disabled and Disfigured Female Bodies in
Contemporary Indian Literature and Culture*

6

Fitting In When Your Body Does Not

Young Girl Characters with Disabilities in Contemporary
Indian English Fiction for Children

ANURIMA CHANDA

Introduction

A few years back, great furor was generated on social media over a chapter on "Major Social Problems in India" in a Class 12 Sociology school textbook from Maharashtra where, under the section "Dowry," a separate case was made for "Ugliness," which read:

> If girl is ugly and handicapped, then it becomes very difficult for her to get married. To marry such girls bridegroom and his family demand more dowry. Parents of such girls become helpless and pay dowry as per the demands of bridegroom's family. It leads to rise in the practice of dowry system.[1]

While this case luckily got reported, numerous others stealthily continue to lie embedded in our culture and practices, generating stereotypical gender expectations regarding physical appearance among women that shape and manipulate their expectations of their bodies. Growing up in an environment surrounded with images that propagate the myth of the beautiful body is difficult enough for women in general, but for women with a disability, it is doubly tortuous. Research shows how girls with disabilities start experiencing a sense of shame toward their bodies from as early as late childhood and early adolescence, when the body becomes a principal site of individuation.[2] Guided by unattainable beauty standards laid down by society—thanks to the homogenizing effect of the "global beauty boom"[3]—contemporary women, especially those with disabilities, across cultures often internalize the belief that their impaired bodies are unfeminine and unattractive, which in turn has grave consequences on their development as healthy physical and sexual beings.

Against such a backdrop, the spate of a bunch of empowered girl characters with disabilities within Indian English children's literature over the last couple of years who have taken upon themselves the task of flouting all bodily expectations has brought about a much-needed discursive change with regard to female embodiment. Under this new articulation, made possible by the new-realist shift that has been noticed within the genre from the late twentieth century onward, along with the advancement of disability activism, a space has been created where dominant discourses around the ideal body type can be challenged and healthier ways of engaging with human subjects can emerge. Through the exploration of two contemporary Indian English books for children centered on girl characters with disabilities—namely, Leela Gour Broome's *Flute in the Forest* (*FIF*) (2010) and Devika Rangachari's *Queen of Ice* (*QOI*) (2014, winner of the Neev Young Adult Book Award), this chapter shows how issues of physical appearance and sexual desirability as dictated by society can have debilitating effects on the developing selfhood of girls with disabilities and how such consciously woven narratives, which challenge problematic body norms, can go a long way in developing newer discourses of celebrating the body in its varied forms and shapes. The attempt here is to demonstrate how these critically unexplored texts do not shy away from displaying the impaired body but make their point by openly flaunting it, thereby subverting dominant standards through a carefully crafted oppositional gaze by bringing back the focus on the functionality of the body irrespective of its state or differences.

Women's Body Aesthetics and the Case of *Flute in the Forest* and *Queen of Ice*

The standards of physical attractiveness and the ideal body vary both inter- as well as intraculturally and across time and space.[4] Yet, with increased globalization, a general consensus seems to be forming throughout the globe about what is considered aesthetically pleasing. Interestingly enough, even though *FIF* and *QOI* are set in different fictional epochs, they still seem to be governed by this dominant beauty standard, perhaps hinting at how deeply ingrained the hegemony of a perfect body is and how little has changed within India. Tellingly, the two lead characters in these novels are female, a fact that proves the claim made by prominent body image scholars that women are more affected by the injunctions of such idealisms and tendencies.[5] Such a body-driven idea of normative femininity, which glorifies an ideal physical type among women, is further backed by an evolutionary logic that almost unanimously abides with most patriarchal sociocultural constructs.[6] As a result, the body as a site of identification for most women becomes dangerously entangled with goals prescribed by both patriarchy and a commodity culture, which in turn might not always align with their own sense of embodiment.

This pressure of fitting into the mold of the ideal body that plagues women across the globe is even more intense for women with physical disabilities. Fighting with both sexism and handicapism, women and girls with special abilities are doubly oppressed.[7] Unfortunately, the struggles of women with physical disabilities often get subsumed within the larger discourse of disability studies, which tends to create a monolithic structure where "disability" and "gender" are treated as mutually exclusive. Specifically in India, where disability studies itself is at a very nascent stage, the general attitude has been to sweep everything under one fold, disregarding differences of kind or degree of impairment, the modes of adaptation to the impairment, and issues of rural-urban divide, class, caste, and gender.[8]

Isolating gender within disability studies, disability studies expert Anita Ghai writes, "In a culture where being a daughter is considered a curse, being a disabled daughter is a fate worse than death."[9] *QOI* echoes this sentiment by addressing conspiracy theories that do the rounds within the royal court when the titular character, Princess Didda of the Kingdom of Lohara from early medieval Kashmir, is not "stifled at birth for being a girl—and a deformed one at that."[10] Here, for being unable to fulfill the ritual value that only a son can within Hinduism, the princess is perhaps forgiven. What cannot be forgiven, however, is her disabled body, which makes her an "imperfect" offering in the institution of marriage. The price of her imperfection has to be borne by her family, primarily her father, who has to arrange for payments in kind to compensate for the supposed lack in his daughter with a disability. In the worst-case scenario, serious compromises have to be made in the choice of the groom irrespective of the daughter's wishes. This is evident in the way Didda's father justifies her marriage trade-off as "He gets Didda, I get a little land . . . after all, a cripple has no value."[11] Despite such compensations and compromises, there is still a huge possibility that the daughter might never find a husband for herself, again proving the huge oppressions of patriarchal values on women who are differently abled.

Defined by their physical appearances and bombarded with images reflecting unattainable beauty standards all the time, women end up objectifying their own bodies and expose themselves to greater dangers of body dissatisfaction and low self-esteem. Unfortunately, it is not an easy cycle to break as such perceptions of the ideal body image are constantly "legitimized and reinforced by social institutions like family, and community and State mechanisms such as education, medicine and popular media."[12] This gendered body, which is purportedly anomalous or differently abled, becomes the site of cultural production of identity through which oppressive cultural structures play out, forcing the woman to conform without any agency of her own. The woman ends up separating her body from her selfhood, giving rise to a skewed sense of identity that is not her own but one projected onto her by masculinist forces, leaving her with very little autonomy and agency over her own body. In this toxic ambit, where selfhood is mistakenly equated with the socially produced female body, any inability to fit in can have a damaging impact on the woman's sense of self.

This is something that has been rampantly observed in women with physical disabilities, who are equally susceptible to the cultural expectations of body aesthetics as every other woman. Women with disabilities are denied even the little semblance of selfhood that is available to their able-bodied counterparts. Their "imperfect" bodies, which are unable to attain physical norms through regular self-fashioning, are not just considered unworthy of the male gaze but also subjected to unkind stares, which "turns the disabled object into a grotesque sight."[13] Both *FIF* and *QOI* strengthen this argument, where one of the protagonists seeks refuge in the depths of the forest and the other wields power as her defense mechanism against unkind stares and insulting attitudes. Both novels demonstrate how the impaired female body ends up distorting a woman's own perceptions of embodiment, leaving her feeling unfeminine and unacceptable. Explaining this phenomenon, Nandini Ghosh appropriately notes, "Socialized into such patriarchal ideologies, disabled girls grow up feeling uncomfortable with their own bodies for being deficient and thus not beautiful."[14]

With global standards of the physically perfect body assuming supremacy, Indian women with physical disability are finding it more and more difficult to fit in. Within this imagination, the ideal female body is one that lacks any extra fat; is tall and slim; has a tiny waist, an accentuated hip, fair skin, and long lustrous hair; and is young, fertile, and agile, among others. There is no focus on the health or functionality of the body as markers of its perfection, but rather an unnecessary fixation on qualities based on appearance alone. Most of the time, these aspirational qualities are completely divorced from a culture's material reality, and the Indian obsession with fair skin or tall and slim bodies proves a case in point. When one adds the aspect of physical disability to this, compliance to these normative prototypes of femininity becomes even more difficult because individuals who are differently abled are often visibly different and even require accommodating devices like wheelchairs or crutches or have restricted physical movements or atypical body parts. This makes the woman with a disability grow up devaluing her impaired body, thereby voluntarily relegating herself to the margins of society, as is seen in Atiya Sardare, the protagonist of *FIF*, who prefers the wilderness over civilization.

While the process of internalizing gendered body norms starts early, it is mainly during adolescence that its effects are fully realized when an individual's body starts undergoing changes. Medically and culturally, women become more concerned about their appearance and shape during this stage onward since appearance and desirability are considered integral to the process of female identity formation. As Nandini Ghosh attests, "Young girls internalise an image of the ideal body and the particular kind of physical beauty, notions of appropriate and acceptable feminine comportment as well as functional capacities that are desirable among women, through the verbal and visual messages projected by other women and the media."[15] The same is true for girls with disabilities, too, who are additionally made to realize their differences from their able-bodied peers and their inadequacy in competing at the same level as the latter—like Atiya, who is teased by her peers as "slow and dim,"[16] and Didda, whose father desires "a strong, healthy son to his name . . . not a weakling girl who was lame."[17] Clearly, living with alternate body abilities is very hard for young women inhabiting cultures obsessed with ideal body aesthetics.

Adolescent Selfhood, Differently Abled Female Bodies, and Young Adult Literature

Girls with disabilities grow up more conscious of their impaired bodies and begin to view them as something deficient and in need of reconstruction.[18] Their immediate reaction is to reduce the visual impact of the disabled body as much as possible, be it through surgery or use of material aids, which again amounts to surrendering to the standards of the perfect body. An example can be taken from Ghosh's study of women with locomotor disabilities from West Bengal, India, where she mentions how one of her subjects chose to shift from frocks to long skirts to hide her calipers because it clashed with her idea of the "feminine self."[19] Despite such efforts, the girl with a disability cannot completely shake off the material reality of her impaired body, which becomes a prime marker in the path of her identity formation. This also means a general internalization of prejudices that "disabled women are 'incomplete' and hence do not require feminine adornments in terms of dress and ornamentation."[20] Ghosh mentions how this leads to young girls downplaying their femininity by underdressing—wearing oversized clothes, using minimal makeup—to avoid taunts and stares from people who find it ridiculous to see a girl with a disability so dressed up.[21]

Unfortunately, for differently abled girls, families are not very supportive in most cases since they are conditioned by the same expectations of feminine body ideal as the society at large. That the pubertal process for girls with disabilities can be the same as that of any other person is looked upon suspiciously, even by mothers. Any delay in the onset of menstruation or the development of breasts is taken as a sign of their difference, making the girls feel less of a woman.[22] The negation of their femininity as a result of an impaired body continues everywhere, including in matters of attracting a romantic partner. Since daughters with disabilities are viewed as desexed, family members feel they are less at risk from sexual predators than their able-bodied counterparts.[23] Naturally, this leaves them with greater risk of and susceptibility toward sexual harassment and violence. These girls also grow up with limited expectations about a "normal" marriage. Yet this does not save them from their responsibilities as women in protecting their reputations through the appropriate social behavior expected of women in general. Such contradictory negotiations with the self leave women who are differently abled uncomfortable in their own skin and with a highly undervalued sense of their own bodies.

This sense of normative femininity is constantly fed via popular media like television or magazine advertisements, popular soap operas or films, and billboards, among others. One among these myriad sources is young adult fiction. Officially categorized as a distinct genre since the 1960s, works of young adult fiction (specifically those targeted at young girls), with their focus on sexuality and sexual development (more often than not in the traditional sense), remain one of the prime sources of providing both information as well as reflection of such body angst among adolescent girls. Interestingly, at the time of the genre's inception, sexuality was a complete taboo within the domain of children's literature. By making sexuality its mainstay, young adult fiction managed to flout all such norms and create a liberal space. Yet, in the manner of the treatment of the subject, it fell back on conventional norms, emerging as sexually liberal but regressive in format, especially on the subject of body image. Within this representation, the ideal feminine body is always the one that fits the dominant patriarchal sociocultural expectations (based on global or Eurocentric formulations)—with insistence on thin bodies, curvaceous form, fair skin, long hair, moderately sized hips, large breasts, and feminine gait—and enormous cultural power is with those who possesses such a body. An example is Judy Blume's *Forever . . .* (1975), which is touted as an iconic young adult fiction for breaking boundaries. And yet, *Forever . . .* , while openly talking about its protagonist's discovery of sexual pleasure, is relatively understated on issues of body weight angst, which is equally embedded within the central narrative.

In India, too, where the idea of young adult fiction is a Western import, a similar tendency can be observed, especially in the case of fiction crafted in English. Although Indian young adult fiction generally follows the status quo even in its handling of sexual subjects when compared to its Western counterpart, on the issue of body image it is mainly regressive, if not worse. Over the last two decades, however, there has been a palpable change within Indian English young adult fiction in terms of challenging such hegemonic body representations by reimagining ways of resisting dominant societal norms, including that of gender. Unfortunately, the majority of works have still not found the adequate vocabulary for such narratives, either falling back on tried-and-tested means or setting up newer gender norms in the process of breaching older ones, thereby proving to be largely counterproductive. One can perhaps take the example of Balaji Venkataramanan's *Flat-Track Bullies* (2013), which does a wonderful job of challenging class politics within Indian society but forgets to do the same while talking about gender. Through the eyes of an eleven-year-old male protagonist, Ravi, readers scan young girls under the lens of preexisting body norms and categorize them as beautiful for adhering to "film-star looks" with flowing hair, fair skin, and a sharp nose; as lucky for having a pretty face; but as inappropriate for wearing skimpy clothes.[24]

While it is evident what effect this might have on a young adult female reader, it will understandably be doubly worse for a young adult female reader with a disability for whom body concerns and limitations are far greater than the former. This is not very shocking since, in reality, there are few Indian young adult works of fiction that are written with such a reader in mind. The adolescent girl with a disability is mostly pushed to the margin and is, in fact, on the receiving end of multiple marginalizations. Even in the rare instance when such a character is given center stage, primacy is given to generating a benevolent attitude toward her rather than her bodily struggles. Under such circumstances, texts like Broome's *FIF* and Rangachari's *QOI* bring in a fresh perspective by attempting the opposite. Not only do they interrogate in depth the challenges of living with an impaired body in a society that gives enormous preference to notions of bodily perfection and explore the problematics of such preferences, but they also try to subvert it through the oppositional gaze—to use the framework of a concept developed by bell hooks— by bringing back the focus on the functionality of the body irrespective of its appearance or form.

Alternate Embodiments / Alternate Beauties in *Flute in the Forest* and *Queen of Ice*

Leela Gour Broome's *Flute in the Forest* is about thirteen-year-old Atiya, who lives with her father, a range forest officer in southern India. Her struggles begin at the age of five when she contracts polio, which leaves her with a weaker and shorter left leg. This results in a huge rift between her parents, causing her mother to leave and her father to immerse himself in work. Atiya is left with no other option but to learn how to take care of herself from a very young age. She grows up a loner, with a busy father, an absent mother, and classmates who make fun of her for being "slow and dim."[25] In this situation, she finds a friend in the forest, where she often escapes alone to undertake short, secret treks on her own. In the course of these expeditions, Atiya crosses path with a sullen old anthropologist and music genius suffering from a degenerative disease (whom she nicknames Ogre Uncle); his daughter, Mishora (a Kurumba girl); and a rogue old elephant, Rangappa. All of them end up forming unlikely bonds with each other that help them self-heal from the various ordeals they are experiencing.

The book starts challenging body norms right at the outset starting with the mother-daughter duo. Sarojini, Atiya's mother, is described as "beautiful" and "lissom"[26]—attributes that make her husband, Ram Deva Sardare, besotted with her in the first place. Atiya, on the other hand, with her "short, straight, black hair and a high forehead," is described to be a "bright young girl" but

> far from good looking [since] her nose was way too long and pointed. Even her chin, was much too sharp in her bony face. She was a long, thin wisp of a girl—made for an athletic outdoor life, but was now trapped by her handicap. Even her ears, though small, stuck out at a ridiculous angle. People often wondered how such good-looking parents could have produced such an ugly child.[27]

It is worth noting here that one of the basic premises that the gendered body norm discourse is based on, as Viren Swami's "Evolutionary Perspectives on Human Appearance and Body Image" attests, is the fact that a beautiful, lithe female body is the harbinger of beautiful and healthy progeny. However, through the case of Atiya, Broome appears to subvert this structure by demonstrating the fallacy of such beliefs. Atiya is neither conventionally beautiful like her mother nor "healthy" (although her disability is not congenital). In addition, Atiya is "slow," as rightly pointed out by her classmates, as anybody walking with a wooden stick is. Yet that does not make her any less "beautiful" or functional, as the world around her claims. Broome proves this not through words but through Atiya's actions. After having delved in depth detailing each of her facial features through the usual societal "gaze," the author spends the rest of the narrative repositioning the reader's gaze so the reader becomes mindful of Atiya's physical beauty not through pre-prejudiced lenses but through articulations where beauty and body functionality are redefined simply owing to their distinctness. What is more important is how, in this process, Broome does not shift the reader's gaze onto the body to focus on some redemptive ability as a compensation for Atiya's so-called lack. Instead, the novelist brings back the focus on Atiya's body itself with all its distinctness as the protagonist limps her way through forests, enlivening the spirits of two old damaged souls (Ogre Uncle and Rangappa) around her. Atiya's body movements are not graceful in the traditional sense here—"limping along on her strong foot, the other being a little shorter"[28]—but that is also because of society's tendency to regard grace through preset constraints. Atiya's beauty, too, is not in tune with the dominant standards, but at the end, when she sits playing the flute with composure, she manages to "charm" a full audience, leaving them in "awestruck silence."[29] By highlighting Atiya's distinct attributes, both of her body and of her mind, the author successfully recrafts the narrative of the body beautiful for an adolescent girl.

The other gender construct that Broome challenges is that of motherhood. Women with disabilities, by virtue of their "imperfect" and hence desexed bodies, are often denied traditional roles assigned to all women (despite having to adhere to traditional female behavior perforce), like motherhood.[30] And when forced into such roles, women with alternate abilities experience a condition called "rolelessness," according to Michele Fine and Adrienne Asch.[31] In *FIF*, however, it is Sarojini who embraces such "rolelessness" by voluntarily rejecting the valorized role of a mother that had been conferred upon her by society and instead choosing a career as a dancer. It is her able-bodiedness that urges her to choose her passion over traditionally consigned roles, thereby reversing those very sociocultural norms that deny women with disabilities the right to even pursue the same. A similar analogy is true for romance/marriage as well in this context. Sardare's love for his wife is solely described as being rooted in the charm of Sarojini's physical beauty. Yet that does not stop them from parting ways, once again nullifying the romantic myth of an aesthetically pleasing woman's eternally blessed marital life. Atiya, on the other hand, manages to find a much-healthier companion in Gopal, the son of Mrs. Naina Pillai, her new geography teacher in school. Although their companionship does not blossom into a conventional romance in the course of the novel, the author leaves us with a promise that in the future it may lead to a meaningful relationship. Their relationship is shown to be based on mutual interests and an easy understanding of each other's aspirations. It does not require Atiya to charm him by converting her body image to something socially acceptable. Instead, we note how Gopal enjoys her company and says "wow!" in admiration to hear her perfectly imitate the Indian pitta bird's two-note call.[32] But at the same time, their bond is also not completely disengaged from physicality. They are shown to be extremely comfortable with each other's bodies, be it spending time together in Atiya's fa-

ther's forest lodge or hurriedly escaping after mistakenly entering a large animal's cave during a secret trek, "holding tightly on to each other."[33] Hence,
if Atiya, with her so-called unattractive body, proves to be a nurturer to Ogre
Uncle and Rangappa, with this same body she makes a loving companion for
Gopal. And in both cases, her body crafts alternate definitions of aesthetic
appeal.

A similar unravelling of the differently abled female body and the politics of embodiment surrounding it can be found in Devika Ranghachari's
historical fiction, *Queen of Ice*. The story revolves around Didda, princess of
Lohara, who was born with a deformed leg and ruled Kashmir from 980/981–
1003 c.e. in early medieval India.[34] It is interesting how Rangachari situates
the narrative in ancient India when the stigma of any kind of body deformity—even in a royal princess, whose physical beauty is supposed to be her
prime asset—would have been quite severe, not just for the individual who
is differently abled but also for her family, especially if her father was the king.
The fact that Didda actually grows up to be a conventional beauty with "big,
dark eyes," "long, curly hair that falls down to the waist," a "wide brow with
prominent cheekbones," "thick, arched eyebrows," a "nose . . . neither long
nor short but . . . perfectly shaped with delicately-flared nostrils," and a "pretty" mouth does not hold much meaning for the king.[35] For him, Didda's disability becomes her chief defining feature owing to which he curses her for
being "one who will never even use her skills to attract a good match."[36] For-
tunately, Didda is allowed to live because of a prophecy made by the royal
astrologer about how she is destined for greatness. The way Didda achieves
this greatness in the novel, not by becoming invisible but through an active
engagement of her apparently desexed, lame body, is a remarkable feat that
the narrative accomplishes. Notably, disability is equated with desexing of
the body within the Indian psyche,[37] but in *QOI* Didda manages to topple and
overcome the very sexist body norms that her father uses to curse her. Through
this process, the narrative shows a way of reimagining female body image by
factoring in differences instead of excluding all different or so-called anomalous bodies as misfits.

To strengthen this point, Rangachari populates the narrative with other
"misfits," one of them being Didda's prime aide, Valga, whose job was to carry the princess around. An ordinary village girl and the eldest daughter born
to a family of many sisters and one brother, Valga is disposed of to her aunt's
quarters in Lohara by her father to reduce the financial burden on the family, which has too many mouths to feed. Valga explains the reason why she
is the one chosen to be cast out:

> It wasn't any surprise that my father had picked on me thus. I knew
> he had no affection for me, his eldest daughter. His eyes sparkled with

derision and anger whenever they rested on me. Perhaps part of the reason was that my heavy features bore no semblance of beauty and he knew I would never make a good match. I am short and stout, my broad face unremarkable, my black hair hanging limply down my back. I do not have anything of my mother's delicate beauty or my father's chiselled features. The only remarkable thing about me is that I am very strong.[38]

Strangely enough, it is her strength that helps Valga make "a good match"—a match to Didda. Disproving dominant patriarchal sociocultural norms that mandate marriage to be a woman's ultimate match, Valga shows that matches can be of other kinds too by finding a match in Didda as a good friend and employer. Through this, Rangachari demonstrates how the imagination of the body ideal and its ultimate functionality can have multiple definitions, not one.

This is more evident in the case of Didda, who is ultimately married as a "trade-off" to Kshemagupta from the alien land of Kashmira. Tellingly, Kshemagupta has a bad reputation due to his hedonistic lifestyle, but Didda is married to him because nobody notable wants to marry a crippled partner. Didda herself attests to this fact when she says, "Who would want to marry a lame woman, however beautiful she may be?"[39] Significantly, if we find Didda internalizing her alleged unattractiveness, we also find her comfortable enough in her alternate corporeality to find both love and acceptance. Hence, she subverts her physical limitations into empowerment when Kshemagupta falls in love with her and gives up all his truant ways to please her. Didda is convinced that her husband falls in love with her mainly because of his fascination with the way she talks, her questions, and her observations about stately affairs in general. However, Valga's accounts of how Kshemagupta's eyes light up in Didda's presence, how he celebrates on knowing of her pregnancy, and how he indulges her materially, including minting coins in her name, seem to suggest that the love is not limited to Didda's mind alone. In fact, Kshemagupta acknowledges as much himself when he proclaims, "I want our love to be known to all. . . . You are my life, Didda, my world."[40] Like Broome, Rangachari also successfully reverses the gendered body politics through a multipronged understanding of the body ideal that is more inclusive of differences. Within this reimagination, Rangachari feels no need to substitute the body deficiencies with some compensatory quality. Indeed, she presents Didda as an astute and graceful person, yet she also highlights the innate beauty of the impaired body itself in all its divergences from the standard, thus showing us ways to reposition the normative gaze.

What is different in the two novels under study from other texts that center on females with disabilities is how they address the differently abled body.

There is a general tendency within the discourse of disability to shift the gaze from the body to other abilities. While this is a well-meaning move made to turn the discourse more ableist than visual, it ends up falling into the same trap as that of standard body image discourse by negating the body and reinforcing the myth of the impaired body as the defective one. Within children's literature, Zai Whitakar has labeled such practices as "the *Taare Zameen Par* phenomenon,"[41] wherein writers get invested in making up for the disability with some special ability in the child to show how the measurement of merit can be multifaceted and how a so-called flaw may be compensated by a strength. This leads us to the question of what happens to those individuals who lack any other ability whatsoever. The problem with the aforementioned representational politics is that it tries to substitute one condition with the other and hence prompts an inevitable negation of at least one "flawed" parameter in individuals with disabilities. For the impaired female body, it is generally the body that gets cancelled out, or invisibilized,[42] for being "inadequate."[43] However, as the body is a special site of identity making for all women mainly because "they are more likely than men to be judged by their appearance and sexual appeal,"[44] such a simplistic this-for-that logic can never work as a permanent solution in matters concerning female body image politics.

The search for an alternative has to therefore begin from within the body and not irrespective of it. It has to begin on the premise that the body is the primary site of identity formation, and the need is to find ways to positively engage with the body in all its uniqueness instead of invisibilizing it. Such positive reimaginations of the body can begin not through a correction of the body but of the gaze, which is the prime determinant in how a body is viewed.[45] Given the patriarchal preponderance in the formulation of this gaze in the case of body image, one way ahead could be to balance it with the oppositional gaze. A concept developed by bell hooks, in the context of black female spectators, the oppositional gaze is based on the premise that "even in the worse circumstances of domination, the ability to manipulate one's gaze in the face of structures of domination that would contain it, opens up the possibility of agency."[46] Exploring the politics of the gaze, hooks notes how resistance begins not just in interrogating the dominant gaze but also in looking back with a critical consciousness. It is in these moments of "looking back," when the viewee turns into the viewer, that the former can find ways of resistance by rejecting being identified by dominant modes of spectatorship as crafted by the latter.

The same can be applied to the present scenario for characters like Atiya and Didda, with a caveat. Seizing back the phallocentric dominant gaze for women with disabilities is not as simplistic as it may seem, as they themselves "become active producers of their bodies through internalization and pursuit of continually shifting ideals of femininity propagated by cultural and media images advocating self-containment, self-monitoring and self-normalization."[47] They are not merely the objects but also the surveyors of their own bodies, which they view as "flawed" objects through the lens generated by the phallocentric norms of viewership. Against such a backdrop, the oppositional gaze can work only after a complete separation of the two gazes has been achieved. This will inevitably create a fresh platform where the body can take ownership of itself on its own terms and create newer imaginations of viewership that are more inclusive of different selfhoods, or, as Ghai would say, a space with "an active integration of differences among and within women."[48]

Conclusion: Celebrating the Body with Special Abilities

Broome's and Rangachari's texts attempt this "integration of differences" in their own way. Instead of cancelling out any gaze, they reposition it at certain angles to bring into focus issues that generally get overshadowed. Within this new frame, the disabled body gets presented as a sum of its parts and not separate from each other. The different parts, like the different fingers of our hands, are not of the same size, form, or strength. Yet, as *FIF* and *QOI* demonstrate, the important thing is not how different these fingers are but what they can do when they come together. Atiya's short left leg or Didda's deformed foot might slow down their movements as compared to others, but that does not keep them from reaching their destinations. Atiya still manages to travel from one end of the town to the other, be it for secret treks or pursuit of music, while overcoming her father's grave displeasure. Didda, on her part, finds ways to maximize the functionality of her body through means of her own choice (like Valga, for one) and manages to combine it with her lethal diplomatic powers to ascend the throne of Kashmira in defiance of all gender norms of her time. Both Atiya and Didda then achieve extraordinary feats not through a negation of their bodies but through active engagement with their bodies, emanating a certain beauty that comes from being able to assert one's own individuality in the face of opposition. Therein emerges the oppositional gaze that creates liberating ways of viewing the disabled female body not in its lack but in acceptance of its distinct functionality inclusive of differences.

NOTES

1. Panicker, "Higher Dowry."
2. Ghosh, "Embodied Experiences," 60.
3. Berry, *Beauty Bias*, 3; Liebelt, "Beauty and the Norm," 1.
4. Berry, *Beauty Bias*, 3.

5. Tiggemann, "Sociocultural Perspectives," 12.
6. Swami, "Evolutionary Perspectives."
7. Ghai, "Disabled Women," 52–57.
8. Ghai, 53.
9. Ghai, 53.
10. Rangachari, *Queen of Ice*, 3.
11. Rangachari, 29.
12. Ghosh, "Experiencing the Body," 103.
13. Ghai, "Disabled Women," 55.
14. Ghosh, "Experiencing the Body," 105.
15. Ghosh, "Embodied Experiences," 59.
16. Broome, *Flute in the Forest*, 1.
17. Rangachari, *Queen of Ice*, 4.
18. Ghosh, "Experiencing the Body," 105.
19. Ghosh, 106.
20. Ghosh, 108.
21. Ghosh, 108.
22. Ghosh, "Embodied Experiences," 60.
23. Ghosh, 62.
24. Venkataramanan, *Flat-Track Bullies*, 23, 119, 49.
25. Broome, *Flute in the Forest*, 1.
26. Broome, 5.
27. Broome, 9.
28. Broome, 2.
29. Broome, 191.
30. Ghai, "Disabled Women," 54.
31. Fine and Asch, *Women with Disabilities*.
32. Broome, *Flute in the Forest,* 59.
33. Broome, 64.
34. Rangachari, *Queen of Ice*, 174.
35. Rangachari, 19.
36. Rangachari, 6.
37. Ghai, "Disabled Women," 55.
38. Rangachari, *Queen of Ice*, 10.
39. Rangachari, 20.
40. Rangachari, 67.
41. Gopalakrishnan, "Children First."
42. Ghai, "Disabled Women," 56.
43. Ghosh, "Experiencing the Body," 105.
44. Taub, Fanflik, and Mclorg, "Body Image among Women," 160.
45. Ghosh, "Experiencing the Body," 102.
46. hooks, "The Oppositional Gaze," 116.
47. Ghosh, "Experiencing the Body," 105.
48. Ghai, "Disabled Women," 64.

BIBLIOGRAPHY

Berry, Bonnie. *Beauty Bias: Discrimination and Social Power.* Westport, CT: Praeger, 2007.
Blume, Judy. *Forever. . .* 1975. Reprint, New York: Simon and Schuster, 2014.

Broome, Leela Gour. *Flute in the Forest*. New Delhi: Puffin Books, 2010.

Cash, Thomas F., and Thomas Pruzinsky, eds. *Body Image: A Handbook of Theory, Research, and Clinical Practice*. New York: Guilford Press, 2002.

Fine, Michele, and Adrienne Asch, eds. *Women with Disabilities: Essays in Psychology, Culture, and Politics*. Philadelphia: Temple University Press, 1988.

Ghai, Anita. "Disabled Women: An Excluded Agenda of Indian Feminism." *Hypatia* 17, no. 3 (2002): 49–66. Available at https://www.jstor.org/stable/3810795.

Ghosh, Nandini. "Embodied Experiences: Being Female and Disabled." *Economic and Political Weekly* 45, no. 17 (2010): 58–63. Available at https://www.jstor.org/stable/2566 4386.

———. "Experiencing the Body: Femininity, Sexuality and Disabled Women in India." In *Disability in South Asia: Knowledge & Experience*, edited by Anita Ghai, 101–117. New Delhi: Sage Publications, 2018.

Gopalakrishnan, Karthika. "Children First: A Summary of the Proceedings." *The Duckbill Blog*, November 14, 2016. Available at https://theplatyplog.wordpress.com/2016 /11/14/children-first-a-summary-of-the-proceedings/.

hooks, bell. "The Oppositional Gaze: Black Female Spectators." In *Black Looks: Race and Representations*, 115–131. New York: South End Press, 1992.

Liebelt, Claudia. "Beauty and the Norm: An Introduction." In *Beauty and the Norm: Debating Standardization in Bodily Appearance*, edited by Claudia Liebelt, Sarah Böllinger, and Ulf Vierke. Cham, Switzerland: Palgrave Macmillan, 2019.

Panicker, Raija Susan. "Higher Dowry Asked for 'Ugly' Brides: Maharashtra Textbook Shocker." *NDTV*, February 2, 2017. Available at https://www.ndtv.com/india-news /families-of-ugly-girls-asked-for-more-dowry-says-maharashtra-schoolbook-1655404.

Rangachari, Devika. *Queen of Ice*. New Delhi: Duckbill Books, 2014.

Swami, Viren. "Evolutionary Perspectives on Human Appearance and Body Image." In *Body Image: A Handbook of Science, Practice, and Prevention*, 2nd ed., edited by Thomas F. Cash and Linda Smolak, 20–28. New York: Guilford Press, 2011.

Taub, Diane E., Patricia L. Fanflik, and Penelope A. Mclorg. "Body Image among Women with Physical Disabilities: Internalization of Norms and Reactions to Nonconformity." *Sociological Focus* 36, no. 2 (2003): 159–176. Available at https://www.jstor.org /stable/20832198.

Tiggemann, Marika. "Sociocultural Perspectives on Human Appearance and Body Image." In *Body Image: A Handbook of Science, Practice, and Prevention*, 2nd. ed., edited by Thomas F. Cash and Linda Smolak, 12–19. New York: Guilford Press, 2011.

Venkataramanan, Balaji. *Flat-Track Bullies*. New Delhi: Duckbill Books, 2013.

7

Pathologies of "Body Fictions"

A Comparative Study of Margarita with a Straw *and* Kuch Bheege Alfaaz

SAMRITA SINHA

The Ontology of the Body-Ego as the Locus of Body Image

Bodies are discursively and ideologically produced. They are entangled in a complicated nexus of power, culture, race, class, caste, and gender. Situated within this matrix is female corporeality, which is a semiotic embodiment of a culture's ideology of the normative and the beautiful. An interrogation of how such normative optics of beauty ordains a standardization of female bodies as an ontological imperative across cultures is the core interest of this chapter. Claudia Liebelt, while examining norms of body image in the introduction to the book *Beauty and the Norm: Standardization in Bodily Appearance*, claims that "as ideological tools, these standards of somatic normalcy continue not only to describe, but also prescribe human bodies today."[1] What therefore can be inferred from this sociocultural modality is that body image precedes bodies. Body image is a mandate of preexistent sociocultural ideals and norms that organize a culture's ways of seeing bodies and consigning their inherent meanings. These organizing ideals are transmitted through a variety of sociocultural apparatuses and are in turn interiorized by subjects, governing paradigms of body satisfaction or dissatisfaction with affective and behavioral corollaries.

Informed by such debates and through the comparative analysis of two recent Hindi films, *Kuch Bheege Alfaaz* (2018) and *Margarita with a Straw* (2014), this chapter interrogates the heterosexist and ableist body image construct to probe and complicate the perpetuation of lookism and scopophobia that affects women with deformities or differently abled corporeality. It examines how two women, one with cerebral palsy and the other with a skin disorder, are represented negotiating body norms and responding to their divergence from normative body aesthetics. Whereas Archana, the central female protagonist in *Kuch Bheege Alfaaz*, has leukoderma, Laila in *Margarita with a Straw* is a queer young woman with cerebral palsy. The focus hinges on a comparison of how the corporeal nonnormativity of both the female protagonists affects their interiorized self-images.

Undeniably, beyond the social, political, and cultural modalities of the body are its psychical dimensions. There are two important paradigms to understanding the hermeneutics of the body—the sociocultural and the psychical. Within the domain of psychoanalysis, the ontology of the body is an important pathway to understanding the psychic dimensions of a subject. Elucidated by Freud, the body as a starting point of mental functioning is at the core of the development of the ego. And as Freud himself famously put it, the ego is "first and foremost a body-ego; it is not merely a surface entity but it is itself the projection of a surface."[2] Resonating Freud's thoughts that the body-self is the predominant foundation for any coherent sense of the self, Lacan tells us that "we are beings who are looked at in the spectacle of the world."[3] What is interesting for us is to understand how the body image construct functions as the Lacanian "master signifier" residing within the socially shared space of the Symbolic register, which is the unconscious repertoire of the multiple available tools of articulation for a subject. Within this matrix of signifiers shared among collective humanity, we see how socially coded messages gain signification in the shaping of subjectivities. The predominant thrust of the Lacanian and Freudian psychical understanding of the role of body schema in a subject's ontological universe is the concept that "we are beings-in-a-body and we are the subject of the other's gaze."[4] This idea of an embodied self and the "looked-at-ness"[5] of the body, along with its culturally mandated visual aesthetics, presents to us the challenge of integrating the meaning of our corporeality into our sense of who we are. In summation, the realization that the self gains cogency in relation to how the body is perceived by others is at the core of how body image can be a hegemonic vector of control in any given culture.

Pathologies of Body Fictions and the Production of Body Image in Women with Deformities/Disabilities

Principally aligned with iterations about the controlling modalities of body image in a given culture, the analysis of *Kuch Bheege Alfaaz*, directed by Onir, and *Margarita with a Straw*, directed by Shonali Bose, engages here with the biopolitics of body image that informs the ontological frontiers of women with disabilities. In all cultures and subcultures, dominant ideological apparatuses such as the media and mass communication disseminate information about the meanings of human appearance. Culturally coded messages transmit acceptable standards, norms, and expectations about appearance—what traits of physical characteristics and appearance are and are not socially deigned and what it means to possess or lack these socially celebrated characteristics. The genesis of this concept can be traced back to the late twentieth century and the beginning of global neoliberalism, as propounded in the works of Susan Bordo and Naomi Wolf. In *The Beauty Myth*, Wolf claims, "In assigning value to women in a vertical hierarchy according to a culturally imposed physical standard, it is an expression of power relations in which women must unnaturally compete for resources that men have appropriated for themselves."[6] Such power relations are embodied in the fact that in a neoliberal consumerist era, the machinery of the beauty and cosmetics industry runs on a fetishization of impossible body ideals with women as the predominant target.

The interrelatedness of beauty ideals and its normative imperatives thus is a historical process of ordering and preordaining bodies into binary categories of desirable and undesirable, claims Bonnie Berry in her compelling book titled *Beauty Bias: Discrimination and Social Power.* Berry argues, "With workplace experience, for example, we see the double standards imposed on women for their appearance that are not similarly imposed on men, in addition to the obvious cases of looks-based discrimination against the not-so-young, the non-white, and the disabled."[7] In a technologically sustained, hyperconsumerist neoliberal world, the female body has therefore emerged as a site of visual consumption, which leads to an inordinate desire for body modification often premised on perceived notions of body flaws.[8] Furthermore, implied in Bonnie Berry's comment is an important idea that women with disabilities are situated within a complex biopolitical assemblage of other oppressive identity markers such as class, caste, gender, race, and heteronormative body image. The perceived deviation from culturally mandated body aesthetics therefore results in the viewing of women with deformities or disabilities as perpetually dwelling within fractured and fragmented bodyselves as they are labeled as women who are "defects and undesirable,"[9] as well as beings who are asexual, unfeminine, and infantile.[10]

In the context of Debra Walker King's notion of "body-fictions," underneath the polysemic layers of culturally constituted specular and fictive body images, "the 'authentic' self gets silenced and lost,"[11] and the body myths of women with physical disabilities are fictively construed as "grotesque spectacle" or "icon of deviance."[12] Further, Susan Wendell tells us that in a culture that equates ableism with body autonomy and control over one's body, a disability "symbolizes failure" and manifests a body image that able-bodied individuals "are trying to avoid, forget, and ignore."[13] In fact, the monolithic sociocultural lexicon of the ideal body image is predicated on ideals and fantasies of youth, slenderness, height, nondisability, and a certain racial primacy.[14] In this context, as a complex assemblage of corporeal, psychical, and social mechanisms, a heteronormative body image construct is a cultural fictionalization of the female body. And this body fiction is a veritable phenomenon of desubjectification of women with deformed/disabled bodies.

The negotiations that women with bodily anomalies make with normative body image discourses need to be further examined within significant epistemological transitions within contemporary optics on disability, not only globally but also in India. That said, it is important to note that there has been a major dissonance among activists, scholars, and persons with disabilities in terms of the remedial social model for the differently abled. The remedial social modality has a circumscribed vision of inclusivity of persons with physical impairment and focuses rather narrowly on their limitations rather than their strengths toward the removal of social barriers in a society ruled by nondisabled persons.[15] This modality has arguably further perpetuated negative body aesthetics for women with body anomalies or disabilities.

From such a commiserative stance—that of a social patronage and decentering of the body within the discourse of disability—several contemporary scholars have recentered the body within the rhetoric of disability, locating in it an epistemological value. In this context, scholars like H-Dirkson L. Bauman and Joseph J. Murray, in a sharp retort to medicalized ideas like "hearing loss," have postulated not oppositional but differential epistemes to the problem that they call "deaf gain."[16] Likewise, Rosemarie Garland-Thomson has conceptualized notions such as "disability gain" to postulate that the very phenomenology of disability should be reframed as a source of gain, rather than a loss, situated in the demand that disability integration be deemed as a resource gain instead of a resource drain.[17] While this approach unsettles, and indeed questions, the social reductionism and devaluation of "disability," it also raises a number of debatable issues around the representational regimes that run the risk of degenerating into a commodification of "disabled" bodies while attempting to represent alternate forms of female embodiment or "alternative beauty."[18] It is through the prism of such a political debate that this chapter interrogates the representational regimes of Bollywood in configuring the body perception of women with deformities or disabilities and posits a need for differential optics toward fostering affirmative and alternative modalities of body positivity of women with nonnormative bodies.

The Normalization of Scopophobia in *Kuch Bheege Alfaaz*

For women with physical impairments, it is their body deficit that becomes a defining parameter of their constitutive selfhood, often leading others to completely ignore their possession of a variety of personal qualities.[19] As a result, the body image of impairment takes over as a predominant paradigm of identity that invisibilizes the other human attributes of the person with a disability. This narrow focus on the limitedness of their functional body is predicated on the stigma-based medical model, which in turn shapes social or identity politics and then reinforces, in a negative way, the notion that bodies of women with disabilities are different.[20] Consequently, women with physical deformities internalize profound anxieties of body dysmorphia and suffer a sense of dissonance from the cultural expectations of appearance aesthetics.[21] This internalized discordance resulting from culture's pejorative reactions to their "anomalous" bodies leads such women to believe that their bodies are a "source of pain, guilt, and embarrassment."[22] Such negative self-images "perpetuate feelings of inferiority, a poor body self-concept, and avoidance of social interactions,"[23] further normalizing scopophobia as an integral part of the ontological negotiations of women with impairments.

The postulations about scopophobia in Onir's *Kuch Bheege Alfaaz* can be reconfigured with the help of the current debates within disability discourses on the praxis of staring, which in turn animates social connection. It is worth turning here to Sarah Böllinger's essay titled "Broken Beauty, Broken Cups: Disabled Bodies in Contemporary African Art," where she argues that "what we can learn from those being stared at is the following: the visibility of their non-normate bodies in public space is of immense importance because society will learn to see and think differently only by being confronted with them, whether this concerns human bodies or artworks."[24] In the parlance of contemporary disability studies, the praxis of staring is predicated on a learning process that gains impetus from the idea of "disability gain."[25] Only if nonnormative bodies did not give way to scopophobia and did not let themselves be dehumanized by the act of being stared at would society be sensitized and learn to include alternate corporealities. According to such a reading, the act of staring is dialogic and carries an immense epistemological potential to foster affirmative and inclusive meanings about alternate and nonnormative bodies. In other words, staring does not necessarily ascribe a victim status to those being stared at; rather, it produces identities in a social matrix.[26] Although such a reading does possess merit, it once again deflects the social and moral onus on nonnormate subjects to shake off scopophobia and engage with a subject position of stared-at-ness in an idealistic manner. Such a reading is precariously premised on a hopeful conjecture of what staring at nonnormate bodies should ideally produce rather than examining the etiological ableist invasive politics of staring. Not all praxis of staring is located in an atmosphere of conviviality and hence scopophobia can be fueled by the hostility of a deeply divisive society toward non-normative bodies. However, Böllinger's reading of the politics of staring should provide a significant alternative pathway if representational apparatuses such as the media begin with fostering a positivist and convivial episteme of staring as a differential modality of learning about persons with disabilities that is meant to forge a culture of body positivity.

In Onir's *Kuch Bheege Alfaaz*, Archana, who is known as Archie, has internalized scopophobia as a result of disparaging reactions she faces toward her skin condition, leukoderma, and because of which she wears a scarf that helps with stigma management. We know that within body image discourse on women with physical deformities, social withdrawal is perceived as a tool of stigma management.[27] In *Kuch Bheege Alfaaz*, we find a strong undercurrent of such disempowering recourses for stigma management as Archana is never seen in socially fostering homosocial company or other alternate social spaces of self-pursuit. And yet, Onir's film is predominantly a love story revolving around Archana's pursuit of ideal love. It is this concatenation of an ideal love, the teleology of existence, and female body image that is at the core of the politics of representation in *Kuch Bheege Alfaaz*. Within the Indian context, it is interesting to note that Bollywood often projects the idea of romantic love as a social reward for women. This ideal of love as a social aspiration therefore is synonymous with the pursuit of ideal body appearance for women in a culture besotted with lookism. In the film, the paradigms of body image are deeply rooted in the female protagonist's pursuit of self-validation through ideal love, defined as a transcendental signified that looks beyond the vagaries of leukodermic patchy skin and superficial beauty. The very sensibility of Onir's film is heavily inclined toward a commiserative patronizing love through which the female protagonist realizes her femininity. In the Indian context, according to Nandini Ghosh, the female fashioning of body appearance is dialectically related to the patriarchally ascribed functionality of the female body. Given the importance of fulfilling the ultimate role of motherhood, female body concepts are transactionally channelized toward fashioning its sexual desirability.[28] The pursuit of love for Archie can therefore be located in this intersection of body anomaly, femininity, and sexuality.

The film opens with a portrayal of the nightscape of the city of Calcutta, when the promise of magical love and its corollary of an exciting life literally hang in the air, with R. J. Alfaaz's seductive voice kick-starting the popular radio show *Kuch Bheege Alfaaz* while belting out old Hindi Bollywood love songs. Archie is shown traveling in a cab to meet her blind date, set up through her Tinder account, and feels spiritually ennobled by the words of Alfaaz and the songs he plays, which the cab driver tunes into as he drives

Archie to her destination. Although it is nighttime, Archie is seen wearing heavy, dark sunglasses, and her head and face are covered up with a scarf. A closer look at Archie gives the viewers hints of white patches around her mouth and eyes. Throughout the movie, Archie is seen wearing her dark sunglasses, and her head is wrapped in a scarf while negotiating public spaces, which normalizes scopophobia around skin disorders, the visibility of which can be controlled by those afflicted by them. This is because the devices of stigma management among women with physical impairments and who negotiate body image ideals primarily depend on the degree of the visibility of their own stigmatic attribute to others. Hence, devices of stigma management for Archie become her "scarf" and the "dark glares." Moreover, it is only the right side of her face that is shown as affected by leukodermic patches, while the left side is clear, and it is mostly her leukodermic profile that the camera focuses on, which in turn becomes a reminder that for women with disfigurements or disabilities, it is their body disorder that is a dominant lens through which their subjectivities are defined and represented.

There is a representational discrepancy in Onir's film, however. On the one hand, Archie is depicted as an independent and feisty young woman who is both self-assured and self-sufficient, and on the other hand, she uses her stigma management tools as her social crutches. She has a moderately successful career as a meme artist, and creativity becomes a pathway for her self-definition. However, there is a pensive aura about Archie as she reflects on love, friendship, and her self-image. Underlying Archie's self-assured exterior disposition, therefore, is a strong element of social isolation because, apart from her coworker and admirer, Apu, she is not seen sharing other social spaces of self-pursuit either through homosocial relations or other relations. The only other close relation is her boisterous, confident, and caring mother, Aruna Pradhan. In fact, the very sociality of Archie's public and social spheres is characterized by her work life and going on blind dates, where one experience after the other leaves her feeling more and more melancholic as she is affected by the look of disappointment on her dates' faces when the realization of her skin condition dawns on them. In due time, however, it is apparent that Archie has come to terms with her suitors' perplexity, as she begins to remove her sunglasses and scarf while talking to them. She even begins to enjoy these moments where she agentively controls the situation by being the surprise factor herself—on the first blind date in the film's opening, Archie good-humoredly asks her dumbfounded date, "Kya hua? Zaada Khubsurat nikli Kya?" (What happened? Did I turn out to be more beautiful than you expected?).[29] Her words here are a testimony to the fact that for women, love and social acceptance are deeply located in their body aesthetics and appearance.

Although a contrarian interpretation of *Kuch Bheege Alfaaz* could be that it problematizes the pursuit of love as an ableist endeavor, by projecting a woman with leukoderma's legitimate claim to it, the contrived manner in which this love is pursued in the film nullifies the validity of such a reading. In fact, in a poignant moment, Archie is seen checking her reflection in the mirror with a wistful and pensive air. This is understandable because in a later scene, where Archie is sitting in a café with Apu, he catches an old man staring at her and in a protective impulse shifts his chair around to block the man's view of her. Archie takes offence at this patronizingly chivalrous behavior and tells Apu that she can handle such situations. Contradictorily, such fleeting moments of Archie's self-assurance are paralleled with an underlying scopophobia owing to which she continuously covers herself up to negotiate with the stigmatic male gaze in public spaces. As the film unfolds, Archie, who is already in love with the disembodied voice and romantic seductions of Alfaaz's persona, serendipitously gets connected with Alfaaz while dialing a date who stood her up. We note that Alfaaz, too, has a conflicted past—while still in high school, in his teenage years, his sixteen-year-old girlfriend, Chavi, had committed suicide after discovering she was pregnant by him.

While Archie is depicted as a conflicted and tormented soul carrying the burden of social stigma, Alfaaz is depicted as a man haunted by his failure to have taken accountability for Chavi's pregnancy and later her death. As a WhatsApp meme creator, Archie is an anonymous creative artist, and she revels in her social anonymity—she also chooses dates who, like her, do not have a profile display picture on their Tinder accounts. By representing Archie's disembodied anonymity both in her workplace and her personal love life (she carries on a telephonic romance with Alfaaz), as a matter of preference and revelry, Onir's film glorifies and valorizes a life of social invisibility as one with ontological value for conflicted individuals like Archie who carry around burdens of internalized social stigma of body appearance.

We further learn of Archie's angsts in a revelatory scene where she is seen recounting to Alfaaz how developing leukoderma changed her life; she claims, "I was like any other girl. Apparently, I was the chosen one."[30] What Archie experiences here has been corroborated by Lennard Davis in his take on disability as a retributory corollary of some vague moral aberration in a previous sinful birth.[31] Hence, Archie tells Alfaaz that in her adolescent years, her friends had played a very cruel prank on her when they had set her up on a blind date with a handsome guy from her class and one look at her patchy face had made him turn and run away because he was expecting a beautiful girl. This incident of bullying foregrounds a socially discriminatory attitude toward women with body deformities. In response, Alfaaz tells her that someday somebody will love her for her inner beauty.

Given that *Kuch Bheege Alfaaz* predominantly projects the pursuit of ideal love as a female quest, it ends up normalizing romantic love as a self-evaluative social mandate for a woman who is leukodermic. This is not to presumptuously claim that the quest for love by the female protagonist makes her appear weak and helpless. Instead, the problematics of Archie's pursuit of love lies in its depiction as a single-minded transcendental quest that is indifferent toward any alternate spaces for self-actualization. The film never emphatically establishes Archie's indefatigable social prowess and her ability to transcend body dysmorphia in claiming social spaces. We never see Archie having any open conversation about her acceptance of leukoderma in the film except at the point where she confesses to an interiorization of the social stigma around leukoderma to Alfaaz. The film celebrates a certain kind of solitariness in which it situates its female protagonist with leukoderma as well as its guilt-ridden male protagonist, perpetuating and normalizing social isolation and seclusion as the archetypal context for such conflicted subjectivities as Archie's and Alfaaz's. This commiserative love toward Archie is therefore borne out of Alfaaz's interiorized guilt over his treatment of Chavi and problematically becomes the source of self-fulfillment for Archie.

In interviews, Onir has claimed that *Kuch Bheege Alfaaz* is about falling in love through a discovery of "inner beauty,"[32] an idea that Alfaaz proclaims before Archie. Such an assertion problematically presupposes that the image of Archie's scarred face is a site of alterity and does not live up to the normative standards of an ideal body image. This reductive and problematically utopic ideology of "inner beauty" desubjectivizes women with nonnormative bodies, subordinating them to an evaluative control of the body image ideal. In the contemporary culture of lookism, which stresses the visibility and tangibility of female corporeality, such abstracted platitudes of "inner beauty" further foreground the lack in that female corporeal frame that must be compensated and/or substituted by ideas of mythic and mystifying notions of inner beauty.

To sum up, the present reading of Onir's film is theoretically affiliated to the contemporary debate in intersectional disability studies, where the presence of "extraordinary bodies"[33] in the new beautyscape of global fashion has been complicated by the idea of a commodification of disability. It draws upon the fact that the inclusion of models with disabilities in the newly emerging topography of capitalist media as well as the global beauty and fashion industry, might not always be about representation of "alternative beauty"[34] since such representational regimes may only end up reinforcing ableist stereotypes of body normativity. Fox, Krings, and Vierke, in a powerful commentary on this phenomenon, claims that a deformed or "disabled body is perfectly able to portray an ableist image if inserted into visual rhetorics that don't challenge conventional stereotypes."[35] In this sense, Archie's representation as a mystified embodiment of "inner beauty" achieving fulfillment through commiserative love is an ableist consignment of meaning onto her physical alterity as a person with leukoderma, which in turn runs the risk of "disability avoidance."[36]

Toward a Positivist Lexicon of Body Aesthetics in *Margarita with a Straw*

Body image norms are particularly confining for women with physical disabilities because they concretize the heterosexist imaginary that women with disabilities are not impacted by body ideals as their bodies are already always interpellated within the ideology of body deviance.[37] What particularly complicates the situation is that in the case of those who use accommodating devices such as wheelchairs, braces, or crutches, women with disabilities are described as "metal . . . hard, cold, angular, and usually ugly"[38] because they are perceived as deviating from normative expectations of appearance ideals. However, Nandini Ghosh tells us that the use of mobility aids is not imbricated with beauty aids but is mobility empowering for women with disability. Disabled women learn to negotiate with these machinic devices as an integral aspect of their body selves. According to Ghosh's ethnographic research in rural Bengal, women with locomotor disabilities are also known to use mobility aids toward a performance of normative femininity to attain a feminine gait, for instance, and to walk straight with the aid of calipers. However, we also know that owing to the hegemony of body image ideals, social encounters of women with physical disabilities are fraught with a perceived compulsion toward concealment of their stigmatized disability aids.[39]

In Shonali Bose's *Margarita with a Straw*,[40] this disability conundrum is highlighted in the initial scenes of the film when Laila, the lead character as a wheelchair user with cerebral palsy, is seen engineering her body appearance on social media by cropping her picture from the waist down, attempting to invisibilize her twisted legs and the fact that she is a wheelchair user. It is worth remembering here that unlike Archie in *Kuch Bheege Alfaaz*, Laila is represented as comfortably steering multiple social relations as she is an active member of a band and has multiple friends who accept her for her talent as a musician. However, there is a gradual transition in Laila as she accepts her wheelchair as radically coterminous with her bodied self. The wheelchair comes to be an important device: a metaphoric locomotive mediating freedom and a tool of Laila's individuation as she is seen negotiating cultural topographies in her wheelchair. Laila's wheelchair radically counters the cultural imaginary that perceives wheelchair users as "wheelchair bound." In this regard, Ann Fox, Krings, and Vierke tell us that "news outlets regularly use language like 'wheelchair bound' to describe wheelchair users when in fact wheelchairs are a device for movement, freedom, and energy conservation for disabled people."[41] Nandini Ghosh's study likewise elaborates that for disabled women, "mobility aids are attuned to not only the needs of their disability but also to the notions of femininity internalized through the processes of socialization."[42] In the light of this—and in the Indian context, especially within an underprivileged scenario—there is a greater burden on women with disabilities to orchestrate their mobility aids toward the performance of femininity for social acceptance. Therefore, as devices of individuation for Indian women with disabilities, mobility aids are socially engineered under the constraint of patriarchal sanction.

In the first half of *Margarita with a Straw*, we see Laila struggling at every step to negotiate with an ableist optics of body morphology mediated through other characters, such as Dhruv, her fellow classmate in Delhi University and also a person with disability. At one instance in the cafeteria, Dhruv is seen ogling another girl's bare midriff, though he claims to Laila jocularly that he would still marry only her. This particular scene establishes the normative body as a sexual body and the body concept of a person with a disability as nonsexual. Hereafter, as Laila tries to explore her sexual awakening, she also explores with the bodily articulations of sexual desire. One day she kisses Dhruv in the university and later musters the courage to declare her love for Nima, the lead singer of the college band for which Laila writes songs. Dhruv, however, takes offense to this and tells her, "Tumhe kya lagta hai? Tum normal logon ke saath rehkar normal ban jayogi?" (What do you think? By mixing with normal people you would become normal?)[43]—manifesting the societal view that Laila's disability is the locus of her body concept, which in turn decimates her social and sexual worth.

With time, Laila secures admission in New York University and moves to the United States with her mother. There she meets Khanum, a Pakistani-Bangladeshi lesbian girl with a visual impairment who completely overhauls Laila's interiorized negative body image and her quest for love. Unlike Laila's conservative perceptions of her own body image, Khanum has a far more positive body optics. She is seen negotiating public spaces in a very self-assured and confident manner. She is also the first person who emphatically tells Laila that she is very beautiful. More importantly, Khanum's touch and her sensual enunciations to Laila about her beautiful body-self establish a significant alternate discourse where a person with disability is enfolded within the lexicon of the body beautiful, an aporic frontier from which persons with disability have been systemically eliminated and alienated. This, as Tobin Siebers states, proves that the hegemonic idea of beauty is integrally congruous with the idea of harmony and wholeness and that standardized beauty is always mediated through uniformity.[44]

Khanum's sexual touch redirects Laila toward an awakening of sensuous pleasures for her own disabled body and an affirmative body aesthetics. Here, as a stroke of feminist strategy, Shonali Bose's film—by making a lesbian woman with a visual impairment the dissenting voice of alternate body image—further destabilizes the heterosexist entitlement to ordering the cultural perceptions of body aesthetics of women with disabilities. And it crafts the symbiotic relation between body image and female sexuality. Khanum takes Laila to all those social spaces that are culturally heterosexist, navigating such spatialities with a greater sense of body autonomy and sexual agency. The film deliberately represents Khanum as a profoundly sexualized being only to establish that her body aesthetics is not governed by her visual impairment, and neither is her sexual worth adjudicated by it. Ideal body image, which generally operates as the Lacanian "master signifier," is debunked here, and other signifiers, such as the moral and social worth associated with body image and resulting in a woman's sexual worth under normative ableist body image discourses, are deconstructed.

Although the application of beauty products generates conflicting arguments within body image studies, in *Margarita with a Straw*, the application of makeup and the use of beauty products are projected as an innocuous self-indulgence, a matter of choice and empowerment, and a way to debunk the misnomer that only able-bodied women with normative bodies can possibly use beauty products. Bonnie Berry, for example, in *The Power of Looks: Social Stratification of Physical Appearance*, claims that there is a difference between the use of cosmetics and that of cosmeceuticals (that bring about more permanent body alterations). Though cosmetics and cosmeceuticals are used for the purposes of attaining social power through cosmetically altered body appearance, the use of cosmeceuticals, unlike cosmetics, portends a kind of obsession with a more permanent nature of body alteration that might foreground body dysmorphia and a more perpetual dissatisfaction with one's body appearance.[45]

Laila's pursuit of beauty in such a context can be interpreted as mediating a particular visual politics, where the visual field of a heteronormative culture only admits beautified and cosmetically enhanced normative female bodies already always inscribed within the paradigms of acceptable and permissible beauty. In the context of *Margarita with a Straw*, therefore, the application of makeup by Khanum and later Laila is not contiguous with the male gaze or the anxieties of lookism. The scene where the audience sees Khanum applying eye shadow and teaching Laila to apply makeup establishes that women with disabilities can have legitimate recourses to claiming their choice to use makeup while negotiating public spaces and social spheres without obsessing with beauty labor. Here, it is Khanum who makes this choice available to Laila.

A certain fulfillment with her "self" at the end of the film, as Laila goes on a date with herself, shows her transcendence over all dependency on the self-evaluative forces of either love or sexual relations while she comes to terms with her nonnormative body image. The film's closure significantly reinforces the self-contentment of a more evolved and empowered Laila reveling in her aloneness borne out of choice and not compulsory isolation. Her agentive reclamation of her body image and its positive hermeneutics are elucidated through the closing scenes as Laila visits a beauty parlor for a ritualistic body-self makeover and tells her friend over the phone that she cannot go out for a movie as she has a date that night. The scene in the beauty salon is a significant intervention in establishing the semantics of beauty labor as not an exclusivist ableist pursuit but to foster the visibility of persons with disabilities in such spaces that have historically been marked by the hypervisibility of only able-bodied women toward a patriarchally legitimated pursuit of beauty. Laila's entry into the beauty parlor is predicated on the idea of the "democratization of beauty."[46]

Furthermore, through the scene in the beauty salon, the film first creates an expectation in the audience that Laila's beauty rituals and her impending date are suggestive of her moving on—perhaps with a new heteronormative relationship after her mother's death and the leaving of Khanum, her lesbian lover. However, such hetero-patriarchal audience expectations are shattered at the end by the mirror scene, in which, while sipping on margarita with a straw, Laila looks at her beautified image in the large mirror hanging opposite and smiles jubilantly, raising a toast to herself. This closing mirror scene is a sharp retort to the hegemonic sociocultural contiguity between the female pursuit of beauty and the pursuit of heteronormative love by replacing it with Laila's self-love, which happens to be with her nonnormate bodied self. This scene, where we see an exuberant, prettified Laila sipping a margarita with a straw on a date with herself, upholds the concept of "alternative beauty,"[47] which does not commodify disability, but rather foregrounds a differential aesthetics of body image within the paradigms of media's representation of disability. The agential reclamation of life and its vagaries is thus mediated through a positivist alteration of body concept with this closing mirror scene.

It is not to say that the ending of *Margarita with a Straw* celebrates a kind of a separatist female utopia, and neither is aloneness being romanticized; in fact, the film makes evident the social needs and the material reality of Laila as a person with a disability. The ending is instead an acknowledgment of the fact that beyond all social spaces exists a spatial ontology of selfhood contiguous with Laila's transition toward body positivity and the film's expansion of the frontiers of human beauty. Laila's transition toward a more coherent internal world, predicated on a consolidated ontology of positive body image, finally enforces an empathetic and sensitive representation where the female protagonist with a disability is not ascribed a perpetual existence of victimhood after the loss of her mother and her lover. The closing scene concretizes the apposite titular implication that sipping a margarita with a straw is not an act of infantile preoccupation for a woman with cerebral palsy but a plea for integration of differential subjectivities with all their non-unitarian body aesthetics.

In conclusion, this chapter sums up the complexities of body image of women with deformities or disabilities, keeping in mind neoliberal India's construction of femininity. Given the nation's patriarchal optics of the functionality of the female body, which is mediated through its reproductive role, body image becomes the mechanism through which the female body is expected to fashion its femininity and sexual desirability. This chapter notes how *Kuch Bheege Alfaaz* posits the submission of the female protagonist to this contrived ideal of body image—where the pursuit of love is imbricated with internalized anxieties about a perceived failure to fulfill reproductive imperatives because of the lack of sexual desirability of a woman with leukoderma. In contrast, *Margarita with a Straw* decouples the pursuit of selfhood from such heteronormatively instrumented body ontology and subverts hegemonic body ideals that normalize ableist semantics of body aesthetics. Hence, whereas, in Shonali Bose's radical film, Laila works toward positive and agentive lexicons of self-articulation that dismantle culturally manufactured pathologies of body fictions around disability, in Onir's film, the female lead is represented as negotiating scopophobia and lookism in a more hetero-patriarchally sanctioned manner that perpetuates the myth of social worthlessness, moral failure, and body dysmorphia around body deformity, rather than debunking it. A comparative reading of both films then becomes important because they address the issue of female body image among women with deformities or disabilities in neoliberal India, which, despite the rhetoric of freedom and choice, largely submits to collusive politics of prescriptive body aesthetics.

NOTES

1. Liebelt, Böllinger, and Verke, *Beauty and the Norm*, 21.
2. Freud, *The Standard Edition*, 26–30.
3. Lacan, *Ecrits*, 81.
4. Lemma, *Under the Skin*, 18–20.
5. Lemma, *Under the Skin*, 18–20.
6. Wolf, *The Beauty Myth*, 3–10.
7. Berry, *Beauty Bias*, 10.
8. Lemma, *Under the Skin*, 15–20.
9. Begum, "Disabled Women," 77.
10. Healey, "The Common Agenda."
11. King, introduction to *Body Politics*.

12. Garland-Thomson, *Extraordinary Bodies*, 285.
13. Wendell, "Toward a Feminist Theory," 268–269.
14. Cash and Smolak, *Body Image*, 3–9.
15. Ghosh, *Interrogating Disability*, 10–16.
16. Bauman and Murray, *Deaf Gain*, 1–10.
17. Garland-Thomson, "Integrating Disability."
18. Liebelt, "Beauty and the Norm," 27.
19. Asch and Fine, "Nurturance, Sexuality."
20. Darling, "Stigma of Disability."
21. Wendell, *The Rejected Body*.
22. Begum, "Disabled Women."
23. Smart, *Disability, Society, and the Individual*, 25.
24. Böllinger, "Broken Beauty," 159.
25. Garland-Thomson, *Staring*, 1–10.
26. Böllinger, "Broken Beauty," 159–160.
27. Taub, Fanklik, and McLorg, "Body Image among Women."
28. Ghosh, *Interrogating Disability*, 142–145.
29. Onir, *Kuch Bheege Alfaaz*.
30. Onir, *Kuch Bheege Alfaaz*.
31. Davis, *The Disability Studies Reader*, 2–10.
32. Onir, *Kuch Bheege Alfaaz*.
33. Fox, Krings, and Vierke, "Disability Gain."
34. Fox, Krings, and Vierke, 105.
35. Fox, Krings, and Vierke, 107.
36. Fox, Krings, and Vierke, 118.
37. Cash and Smolak, *Body Image*, 3–10.
38. Bogle and Shaul, "Body Image," 93.
39. Ghosh, *Interrogating Disability*, 140–142.
40. Bose, *Margarita with a Straw*.
41. Fox, Krings, and Vierke, "Disability," 118.
42. Ghosh, *Interrogating Disability*, 141.
43. Bose, *Margarita with a Straw*.
44. Siebers, "Disability Aesthetics."
45. Berry, *The Power of Looks*, 63–65.
46. Berry, 68.
47. Fox, Krings, and Vierke, "Disability Gain," 120.

BIBLIOGRAPHY

Asch, Adrienne, and Michelle Fine. "Nurturance, Sexuality and Women with Disabilities: The Example of Women and Literature." In *The Disability Studies Reader*, edited by Lennard J. Davis, 241–259. London: Routledge, 1997.

Bauman, H-Dirksen L., and Joseph J. Murray. *Deaf Gain: Raising the Stakes for Human Diversity*. Minneapolis: University of Minnesota Press, 2014.

Begum, Nasa. "Disabled Women and the Feminist Agenda." *Feminist Review* 40, no. 1 (1992): 70–80.

Berry, Bonnie. *Beauty Bias: Discrimination and Social Power*. Westport, CT: Praeger, 2007.

———. *The Power of Looks: Social Stratification of Physical Appearance*. London: Ashgate, 2008.

Bogle, Jane Elder, and Susan L. Shaul. "Body Image and the Woman with a Disability." In *Sexuality and Physical Disability: Personal Perspectives*, edited by David G. Bullard and Susan E. Knight, 91–95. St. Louis, MO: Mosby Press, 1981.

Böllinger, Sarah. "Broken Beauty, Broken Cups: Disabled Bodies in Contemporary African Art." In *Beauty and the Norm: Debating Standardization in Bodily Appearance*, edited by Claudia Liebelt, Sarah Böllinger, and Ulf Vierke, 127–154. New York: Palgrave Macmillan, 2019.

Bordo, Susan. *Unbearable Weight: Feminism, Western Culture, and the Body*. Berkeley: University of California Press, 1993.

Bose, Shonali, dir. *Margarita with a Straw*. (Viacom18 Motion Pictures, Mumbai, 2014).

Cash, Thomas F., and Linda Smolak, eds. *Body Image: A Handbook of Science, Practice, and Prevention*. 2nd ed. New York: Guilford Press, 2011.

Darling, Rosalyn Benjamin. "Stigma of Disability." In *Encyclopaedia of Criminology and Deviant Behaviour*, edited by Clifton D. Bryant, 482–485. London: Routledge, 2001.

Davis, Lennard J. *The Disability Studies Reader*. London: Routledge, 1997.

Fox, Ann M., Matthias Krings, and Ulf Vierke. "'Disability Gain' and the Limits of Representing Alternative Beauty." In *Beauty and the Norm: Debating Standardization in Bodily Appearance*, edited by Claudia Liebelt, Sarah Böllinger, and Ulf Vierke, 105–109. New York: Palgrave Macmillan, 2019.

Freud, Sigmund. *The Standard Edition of the Complete Psychoanalytical Works of Sigmund Freud*. London: Hogarth Press, 1923.

Garland-Thomson, Rosemarie. *Extraordinary Bodies: Figuring Physical Disability in American Culture and Literature*. New York: Columbia University Press, 1997.

———. "Integrating Disability, Transforming Feminist Theory." *NWSA Journal* 14, no. 3 (2002): 1–32.

———. *Staring: How We Look*. Oxford: Oxford University Press, 2009.

Ghosh, Nandini. *Interrogating Disability in India: Theory and Practice*. New Delhi: Springer, 2016.

Healey, Shevy. "The Common Agenda between Old Women, Women with Disability and All Women." *Women and Therapy* 14, no. 3–4 (1993): 65–77.

King, Debra Walker. Introduction to *Body Politics and the Fictional Double*, edited by Debra Walker King, 10–20. Bloomington: Indiana University Press, 2000.

Lacan, Jacques. *Ecrits*. 1st complete ed. in English. Translated by B. Fink. New York: Norton, 2006.

Lemma, Alessandra. *Under the Skin: A Psychoanalytic Study of Body Modification*. London: Routledge, 2010.

Liebelt, Claudia. "Beauty and the Norm: An Introduction," in *Beauty and the Norm: Debating Standardization in Bodily Appearance*, edited by Claudia Liebelt, Sarah Böllinger, and Ulf Verke (New York: Palgrave Macmillan, 2019).

Liebelt, Claudia, Sarah Böllinger, and Ulf Vierke. *Beauty and the Norm: Debating Standardization in Bodily Appearance*. New York: Palgrave Macmillan, 2019.

Onir, dir. *Kuch Bheege Alfaaz*. (Yoodlee Films, Mumbai, 2018).

Siebers, Tobin. "Disability Aesthetics and the Body Beautiful: Signposts in the History of Art." *ALTER—European Journal for Disability Studies* 2, no. 4 (2008): 329–336.

Smart, Julie. *Disability, Society, and the Individual*. Gaithersburg, MD: Aspen, 2001.

Taub, Diane E., Patricia L. Fanklik, and Penelope A. McLorg. "Body Image among Women with Physical Disabilities: Internalization of Norms and Reactions to Nonconformity." *Sociological Focus* 36, no. 2 (2012): 159–176.

Wendell, Susan. *The Rejected Body: Feminist Philosophical Reflections on Disability*. London: Routledge, 1996.

———. "Toward a Feminist Theory of Disability," in *The Disability Studies Reader*, edited by Lennard J. Davis (London: Routledge, 1997).

Wolf, Naomi. *The Beauty Myth: How Images of Beauty Are Used against Women*. New York: William Morrow, 1991.

IV

Scopophilic Cultures

Female Body Image in Contemporary Indian Cinema

8

Unjust Gradations of Fairness

Gender, Looks, and Colorism in Postmillennial Hindi Cinema

Shailendra Kumar Singh

Introduction

Amid a global pandemic that severely crippled multiple economies, daily routines, and familiar lifestyles, the consolidation of online platforms and digital landscapes was only inevitable. While this definitely led to increased screen time and unprecedented levels of binge-watching, a concomitant phenomenon that also dominated this particular phase of our "new normal" was the pronounced proliferation of Internet chatterati. It therefore was not at all surprising that when a Hindi song with a chorus "Tujhe dekh ke goriya, Beyoncé sharma jayegi" (On seeing you, o fair lady, Beyoncé will pale in comparison) was released on YouTube in 2020, it received considerable critical backlash for promoting skin color prejudices and discrimination. Predictably enough, the lyrics of the song were adjusted to make it relatively less controversial. Nonetheless, what stood out in this entire sequence of events was the way the director and the lyricist still chose to defend their ground by pointing out how the term *goriya* (a fair maiden) has been so often used to refer to a girl that it did not occur to them to interpret it in the literal manner (*Rolling Stone India* 2020).

The glaring contradictions of the Hindi film industry were also exposed when many of the filmmakers were accused of hypocrisy and double standards for supporting the Black Lives Matter movement following the killing of George Floyd on May 25, 2020. Celebrities like Priyanka Chopra Jonas, whose espousal of Black Lives Matter on social media was probably aimed at her Western fan base, nevertheless incurred the wrath of Bollywood enthusiasts who swiftly seized on her post to highlight her appearance in an advertising campaign for skin-lightening products (Waheed 2020). Chopra's case is especially curious since in the movie *Fashion* (2008), her dreadful descent into the world of drugs, alcohol, and moral bankruptcy reaches a climactic point when she sleeps with a dark-skinned person! Even historically, Hindi cinema has deployed darkness as a formulaic marker of villainy, wickedness, and duplicitous behavior. Iconic characters such as Birju in *Mother India* (Khan 1957) and Gabbar Singh in *Sholay* (Embers) (Sippy 1975) sufficiently corroborate this premise. Similarly, when it comes to the representation of women, all that was repressed in the Hindu woman resurfaced in her white counterpart—the racial, sexual "Other" onto whom everything repressed within the self could be projected (Mubarki 2016). However, in the postmillennial period, the overtly promiscuous and sexually available figure of the westernized vamp has receded into anonymity and insignificance. Instead, leading actresses (most notably Katrina Kaif and Kareena Kapoor) have themselves performed *item songs* (sexually provocative dance sequences for movie songs that may or may not have any relevance to the main plot) for their films. But the one thing that has remained constant for the film industry is the kind of stigma, invisibility, and erasure that is often linked with dark skin tone.

Cinematic representations such as *Parched* (Yadav 2015) and *Vivah* (Marriage) (Barjatya 2006) clearly attest to this since not having fair skin is tantamount to not being attractive or desirable. In light of these existing blemishes, predilections, and dichotomies, this chapter examines the discursive politics of representation that crystallizes around the theme of colorism in two films, namely *Udta Punjab* (Punjab on a high) (Chaubey 2016) and *Bala* (Kaushik 2019). It demonstrates how the composite dynamics of gender, appearance, and skin tone, in these two films, borrow heavily from the prejudicial discourses and reductive stereotypes that dominate popular cultures in contemporary India. Color-based discrimination that was earlier evident through the formulaic portrayals of villains and vamps in Hindi cinema has increasingly been associated with urban slums or small towns, which in turn become synonymous with lack of growth, progress, and opportunity. The dark-skinned female protagonist is thus either delineated as an archetypal marker of a much-maligned regional identity (often far removed from the celebratory accounts of various "India Shining" narratives) or simply posited with a somewhat dichotomous and half-baked rhetoric of self-acceptance that problematizes any straightforward interpretations of such ostensibly innocuous cinematic representations. The problem of colorism in Indian culture is a deeply entrenched and pervasive one, especially with regard to female body image and aesthetic capital (D'Mello 2016; Jha and Adelman 2009;

Parameswaran and Cardoza 2009a; Vaid 2009). As such, decoding the various nuances and subtleties of these two postmillennial Hindi films can provide important clues about how social prejudices organized around skin tone can either be interrogated or buttressed through popular modes of entertainment.

Dark Skin, India Shining, and the Outrageous North Indian Stereotype

The slim, tall, and fair female subject that has been unequivocally valorized through films, advertising, television, and mass media is a bitter reality of the postliberalization period in India. Radhika Parameswaran and Kavitha Cardoza observe that even though dark skin was a source of stigma for Indian women long before the arrival of globalization, "a slew of facial-lightening products in the global Indian marketplace renewed age-old associations between light skin color and its embodiment of higher social and economic status" (2009b, 217–218). This palpable shift was further buttressed by the fact that Western body ideals now fueled the popular imagination of the masses in India because of the global success and fame that South Asian models had begun acquiring in prestigious beauty pageants. One of the most damaging consequences of such a Procrustean standard of attractiveness was the blatant rejection of women who failed to conform to this stereotype (that is, women who were either fat, little, or dusky) (Parameswaran 2004). The rhetoric of the hard-working, self-made, and fair-complexioned celebrity from the global South who could also make a somewhat kindred transition toward a career in cinema neatly resonated with India's increasing presence in world politics and international affairs. As a result, the dark-skinned rural migrant workers from several underdeveloped North Indian states, such as the tribal belts of Jharkhand, the rural parts of Uttar Pradesh, Rajasthan, Bihar, and even Odisha, are perceived according to an untenable logic that equates fairness with growth, prosperity, abundance, and empowerment. In this section, I argue that the portrayal of the dark-skinned migrant worker from Bihar in Abhishek Chaubey's film *Udta Punjab* unapologetically relies on a certain set of stereotypes that have become common knowledge in contemporary North India.

The principal plot that gravitates around the problem of drug addiction and trade shows it to be a menace that has plagued the entire state of Punjab—and more specifically its male youth. Meanwhile, Kumari Pinky, a former district-level hockey player, has been forced by her familial circumstances to migrate from Bihar to work as a laborer in the Sarhota fields. When she accidently comes across a package that contains three kilos of heroin, she decides to sell it to a prospective buyer in an attempt to ameliorate her financial fortunes. However, things take a dramatic turn when she is kidnapped and held captive by the drug dealers, who sexually assault her on multiple occasions. The rest of the film engages with Pinky's personal struggles as a drug addict and how her indomitable spirit brings about a desirable change in Tommy Singh, a young, popular, and successful Punjabi musician whose proclivities for substance abuse constantly land him into trouble with the police and the media. It is my contention here that the delineation of the dark-skinned character who not only belongs to the working classes but also to one of the poorest and most underdeveloped states of India is not merely incidental. This is because, within the subcontinent, the linguistic and cultural references that are often employed at an ordinary, everyday register are at best derogatory when it comes to identifying darkness with poverty and backwardness (Jha 2015; Kulkarni 2016). Just as dark skin is portrayed in commercials as blemished and backward, India's economic reforms have irreversibly distorted the country's developmental priorities so that the questions of inequality, poor infrastructure, poverty alleviation, and broad-based growth are contemptuously dismissed by elites and policymakers as something belonging to an older provincial order: one of nepotism, corruption, and endless red tape (Nadeem 2014).[1] In other words, if fairness signifies a global yardstick of beauty that neatly resonates with "India Shining" narratives,[2] then dark skin tone, its obverse, is symbolically associated with the veritable roadblocks that impede the country's growth rate. The acronym BIMARU (literally meaning "sick"), which is often used to refer to the Indian states of Bihar, Madhya Pradesh, Rajasthan, and Uttar Pradesh, also seems to serve a similar function. Dark-skinned girls and women in the postmillennial context of India definitely do not make it to the list of global/transnational citizens and subjects in the same way that the term "Bihari" is frequently equated with a lack of etiquette, refinement, sophistication, and cosmopolitanism. Both a dark skin tone and the overarching category of being a "Bihari" are predictably conflated in *Udta Punjab* to communicate a stereotype that has almost become synonymous with a regional slur characterized by acute indigence, sheer wretchedness, and a lack of desirability.

From high levels of arsenic in the groundwater to annual flooding and the devastation of lives and livelihoods, from poor infrastructure and the acute shortage of power to high levels of crime, the state of Bihar remains the discursive figurehead of underdevelopment (Kumar 2018). This may indeed be compared with Alia Bhatt's decision to go three shades darker for the film in order to play the role of a Bihari girl (*The Statesman* 2016). The brownface/blackface debate that is lately turning out to be a sore point for many Bollywood films reflects an incipient and tentative interrogation of the deep-seated prejudices that relate to skin tone and have consistently plagued Hindi cinema in the postindependence period. Films such as *Brahmachari* (Bachelor) (Sonie 1968), *Doosri Sita* (The second Sita) (Anand 1974), and *Apne Rang Hazaar* (Our thousand colors) (Tandon 1975) featured dark-skinned actresses who were either treated with contempt or simply considered undeserving of love. In recent years, however, the reemergence of narratives revolving around rural areas and small towns has also convinced filmmakers about the so-called veracity of a class position that is often understood through the lens of colorism in India. Sanjay Srivastava sums it up quite neatly when he says that in India, "fair skin tone is aspirational while dark skin tone is associated with people who are lower on the caste and class hierarchy and popular culture just perpetuates this stereotype" (quoted in Bedika 2019). The convenient pretext to lend authenticity and verisimilitude to a character in *Udta Punjab* is nothing but a reiteration of the stereotype that equates darkness with underdevelopment. And though one may discursively argue here that male characters too are subject to the brownface/blackface practice, the pejorative categorizations that surround the term "Bihari" in North India are way too culturally loaded for us to ignore its import or significance vis-à-vis Chaubey's film. Its recurrent identification with epithets such as *gawaar/dehaati* (a villager) and *jaahil* (uncivilized and boorish) in the urban spaces of metropolitan cities like New Delhi often involves a gratuitous disdain for working-class migrants. This is only made worse by derisive and scornful references to their *gamachhas* (a traditional thin, coarse cotton towel), while those from the educated sections who are able to conduct themselves with flair, grace, and a chaste English accent are received with surprise as they do not conform to the dominant compartmentalizations. The pervasive and deeply entrenched anti-Bihari sentiments that one finds in Maharashtra (*Two Circles* 2008), Rajasthan, Gujarat, and the northeast states have by and large eclipsed the other narrative according to which Biharis qualify in significant numbers for joining Indian Administrative Services, Indian Institutes of Technology, and Indian Institutes of Management (Verma 2019). Viewed in this context, even though the character of Kumari Pinky occupies diegetic centrality, an irreducible component of tokenism (evident most conspicuously by the dark skin tone) cannot be denied.

Having said this, what is also important is that once we move past the overt connection that is drawn between dark skin and a Bihari girl, we realize that Chaubey also manages to capture certain finer nuances and subtleties about Bhatt's character. For instance, her resilience, tenacity, and self-determination in the face of overwhelming odds contrast sharply with Tommy's desire to commit suicide. The fact that her captors periodically inject her with intoxicating doses of heroin (so that they can take turns while forcing themselves upon her or even collectively rape her) is met with an extraordinary strength of character that in turn presents her in a positive light. Not one to give in too easily to despair, Pinky draws comfort and consolation by staring endlessly at the big billboard (an advertisement for a Goa holiday) that is visible from her window. The billboard that symbolically represents her idea of a good time lends her a firmness of purpose since she refuses to succumb to her impossibly difficult circumstances and fights her way out of both addiction and incarceration. This too is quite commensurate with the academic literature that is available on Biharis and according to which Biharis were discursively sensitive toward others' feelings, cared for relationships, and were intelligent, hardworking, and patient (Verma 2019). More importantly, though, the fact that the possibility of heterosexual romantic love is not foreclosed for the dark-skinned female protagonist in the film is a welcome change for an industry where more often than not it is only the tall, slim, and fair characters who are promised a happy ending in the concluding sections of any cinematic representation.

Lest it may appear as if colorism is merely a region-specific phenomenon, a few qualifications are in order here. The first is that it is a systemic discrimination, historically practiced all over India and integral to the social, institutional, and cultural fabric of Indian society (Jha 2015). Thus, even South Indians are repeatedly portrayed in a derogatory capacity, and often their presence seems to serve a comic function. From *Padosan* (Female neighbor) (Swaroop 1968) to *Chennai Express* (Shetty 2013) and *2 States* (Varman 2014), South Indians have had a contemptuous and disdainful representation—dark skinned, wearing a lungi, and speaking in a comically heavy South Indian accent (Bhattacharya 2018). What is equally worse, if not more, is that even in Tamil cinema, there is a clear propensity toward fair-skinned actresses who do not even hail from the state (Nair 2019). These arbitrary, relative, and unjust gradations of fairness are uniquely preposterous in a country where "most people are varying shades of brown and black" (Parameswaran and Cardoza 2009b, 228). And yet, in this section I have tried to underscore the eccentric parallels and damaging stereotypes that exist vis-à-vis dark skin tone and the unpalatable realities of destitution, backwardness, and underdevelopment in contemporary India.

The Paradoxes of Portraying Color Prejudice

If Abhishek Chaubey's *Udta Punjab* draws on popular perceptions surrounding darkness and Biharis, then Amar Kaushik's film *Bala* involves a dark-complexioned lawyer who has had to constantly grapple with disparaging remarks and nasty comments since her childhood. Latika Trivedi has an acrimonious relationship with Bala, one of her neighbors, who not only prides himself on his good looks and impressive hairstyle but is also downright vitriolic and cruel when it comes to making fun of her skin tone. But with a receding hairline at the mere age of twenty-five, Bala realizes, almost in a form of karmic retribution, what it means to be ridiculed on the basis of one's looks and appearance. When Pari Mishra, a fair-skinned model, walks out on him after discovering the truth behind his wig, Bala seeks legal assistance from Latika, who gradually also helps him come to terms with his own sense of self-perception. While Bala's marriage to Pari is annulled in a court of law, the movie concludes with a rhetoric of self-acceptance and a resumption of friendship between the two neighbors.

Kaushik's film raises important issues regarding the complex interplay of gender, skin tone, and desirability in postliberalization India. It demonstrates how a woman's fairness or lack of it is inextricably intertwined with her worth and value as a potential bride. This is consistent with the research findings on the subject because "light skin tone is interpreted as beauty, and beauty operates as social capital for women" (Hunter 2005, 37). Besides, Thompson and Keith argue that "although colorism affects attitudes about the self for both men and women, it appears that these effects are stronger for women than men" (2001, 338).[3] Similarly, Parameswaran and Cardoza observe that in a patriarchal culture that is preoccupied with channeling Indian women's sexuality through the institutions of marriage and domesticity, "beauty becomes the password to unlock the gateways to normative structures of romance, courtship, and marriage" (2009b, 256). Even though Bala himself is quite conscious about his self-image, he unapologetically preys upon the anxieties and plummeting self-esteem of girls and women in the neighborhood to sell Pretty You, a fairness product. As opposed to this, we have Latika, who does not have a problem with her complexion and is literally comfortable in her own skin. In fact, she sternly rebukes Bala for using skin filters to make her photos fairer and more attractive on Instagram. But the real tragedy that befalls Bala is when he is defeated by his own conservative attitude and mentality. Always so finicky and condescending about other people's appearance and desirability, he gets a taste of his own medicine when Pari refuses to live with him after finding out about his premature hair loss. As a result, when his boss tells him that selling beauty to this ugly country is like selling water coolers in deserts, heaters on the Himalayas, liquor in Bihar, and fresh air in Delhi, he realizes how he is himself part of the problem that affects his own sense of self-worth.

The Indian fairness cream market, which was reportedly worth around ₹3,000 crores in 2019, is expected to reach ₹5,000 crores in 2023 (Krishnankutty 2020). Persuasively advertised as "alchemic agents of self-transformation" (Nadeem 2014, 224), these fairness creams are critiqued in the film for promising shallow and ineffective solutions to one's own apprehensions and misgivings vis-à-vis self-image. At a metathematic register, the film also appears to take a serious stand against celebrities who promote these products.

This is because the role of Pari is played by Yami Gautam, an Indian actress who has acquired fame as well as notoriety for starring in a number of commercials for Fair & Lovely (now renamed Glow & Lovely), an Indian skin-lightening product that has captured the imagination of masses for more than four decades. As a local celebrity and TikTok star who is simply obsessed with popularity and distinction, Pari is presented as a frivolous and insincere character whose pronounced disgust for Bala's receding hairline single-handedly outweighs his otherwise sensitive, emotional, and caring nature. There is an implicit critique of her predilections since in the ultimate analysis, all she seems to care about are fancy hairstyles and outward appearances. But the one area where the film excels is its spirited refusal to slide into the mode of sentimentality and melodrama. Bala tries his level best to impress Latika even as the latter resolutely rejects his advances in favor of Rohan, an Australia-based NRI (Non-Resident Indian). Here too the possibility of romance, courtship, and marriage is not denied to the dark-skinned female protagonist, which is indeed a rarity in Hindi cinema. Latika's character is also crucial because, through her subjective experiences, she is able to educate and sensitize Bala toward his own complicity in perpetuating colorism. When Bala tells her that she will never be able to understand what he is going through, Latika retorts by revealing her own apprehensions about her looks, the comments on her skin tone, and the sheer embarrassment and suffocation she had to endure from an early age. Turning the accusation on its head, she further adds that it is he who will never be able to make sense of the mental and emotional trauma that a ten-year-old girl has to put up with when she is called "dark-skinned." Not stopping there, when she fights his case, she sympathizes with his sense of uneasiness and his fear of humiliation. As a friend, she also lends him the necessary validation when she not only urges him to accept himself but also assures him that he looks good the way he is. This convinces him to stop making any efforts to change himself, which in turn allows him to quit his job, which otherwise blatantly relied on color prejudices for its sales.

However, the film itself succumbs to certain conventions that have been a part of Bollywood for many years. The offensive practice of using blackface, which can be historically traced through various cinematic representations like *Meri Surat Teri Aankhen* (My face, your eyes) (Rakhan 1963), *Mai Bhi Ladki Hoon* (I too am a girl) (Tirulokchandar 1964), *Souten* (Co-wife) (Tak 1983), *Razia Sultan* (Amrohi 1983), and *Naseeb Apna Apna* (Each person has their own fate) (Rao 1986), is also true of *Bala*. Bhumi Pednekar, who is otherwise quite fair faced, had to use heavy makeup in order to play Latika. In other words, the dark-skinned actress is still conspicuous by her very absence, which reinscribes the superiority of her fair-skinned counterpart over her. This particular issue is also a gendered question because male actors with relatively darker skin tones (actors like Nawazuddin Siddiqui) have been eventu-

ally incorporated within the folds of mainstream Hindi cinema as both powerful character actors as well as convincing male leads. By contrast, dusky
actresses such as Konkona Sen Sharma and Bipasha Basu have been essentially marginalized and written off in recent times. What is also noteworthy
is that while Bhumi was generally lauded for putting on weight for her debut
film, *Dum Laga ke Haisha* (Give in all your energy) (Katariya 2015), she incurred the critics' ire for her blackface in *Bala* and for playing a sharpshoot-
er older than sixty in *Saand Ki Aankh* (Bull's eye) (Hiranandani 2019). Even
though all three films mentioned here continue to discriminate against either fat, dark-skinned, or older actresses, there is a qualitative difference between the three. This is because weight gain is not the same as makeup—or,
for that matter, taking recourse to a fat suit—since it is a corporeal experience that we do not find in the other two cases. The essential point to keep
in mind here is that the controversy surrounding *Saand Ki Aankh* became
a subject of discussion mainly after Neena Gupta, a senior artist, tweeted a
request that directors and producers consider older actresses for roles that
dealt with elderliness (*India Today* 2019). Moreover, critics like Pankhuri Shukla (2019) have rightly pointed out how Bhumi's character is purely a plot point
in *Bala* with the sole intention of helping the male protagonist realize his own
problem. And yet, the most glaring and fundamental contradiction that can
be discerned in the concluding sections of the film is that Bala continues to
make fun of fat, short, and dark-skinned people, which problematizes any
real, concrete claims to overcome color prejudice. The rhetoric of self-acceptance and the practice of offensive comedy do not appear to be mutually exclusive to him even at the very end.

In India, color prejudice is a pervasive and persistent issue that has serious implications for girls and women both in terms of personal assessment
of one's worth as well as professional growth. A fair complexion is seen as a
kind of visible asset that opens up multiple opportunities related to marital
prospects and desirable careers. As such, the transformational imperatives
vis-à-vis fairness are often packaged not only as a reliable route to success,
visibility, and recognition but also simultaneously equated with grace, confidence, and individuality. In the two films analyzed previously, one finds a
familiar logic of either associating darkness with underdevelopment or a simplistic blackface that clearly does not convey a reassuring message of self-love
to dark-skinned fans. For instance, Krishna Priya Pallavi (2019) writes, "I am
not a gori ladki [a fair-complexioned girl]. *Bala* left me feeling cheated." Similarly, Rohini Chatterji (2019) states how Bhumi's makeup is infuriating to
watch as a dark-skinned woman. One finds a comparable absence of dark-
skinned actresses in soap operas such as *Sapna Babul Ka . . . Bidaai* (A father's dream to have his daughter happily married; see Shahi et al. 2007–2010).
The overwhelming presence of fair-skinned female artists in daytime dra-

mas is a discriminatory but established fact. Soap operas, like films, thus contribute to a reinscription of perpetually polemical discourses surrounding epidermal fascinations in India. Examining how aspects of women's bodies such as menstrual fluids, lumps of fat, and lines in the skin that indicate aging are often stigmatized in art and popular culture (as something fundamentally disgusting), Joan C. Chrisler (2011) offers a tripartite structure through which gendered corporeal anxieties and prejudices can be better understood. However, in addition to leaks (menstrual cycle), lumps (corpulence), and lines (that indicate aging)—the three major facets of body shaming that Chrisler identifies—a dark skin tone is also constructed as a social and cultural stigma that privileges pigmentocracy over actual merit.[4] The unrealized potential of films such as *Udta Punjab* and *Bala* can only be read as a classic case of lost chances and missed opportunities considering how cinema can initiate a powerful discourse of contestation vis-à-vis long-standing orthodoxies and can decisively demystify discriminations based on skin color.

Color prejudice can almost be viewed as a fait accompli in India, where, apart from contemporary newspaper articles, "the issue has not been subjected to sufficient academic debate like its parallel phenomenon in black society and culture" (Johnson 2002, 216). However, significant measures are being taken by select groups and organizations that feel strongly committed to the cause of fighting colorism at a quotidian register. For instance, Nandita Das, a Bollywood actress and social activist, has vehemently supported the crusade against the fetishism of skin-lightening products and has urged people to love themselves not in spite of their complexion but because of it (Dhillon 2013). The Dark Is Beautiful campaign started by Women of Worth in Chennai has become a national forum that allows women to express their values of self-worth and self-love and discourages discrimination against and maltreatment of dark-skinned women (Sims and Hirudayaraj 2016). In the realm of popular culture, the Hindi television serial *Saat Phere: Saloni Ka Safar* (Seven rounds of marriage: Saloni's journey) (Sarang 2005–2009) established a radical precedent by casting Rajshree Thakur, a dark-complexioned actress, in the lead role. Efforts of the kind mentioned here can bring about a constructive dialogue, awareness, and sensitivity about combating color prejudice in India even as they discursively challenge the immutable rigidities and stubbornness of Hindi cinema.

ACKNOWLEDGMENTS

The author is grateful to Yuvaan, Santosh, and Pooja for their comments on earlier versions of this chapter. The author is also thankful to the editors and reviewers of this volume for their suggestions. A special thanks to Aditi, Ashima, Naqiya, and Saumya for engaging with successive versions. The responsibility for any error, however, remains entirely with the author. This chapter is humbly dedicated to the author's late parents.

NOTES

1. Mohan Guruswamy (2020) astutely observes that as opposed to an all-India per capita developmental expenditure of ₹7,935 for the period between 2017 and 2019, Bihar's is less than half at ₹3,633.

2. The hype around an increasingly affluent India and its booming high-tech industry—which has yet to result in an upgrade in the nationwide standard of living—was almost entirely built around the slogan "India Shining" (Mendes 2010). Mendes further points out how this political motto was coined for the 2004 Indian general election campaign by the then ruling nationalist Bharatiya Janata Party to sell an idea of economic optimism and advertise the country's achievements abroad.

3. On a related note, Evelyn Nanako Glenn pertinently points out how the "relation between skin color and judgments about attractiveness affect women most acutely, since women's worth is judged heavily on the basis of appearance" (2008, 282).

4. For more on pigmentocracy, see Telles (2014).

REFERENCES

Amrohi, Kamal, dir. 1983. *Razia Sultan*. Mumbai: Rajdhani Films.

Anand, Gogi, dir. 1974. *Doosri Sita*. Mumbai: B. K. Khanna Productions.

Barjatya, Sooraj, dir. 2006. *Vivah*. Mumbai: Rajshri Productions.

Bedika. 2019. "Racism in Cinema: Bollywood Mirror on the Wall, Who's the Fairest of Them All." *PTI News*, June 8, 2019. Available at http://ptinews.com/news/10625235 _Racism-in-cinema--Bollywood-mirror-on-the-wall--who-s-the-fairest-of-them-all .html.

Bhattacharya, Uttara. 2018. "*Thackeray*'s Trailer Triggers Row." *Asian Age*, December 29, 2018. Available at https://www.asianage.com/entertainment/bollywood/291218/thac kerays-trailer-triggers-row.html.

Chatterji, Rohini. 2019. "Bhumi Pednekar's Brownface in *Bala* Is Infuriating to Watch as a Dark-Skinned Woman." *Huff Post*, November 12, 2019. Available at https://www .huffpost.com/archive/in/entry/bhumi-pednekar-brown-face-bala-infuriating_in _5dca4370e4b0fcfb7f6bdf71.

Chaubey, Abhishek, dir. 2016. *Udta Punjab*. Mumbai: Balaji Motion Pictures.

Chrisler, Joan C. 2011. "Leaks, Lumps, and Lines: Stigma and Women's Bodies." *Psychology of Women Quarterly* 35 (2): 202–214.

Dhillon, Amrit. 2013. "Women Take on Shah Rukh Khan for Promoting Skin-Lightening Cream." *National News*, August 5, 2013. Available at https://www.thenationalnews.com /lifestyle/women-take-on-shah-rukh-khan-for-promoting-skin-lightening-cream-1 .659435.

D'Mello, Rosalyn. 2016. "Black." In *Walking towards Ourselves: Indian Women Tell Their Stories*, edited by Catriona Mitchell, 57–66. New Delhi: Harper Collins.

Glenn, Evelyn Nanako. 2008. "Yearning for Lightness: Transnational Circuits in the Marketing and Consumption of Skin Lighteners." *Gender and Society* 22 (3): 281–302.

Guruswamy, Mohan. 2020. "How Bihar Has Been Economically Strangulated." *National Herald*, July 12, 2020. Available at https://www.nationalheraldindia.com/opinion /how-bihar-has-been-economically-strangulated.

Hiranandani, Tushar, dir. 2019. *Saand Ki Aankh*. Mumbai: Reliance Entertainment and PVR Pictures.

Hunter, Margaret L. 2005. *Race, Gender, and the Politics of Skin Tone*. New York: Routledge.

India Today. 2019. "Neena Gupta on 30-Year-Olds Playing 60 in *Saand Ki Aankh*: Hamari Umar Ke Role Toh Humse Kara Lo." September 24, 2019. Available at https://www .indiatoday.in/movies/celebrities/story/neena-gupta-on-30-year-olds-playing-60-in -saand-ke-aankh-hamari-umar-ki-role-toh-humse-kara-lo-1602677-2019-09-24.

Jha, Meeta Rani. 2015. *The Global Beauty Industry: Colorism, Racism, and the National Body*. New York: Routledge.

Jha, Sonora, and Mara Adelman. 2009. "Looking for Love in All the White Places: A Study of Skin Color Preferences on Indian Matrimonial and Mate-Seeking Websites." *Studies in South Asian Film and Media* 1 (1): 65–83.

Johnson, Sonali Elizabeth. 2002. "The Pot Calling the Kettle Black? Gender-Specific Health Dimensions of Colour Prejudice in India." *Journal of Health Management* 4 (2): 215–227.

Katariya, Sharat, dir. 2015. *Dum Laga Ke Haisha*. Mumbai: Yash Raj Films.

Kaushik, Amar, dir. 2019. *Bala*. Mumbai: Maddock Films.

Khan, Mehboob, dir. 1957. *Mother India*. Mumbai: Mehboob Productions.

Krishnankutty, Pia. 2020. "Before Fair and Lovely, There Was Afghan Snow—All About the Fairness Creams Market in India." *The Print*, June 26, 2020. Available at https:// theprint.in/theprint-essential/before-fair-lovely-there-was-afghan-snow-%E2%81%A0 -all-about-the-fairness-creams-market-in-india/449045/.

Kulkarni, Damini. 2016. "In the Movies, Fair Equals Lovely While Dark Equals Backward, Villainous, Savage (Take Your Pick)." *Scroll*, October 22, 2016. Available at https:// scroll.in/reel/819289/in-the-movies-fair-equals-lovely-while-dark-equals-backward -villainous-savage-take-your-pick.

Kumar, Akshaya. 2018. "*Deswa*, the Film and the Movement: Taste, Industry and Representation in Bhojpuri Cinema." *Contemporary South Asia* 26 (1): 69–85.

Mendes, Ana Cristina. 2010. "Showcasing India Unshining: Film Tourism in Danny Boyle's *Slumdog Millionaire*." *Third Text* 24 (4): 471–479.

Mubarki, Meraj Ahmed. 2016. "Brown Gaze and White Flesh: Exploring 'Moments' of the Single White Female in Hindi Cinema." *Contemporary South Asia* 24 (2): 164–183.

Nadeem, Shehzad. 2014. "Fair and Anxious: On Mimicry and Skin-Lightening in India." *Social Identities* 20 (2/3): 224–238.

Nair, Nandana. 2019. "What Is With Tamil Cinema's Bias for Only Fair Skin Actresses Who Are Not Even from the State." *ED Times*, October 17, 2019. Available at https:// edtimes.in/what-is-with-tamil-cinemas-bias-for-only-fair-skin-actresses-who-are-not -even-from-the-state/.

Pallavi, Krishna Priya. 2019. "I Am Not a Gori Ladki. *Bala* Left Me Feeling Cheated." *India Today*, November 11, 2019. Available at https://www.indiatoday.in/movies/standpoint /story/i-am-not-a-gori-ladki-bala-left-me-feeling-cheated-1617792-2019-11-11.

Parameswaran, Radhika. 2004. "Global Queens, National Celebrities: Tales of Feminine Triumph in Post-Liberalization India." *Critical Studies in Media Communication* 21 (4): 346–370.

Parameswaran, Radhika, and Kavitha Cardoza. 2009a. "Immortal Comics, Epidermal Politics: Representations of Gender and Colorism in India." *Journal of Children and Media* 3 (1): 19–34.

———. 2009b. "Melanin on the Margins: Advertising and the Cultural Politics of Fair/ Light/White Beauty in India." *Journalism and Communication Monographs* 11 (3): 213–274.

Rakhan, R. K., dir. 1963. *Meri Surat Teri Ankhen*. Mumbai: Gee Pee Films.

Rao, T. Rama, dir. 1986. *Naseeb Apna Apna*. Mumbai: BMB Productions.

Rolling Stone India. 2020. "Controversial Song 'Beyoncé Sharma Jayegi' Has Been Rechris- tened 'Duniya Sharma Jayegi.'" September 16, 2020. Available at https://rollingstone india.com/khaali-peeli-beyonce-duniya-sharma-jayegi/.

Sarang, Rakesh, and Rajan Shahi, dir. 2005–2009. *Saat Phere: Saloni Ka Safar*. Mumbai: Sphere Origins. Aired on Zee TV.

Shahi, Rajan, Romesh Kalra, Sunand Baranwal, Neeraj Baliyan, Sharad Pandey, Mayank Gupta, and Ismail Umar Khan, dir. 2007–2010. *Sapna Babul Ka . . . Bidaai*. Mumbai: Director Kut's Productions. Aired on StarPlus.

Shetty, Rohit, dir. 2013. *Chennai Express*. Mumbai: UTV Motion Pictures and Red Chil- lies Entertainment.

Shukla, Pankhuri. 2019. "Bhumi's Blackface Is the Real Culprit of Ayushmann-Starrer *Bala*." *The Quint*, November 9, 2019. Available at https://www.thequint.com/neon /bhumi-pednekar-blackface-real-culprit-of-ayushmann-starrer-bala.

Sims, Cynthia, and Malar Hirudayaraj. 2016. "The Impact of Colorism on the Career As- pirations and Career Opportunities of Women in India." *Advances in Developing Hu- man Resources* 18 (1): 38–53.

Sippy, Ramesh, dir. 1975. *Sholay*. Mumbai: United Producers and Sippy Films.

Sonie, Bhappi, dir. 1968. *Brahmachari*. Mumbai: Sippy Films.

The Statesman. 2016. "Alia Bhatt Goes Three Shades Darker in *Udta Punjab*." April 15, 2016. Available at https://www.thestatesman.com/lifestyle/alia-bhatt-goes-3-shades -darker-in-udta-punjab-136617.html.

Swaroop, Jyoti, dir. 1968. *Padosan*. Mumbai: Mehmood Productions.

Tak, Saawan Kumar, dir. 1983. *Souten*. Mumbai: Mercury Productions.

Tandon, Ravi, dir. 1975. *Apne Rang Hazaar*. Mumbai: Ravi Tandon Productions.

Telles, Edward E. 2014. *Pigmentocracies: Ethnicity, Race, and Color in Latin America*. Cha- pel Hill: University of North Carolina Press.

Thompson, Maxine S., and Verna M. Keith. 2001. "The Blacker the Berry: Gender, Skin Tone, Self-Esteem, and Self-Efficacy." *Gender and Society* 15 (3): 336–357.

Tirulokchandar, A. C., dir. 1964. *Main Bhi Ladki Hoon*. Mumbai: AVM Productions.

Two Circles. 2008. "Biharis Are an Affliction, Says Bal Thackeray." March 6, 2008. Avail- able at http://twocircles.net/2008mar05/biharis_are_affliction_says_bal_thackeray .html?amp.

Vaid, Jyotsna. 2009. "Fair Enough? Color and the Commodification of Self in Indian Mat- rimonials." In *Shades of Difference: Why Skin Color Matters*, edited by Evelyn Nakano Glenn, 148–165. Stanford, CA: Stanford University Press.

Varman, Abhishek, dir. 2014. *2 States*. Mumbai: Dharma Productions and Nadiadwala Grandson Entertainment.

Verma, Jyoti. 2019. "Bihari Identity: An Uncharted Question." *Psychology and Develop- ing Societies* 31 (2): 315–342.

Waheed, Alia. 2020. "Glamour, Glitz and Artificially Light Skin: Bollywood Stars in Their Own Racism Row." *The Guardian*, June 28, 2020. Available at https://www.theguardian .com/film/2020/jun/28/glamour-glitz-and-artificially-light-skin-bollywood-stars-in -their-own-racism-row.

Yadav, Leena, dir. 2015. *Parched*. Mumbai: Ajay Devgn Films.

9

Fetishism, Scopophilia, and the Fat Actresses of Bhojpuri Cinema

Shailendra Kumar Singh

Introduction

Often existing as a discursive presence to the dominant Hindi film industry in contemporary North India, Bhojpuri cinema constitutes a principal source of entertainment for the working-class migrants of eastern Uttar Pradesh and western Bihar. It is a vibrant industry that has thrived not despite but because of its formulaic representation of the action hero, the classic conflict between the rural values and the urban ethos, and the alternative visual pleasures it offers its spectators through a predictable commodification of the fat actress. The body image that the music videos of this vernacular cinema offer is one that is quite consistent with the provincial standards of beauty in these regions where fatness is not stigmatized or scoffed at. Instead, it is seen as normative and desirable. But this apparent acceptance of corpulent bodies ultimately does not translate into any fat-positive messages or discourse since the bawdy fetishism and erotic scopophilia of these videos combine with a number of scandalizing puns and obscenities in order to pander to the fierce and voracious appetite of its predominantly male audiences.

In other words, although the plump and well-rounded actresses of Bhojpuri cinema enjoy considerable stardom, prominence, and recognition, their body image still serves a routine purpose, namely that of providing entertainment and titillation. This chapter investigates the various aesthetic contours and thematic templates that determine the visual and verbal content of Bhojpuri music videos. It demonstrates how even though these portrayals situate themselves in opposition to the dominant body ideals of Hindi cinema and the Hindi music industry, they still fall short of providing an alternative, meaningful, or deobjectified representation of fat female bodies. For all its differential vectors of demands and expectations of its perceived audiences and viewers, the implicit promise and potential of this subaltern entertainment industry to foreground a disparate and contrasting model of beauty, sexuality, romance, and body politics thus remain fundamentally unrealized and unfulfilled. What could otherwise have been a liberating paradigm for visual cultures in India eventually ends up perpetuating outrageous discourses of gendered violence through a pathological fixation on verbal misogyny and fat female body parts.

Fatness as an Index of Vernacular Idiosyncrasy

The phenomenal visibility and exponential growth of Bhojpuri cinema in postmillennial North India is a story for the ages. Having been forced to contend with moderate success during the first two chapters of its prolonged gestation, this industry finally came into its own through a complex interplay of different albeit interrelated factors. The first period, which roughly spans the better part of the 1960s, includes movies such as *Ganga Maiyya Tohe Piyari Chadhaibo* (Oh mother Ganges, I will offer you a yellow sari) (Kumar 1962) and *Hamaar Sansaar* (Our world) (Hussain 1965), which in turn contributed significantly to the consolidation of a provincial and vernacular identity (Ghosh 2012). The second era begins around the late 1970s and early 1980s and, like its predecessor, had variable fortunes right until the turn of the century. However, with the arrival of the multiplexes in the protracted aftermath of the liberalization and globalization of the Indian economy, Bhojpuri cinema received a new lease on life through the single-screen exhibition spaces that earlier leaned on fringe genres involving sleazy content such as the B-grade horror films made by the Ramsay brothers (Kumar 2016a). The superlative response that a film like *Sasura Bada Paisawala* (The rich father-in-law) (Sinha 2004) met with marked the beginning of an era of unprecedented growth that also precipitated an elaborate network of actors, producers, and distributors. The other pivotal determinants that worked in favor of Bhojpuri cinema were the increasingly urban and globalized rhythms, lifestyles, and sensibilities that had come to characterize Hindi cinema, most prominently in the late 1990s and early 2000s. As such, conventional migrant workers from the Bhojpuri-speaking regions of North India want a slice of the larger, more lavish world that they see around them—not in "Bollywood" style, which they find alien, but something that is given to them on their own terms, in a milieu they are able to identify with, and in a language they are most familiar with (Ghosh 2012). In keeping with this set of distinctive provincial

expectations, the Bhojpuri audience does not want heroines with toned bodies and size-zero figures (Ghosh 2012). Instead, they hanker after women who
are big and fleshy, with oversized breasts accentuated by colorful cholis or
blouses (Ghosh 2012). It is to these deviant and anomalous proclivities that
I turn in this particular section (especially with respect to the fat female actresses of Bhojpuri cinema).

Despite the fact that gender codes are either historically or culturally determined, what has nevertheless still been recognized within the larger remit
of feminist studies is that these codes mirror performances that subscribe to
dominant formulations of masculinity and femininity (Butler 1990; West and
Zimmerman 1987). Questions of looks, appearances, and desirability therefore have a gendered configuration so that women are often held to a thin and
therefore unbending ideal (Bordo 1993; Wolf 2002). Not surprisingly, then,
fat women become archetypal victims of sustained prejudice and discrimination because of punishing body ideals that have been culturally legitimized
in the West (Puhl and Brownell 2004). With the opening up of the Indian
economy in the 1990s and the deregulation of markets, cable television, Internet access, and persuasive advertising took over the imagination of the elite
and middle classes in the urban spaces and cemented these notions about body
size in South Asia. Consequently, actresses such as Kajol, Karisma Kapoor,
Raveena Tandon, Urmila Matondkar, Shilpa Shetty, and Sonali Bendre redefined the hitherto existing paradigms of beauty for Hindi cinema.

This palpable change can be better understood if one takes into consideration the earlier parameters and yardsticks that existed for mainstream Hindi
film actresses such as Meena Kumari, Nargis, Asha Parekh, Hema Malini,
and Mala Sinha, all of whom were never rejected because they grew fat with
age (Kishwar 1995). Similarly, during the 1970s, English-language fan magazines commonly referred to Sridevi (a curvy actress) as "thunder thighs" without too much disapproval or contempt (Derné 2008). The phenomenal emergence of the beauty queen in postliberalization India should thus be construed
as an irreversible shift that unapologetically camouflaged the exclusion of
certain subjects—short, very dark-skinned, or large women, as well as women
who cannot speak English (Parameswaran 2004)—from these evolving standards of beauty. Be that as it may, the remit of Bhojpuri cinema and music
videos reveals a normative celebration of fatness as an index of vernacular
idiosyncrasy. All the leading actresses of Bhojpuri cinema, such as Amrapali
Dubey, Kajal Raghwani, and Akshara Singh, boast of a rather healthy, plump,
and well-rounded figure that essentially differentiates them from their representative counterparts in Hindi cinema. And though one may argue here
that a similar emphasis on the pudgy and buxom figures of South Indian actresses could serve as a comparable corporeal reality, what renders uniqueness to the presence of the fat female body in the Bhojpuri entertainment

industry is that it does not extend the same latitude to the current crop of Bhojpuri actors, whose diligently sculpted bodies become tailor-made for gravity-defying stunts and hypermasculine action sequences. On the contrary, for any young, aspiring actress in Bhojpuri cinema, fatness is not optional but rather a necessary prerequisite that ensures cinematic success, fame, and popularity. For instance, in an interview, actress Monalisa (Antara Biswas) revealed how she used to be very thin before she arrived in this industry (Husselbee 2023). However, several directors advised her, in no uncertain terms, to put on more weight since people here prefer to see women with a fuller figure.

On the surface, it may appear as though a vernacular cinematic stereotype that embraces fatness to a point of unspoken indispensability posits an alternative organizing principle that challenges the largely fatphobic discourses of Hindi cinema. Whereas Bollywood actresses such as Vidya Balan and Huma Qureshi are routinely subjected to fat-shaming questions and comments over and over again, the leading ladies of Bhojpuri cinema are able to enjoy stardom and visibility precisely because of their well-endowed physiques. But this acceptance is only a necessary and not an adequate litmus test of fat activism. This is because even a cursory look at some of the most popular and influential music videos of this entertainment industry reveals some seriously disconcerting paradoxes. In "Chhalakata Hamro Jawaniya" (My brimming youth spills all over), a song that has had more than four hundred million views on YouTube, multiple close-ups of Kajal Raghwani's body parts, particularly around the navel, breasts, and gyrating hips, ultimately end up fetishizing fatness for the predominantly male gaze of its viewers (Worldwide Records Bhojpuri 2016a). And while one may argue that a similar commodification of slim Hindi film actresses such as Katrina Kaif and Kareena Kapoor also takes place when they perform raunchy item numbers, the insatiable rapacity and explosive sexual appetite of Bhojpuri songs are unmistakably established through the clumsy and provocative mannerisms of the male star. In this video, for example, Pawan Singh begins by repeatedly putting his index finger in the hollowed area of the belly button of the female star. This is followed by another sequence in which Kajal is shown lying on a cot while Singh salaciously moves his lower body back and forth in a manner that overtly insinuates the act of sexual intercourse followed by ejaculation. This outlandish, immoderate, and avoidable gesture is formulaically repeated at the end of the video as well. Other representative music videos, such as "Bhar Jata Dhodi" (My navel gets filled; see Wave Music 2017), and "Meri Jawani Hai Made in Bihar" (My youth is made in Bihar; see Worldwide Records Bhojpuri 2020), reiterate the familiar motif of the sexually starved and hence uncontrollably desperate male protagonist.

The fundamental reason behind making such videos is that they immediately resonate with the plight of countless working-class migrants belonging to the Purvanchal (eastern end of Uttar Pradesh) and other Bhojpuri-speaking regions. These migrants "work across the country as construction laborers, porters, rickshaw-wallahs, and taxi-drivers" (Kumar 2016a, 151). In a somewhat accurate though sweeping rejoinder to a question asked on Quora (as to why the Bhojpuri heroine is so fat), a respondent reveals how Bhojpuri viewers "drool over such fleshy bodies on screen and sometimes these over-fleshy bodies are the sole reason they throng to cinema halls" (Malhan 2019). Since the female characters of this regional cinema invariably belong to the upper class as opposed to the subaltern masculinity the hero comes to symbolize in these narratives about social ranks and hierarchies, the reason behind this particular fetish also involves an element of fanciful wish fulfillment for working-class migrants. This is because the fat female body is traditionally viewed as a symbol of prosperity and fecundity in Bihar, which implies that male desire ultimately exceeds beyond the straightforward confines of the sexual and is additionally organized around the fictive likelihood of an interclass romance. More importantly, though, the functional albeit run-down, decrepit single-screen theaters remain the only entertainment venues available to the working classes in cities where they can barely afford any other form or variety of leisure (Kumar 2016a). As Akshaya Kumar succinctly puts it, "The rundown theatres screening films only watched by a male audience, have thus earned their place—devoid of respectability and female participation" (160). It is this missing female audience that clearly spells out a discourse of fat fetishism and erotic scopophilia. Often these migrant workers are geographically estranged from their spouses and other family members, who either cannot afford to live in the city throughout the year or have to manage the household affairs back home in the countryside. Add to this the sheer drudgery of the work profile of these migrants and the stultifying/defamiliarizing rituals, rhythms, and routines of the urban spaces and what remains is a totally insipid and monotonous lifestyle that offers little escape, respite, or diversion to these urban subalterns. Bhojpuri music videos that are primarily intended for male consumption thus demonstrate a blatant disregard for gender sensitivity and exploit this avenue for commercial success through outrageous instances of visual as well as verbal aesthetics. As such, despite subverting a number of hegemonic fallacies/stereotypes, such as that fat women are typically unattractive (Murray 2004), that they are largely asexual (Thomas and Wilkerson 2005), or that the media often presents only young and slender women who are good looking (Holtzman 2000), this industry also contributes to the consolidation and reification of its own image and status as borderline pornographic (*Times of India* 2014; Sharma 2017). This particular assessment is not entirely off the mark because even scholarly research in the field of feminist porn studies reveals how fat female bodies are hypersexualized because these women's bodies must have large breasts, hips, and butts, which satisfy the male gaze (Jones 2019). The inherent duplicity and contradiction become increasingly apparent: though fat women are often considered asexual by fatphobic cultures, they are invariably hypersexualized and fetishized for their fatness in pornography (Braziel 2001). Therefore, despite the emerging presence of feminist scholarship that recognizes the "pleasures of fetishization" (Jones 2019, 280) and theorizes "new forms of non-normative pleasure" (Khan 2017, 25), in the case of Bhojpuri music videos, such a line of reading is rendered untenable precisely because of the glaring absence of female viewers.

Of Puns, Obscenity, and Sexual Commodification

In this section, I examine the overwhelming presence of puns, obscenity, and sexual commodification that often undergirds the popular music of this industry. Drawing on an extensive range of sartorial and bodily metaphors, I argue that the considerations of logic, reason, and propriety are categorically sidestepped in favor of the appalling and the preposterous. The bawdy humor, the euphemistic idiom, and the sensational, titillating, and melodramatic registers thus constitute an organizing principle that almost becomes synonymous with a publicity stunt designed exclusively for vicarious entertainment and mass consumption. Here I largely focus on those video songs that even feature the mainstream actors and actresses of the Bhojpuri industry, the implicit suggestion being that the nature of the puns, and the degree of obscenity and sexual commodification, only gets worse in the case of local artists and musicians. So, for instance, in 2017, Dinesh Lal Yadav "Nirahua" (hereafter Nirahua) and Amrapali Dubey, two of the top celebrities in this trade, released a song titled "Holi Mein Chuve Lagal Gagri" (My skirt is coming down because it's Holi).[1] The abiding popularity of this song can be easily gauged by the fact that it garnered more than two hundred seventy-eight thousand views on YouTube (despite being released on the video sharing platform after a period of four years), a figure that is fairly respectable according to the Bhojpuri standards of musical reception (Bipl 2021). The song is an eclectic variety of themes pertaining to *sringara* (romantic love), *viraha* (longing in separation), and nostalgia from the Indian aesthetic tradition. It describes a telephonic conversation between two lovers who are miles apart but are equally desirous of and almost desperate about meeting each other on the occasion of Holi. It specifically captures the moods and anxieties of the thousands of migrant workers who are compelled by their financial circumstances to leave their families and hometowns in search of better employment opportunities and are able to manage only one or a couple of trips back home in a calendar year (Tripathy 2007; Hardy 2010). However, the elements of pun, innuendo, and wordplay are almost perversely expressed through the figure of the *pi-*

chkari, or the water gun, which, in turn, is unmistakably meant to evoke phallocentric images and associations. At various points, the male singer uses expressions like "Pichkariya se daalam ras sagari ho roka ghaghari" (Hold on, with your skirt, for I'll certainly make you wet with my water gun), "Pichkariya hamaar khoje ghaghari ho tohar ghaghari" (My water gun is on the lookout for a skirt, your skirt), and "Pichkariya ke pai jab ghaghari ho tabhe taghari" (Your skirt will only come down when it'll find my water gun). The literal meaning of playing with wet colors during Holi is virtually pushed out of its context in order to accommodate verbal obscenity and sexually demeaning innuendoes. Here, the fat female body that is otherwise shown to be worthy of heterosexual male desire and attention is nevertheless subjected to an aggressively risqué and concupiscent vocabulary, which hardly makes a compelling case for a body positive discourse or representation.

Another illustration that neatly captures one of the most important thematic concerns of this popular music industry is the kind of oral violence that one finds in music videos relating to relationships between the *devar* (the brother-in-law) and his *bhabhi* (his elder brother's wife) (Manuel 2014). As Charu Gupta rightly points out, "In UP [Uttar Pradesh], as elsewhere, devar-bhabhi relationships have provoked many responses and meanings and have been a subject of stories, songs, proverbs and jokes" (2001, 151).[2] In 2016, Khesari Lal Yadav, another Bhojpuri superstar, released an enormously popular (though unequivocally problematic) song titled "Bhouji Ko Dudh Nahi Hota He" (My sister-in-law does not yield milk), which again is nothing but a reductive, disconcerting, and sexist take on women as cows that yield milk![3] The entire song sequence revolves around the idea that the sister-in-law's young child is only crying because she is reluctant to breastfeed (Wave Music 2016). This point is strongly reinforced when the male speaker uses expressions such as "Dekhla mein laagata ki bhar dihey baalti / Naikhi piyaawat ki ghati personality" (It appears as if she could fill an entire bucket [with milk] / But she doesn't breastfeed because it will ruin her figure and personality). He further comments: "Babua janmawte e tah bhaili bakena / Doodhwa chorawat baari pharihey ka chhena" (The moment she gave birth to a child, she was like a milk-giving cow or buffalo / So, is she stealing milk because she wants to prepare curd?). The song's implicit critique of urban modernity—because of which women apparently become averse to the very idea of breastfeeding, already a problematic position to begin with—is itself comprehensively defeated by the oral violence, misogyny, and bias propagated in its name.[4] Once again, sexism, misogyny, and objectification exclude any possibility of fat-positive portrayal. Instead, the implicit suggestion that breastfeeding one's child could ruin one's personality insinuates a tacit hierarchy of corpulence that draws a somewhat vague distinction between acceptable portliness and revolting fat (more about this later).

The appalling obscenity of the verbal medium is matched only by the outrageous comparisons and stultifying logic of the visual content. There is an irreducible presence of sexual commodification of women in these music videos that often takes place through sartorial as well as bodily metaphors. In *Sajan Chale Sasural 2* (Husband goes to his in-laws' 2) (Singh 2016), Khesari and Akshara Singh (one of the most popular actresses of the industry) are shown dancing to a song titled "Tohar Dhodi Ba Phulaha Katori Niyan" (Your navel is like a small bronze bowl). The close-up of the female protagonist's navel and the way it is lustfully grabbed by Khesari clearly epitomize the dominant trend of this music industry that almost reveals a quasi-pathological fixation with body parts (Worldwide Records Bhojpuri 2017). As Barbara L. Fredrickson and Tomi-Ann Roberts perceptively point out, sexual objectification/commodification "occurs whenever a person's body, body parts, or sexual functions are separated out from his or her person, reduced to the status of mere instruments, or regarded as if they were capable of representing him or her" (1997, 175). In addition, the choli (blouse) and the *lehnga* (skirt) are the other two commonly used metaphors that are almost as obsessively employed as the belly button. The songs often portray the male protagonist as someone who either mischievously refers to the way his female counterpart takes off her clothes or roguishly reveals how he himself will lift her skirt. In another song sequence ("Sakhi Salai Rinch Se Kholela") from the same film, Khesari uses an outlandish and somewhat unsettling logic that seems to imply that his friend unbuttons her blouse with a "salai rinch" (pipe wrench) (Worldwide Records Bhojpuri 2016b)! Similarly, the refrain of another famous Bhojpuri song ("Lehnga Utha Deb Rimot Se") describes the hero's ability to lift a young woman's skirt with a remote (T-Series Hamaar Bhojpuri 2012)! The pipe wrench and the remote-like stick can undoubtedly be construed as phallic symbols even as they further corroborate the impression that this popular music industry fundamentally thrives on offense, melodrama, and shock value. In all three music videos, even though fatness is deemed attractive and devoid of stigma, the raging hormones, lascivious overtures, and formulaic hypersexuality of the male protagonists leave a lot to be desired before any meaningful engagement with gendered concerns could be identified in this film industry.

The verbal obscenity and visual absurdity of Bhojpuri songs are even more surprising when compared with the equally baffling though conservative portrayal of women in Bhojpuri films (Kumar 2014). As Madhusri Shrivastava succinctly puts it, "It is the screen representations of wives, mothers, sisters and daughters in the films that set the standards of behavior considered appropriate for women" (2015, 92). Similarly, Akshaya Kumar draws attention to the way Bhojpuri films "privilege the subaltern and allow her the opportunity to speak for the larger whole she represents" (Kumar 2014, 197).[5] Bhojpuri songs, on the other hand, largely steer clear of community values and traditional morality. Instead, the very usage of words such as "remote" and "lollipop" ("Lollypop Lagelu"; see Wave Music 2015) connotes a sense of legitimacy that is accorded to modern taste, individual pleasure, and personal fantasy. To borrow Linda Williams's terms, albeit from a different context, it bears a striking analogy to the very idea of "on/scenity: the gesture by which a culture brings on to its public arena the very organs, acts, bodies, and pleasures that have been designated ob/scene and kept literally off the scene" (2004, 3). Women in the Bhojpuri entertainment industry can therefore be both revered/idealized as well as degraded/commodified—they can be both veritable repositories of custom and tradition as well as strategic appropriations that legitimize "men's cultural domination, in particular, the creation of women as the objects of their sexual fantasies" (Lorber 1994, 100). All three examples cited prior neatly dovetail with Laura Mulvey's emphatic assertion that "the woman's body exists as the erotic, spectacular and exhibitionist 'other'" (1987, 6). Over the years, Mulvey's observations have, of course, been contested and found to be plagued with essentialism (Rodowick 1991), heterosexual assumptions (Gamman 1988), and a rigid understanding of gender that does not leave much scope for fluidity/flexibility (Hines 2018). And yet, the familiar and habitual objectification of the fat female body in Bhojpuri music videos could be construed through her insightful theoretical postulations. The vicarious entertainment, the mass consumption, and the subversive pleasures that often constitute the key components of this popular music industry are thus able to offer a grammar of alternative aesthetics to the constructive paradigms of the socially relevant and politically correct Bhojpuri films.

Heightened Affects through Erotic Scopophilia

In what can only be described as one of the most seminal and compelling scholarly interventions within the remit of cinema and gender studies, Laura Mulvey argues that scopophilia or voyeurism implies "using another person as an object of sexual stimulation through sight" (1988, 61). Drawing her conclusions and findings based on psychoanalytic theory, she observes that the "determining male gaze projects its phantasy on the female figure" (62), thereby subjecting it to a "controlling and curious gaze" (59). The underlying assumption behind her theoretical premises is that films' "preoccupations reflect the psychical obsessions of the society" (59) that produces them, even as the on-screen woman functions "on two levels: an erotic object for the character within the screen story, and as the erotic object for the spectator within the auditorium, with a shifting tension between the looks on either side of the screen" (62). It is clear that some of the aesthetic conventions and vi-

sual strategies that are frequently mobilized in Bhojpuri music videos to produce erotic scopophilia for the sexually starved working-class migrants in
urban spaces prove to be a stock-in-trade formula for the commercial success of this entertainment industry. But a more heightened affect being created in the last few years has to do with ideas of the French kiss, the wet sari
sequences, and the repositioning of the male star as a nationalist subject who
could also have global aspirations and transnational desires.

One of the first on-screen couples to have normalized/popularized all
three aforementioned elements is the dynamic duo of Nirahua and Amrapali. In *Nirahua Hindustani* (Nirahua: The Indian) (Jain 2014), a film that, in
many ways, introduces a vernacular subject of nationalist importance, there
is a heavily fetishized song sequence that is exclusively shot in the rain ("Naee
Jhulani Ke Chhaiyan") (Nirahua Music World 2014a). It is a direct imitation
of the "wet sari" sequences that have had a long historical trajectory in Hindi
cinema. While analyzing the erotics of such excessively charged segments,
Rachel Dwyer argues that "the sari is the perfect garment to accentuate this
body, its drape drawing attention to the 'acceptable' erotic zones of the breasts,
waist and hips even while covering them" (2000, 150–151). Moreover, a year
later, in *Nirahua Rickshawala 2* (Nirahua: The rickshaw wallah 2) (Jain 2015),
this erotic scopophilia acquires a much more pronounced disposition and
literally spills over into the diegetic space of the film. In a somewhat familiar,
repetitive, and predictable scene, the male protagonist is publicly humiliated
by the heroine's father because of his subaltern identity as a rickshaw wallah,
to which the former responds by kissing his love interest on the lips before
everyone around him. It almost appears as if the initial slap in the face could
only come full circle through a proportionately unapologetic articulation of
subjective desire in the public sphere. The moral justification of the French
kiss that follows the slap immediately recedes into the background and opens
up a distinctly erotic experience for its male viewers both within the diegetic
space as well as outside it. These global rhythms and transnational sensibilities are not unique to Bhojpuri cinema since, in the Hindi heartland, comic
books and detective novels also offer their readers a similar variety of descriptive and visual pleasures through erotic fantasies, consumerist modernity, foreign lands, international settings, wondrous escape routes, and spectacular make-believe worlds (Kaur and Eqbal 2015; Srivastava 2013).

However, critics such as Akshaya Kumar have discursively argued that
Khesari's performance as a *launda* (female impersonator) not only arranges
a plethora of pleasures around the figure of the male star but also vanquishes
the "othered" urban values that are often resident in the woman's body (Kumar 2016b). This alternative reading also finds somewhat of a theoretical
equivalence seeing that Mulvey's formulations of the male gaze have been
interrogated from different perspectives, such as that of the female spectator

(Doane 1982), masculinity as spectacle (Neale 1983), the oppositional gaze (hooks 2003), and the lesbian film (Hollinger 1998). And yet, one must not lose sight of the fact that in the Bhojpuri-speaking regions of North India, the festive spirit of wedding ceremonies immediately becomes a convenient pretext through which *laundas* are unapologetically touched and groped without consent and frequently subjected to rape, prostitution, and sexual assault (Rawat 2020). Besides, in recent times there has been a perceptible decrease in the frequency of Khesari's live concerts as a *launda*. His latest bodily transformation, which has earned him comparisons with Salman Khan (Khushboo 2019), can also be read as a conscious attempt to outgrow this image. This is because when Chhotu Chingari, a YouTuber, called him a eunuch, Khesari defended himself by admitting that his performances were a matter of sheer economic necessity as opposed to a question of personal choice and individual autonomy (People Biography 2019). This itself severely limits the notion of rebellious and native masculinity (Kumar 2016b) that was ostensibly supposed to provide a formidable and counterhegemonic challenge to the fat female actresses of Bhojpuri cinema.

Cute and Chubby versus Distasteful Fat

Before making an impressive and arresting debut in Bhojpuri cinema with a leading role in *Nirahua Hindustani* opposite Dinesh Lal Yadav, Amrapali Dubey had acted in a number of Hindi soap operas and television shows such as *Rehna Hai Teri Palkon Ki Chhaon Mein* (I want to stay in the shadow of your eyelids) (Kumar 2009–2010) and *Saat Phere: Saloni Ka Safar* (Wedding rituals: Saloni's journey) (Sarang and Shahi 2005–2009). Her strategic transition from being a television actress to becoming a movie star, albeit of a vernacular film industry, provides a definitive indication of the varying yardsticks of attractiveness and desirability that govern the visual templates of Bhojpuri movies and music videos. For instance, in her first film, her physique and overall appearance are more in line with the accepted standards of Hindi TV shows, which, like Hindi cinema, prioritize the mainstream presence of young, slim, and curvaceous leading actresses and where slenderness is still very much a corporeal virtue. It therefore comes as no surprise that in response to one of the songs ("Ud Jaibu Ye Maina") in the film, a fan compares Amrapali to Priyanka Chopra in the YouTube comments section (Nirahua Music World 2014b). Chopra, who is a Bollywood actress, singer, and film producer in addition to being one of the highest-paid and most popular entertainers of contemporary South Asia, was also the winner of the Miss World 2000 pageant. Here Amrapali's fitness is not being outrightly rejected by viewers precisely because the movie constantly attempts to integrate

Nirahua's Bhojpuri identity as a Hindustani. On the contrary, it neatly dove-tails with the idea of this native beauty (Amrapali is originally from Go-rakhpur, a city along the banks of the Rapti River in the northeastern part, or the Purvanchal region, of Uttar Pradesh) who can aspire to have a pan-Indian appeal.

However, due to her meteoric rise in an industry that immediately sought to cash in on her good looks and considerable acting credentials, Amrapali did several films in quick succession, which incidentally left her with little time for anything else, to say nothing of maintaining body fitness through a strictly regimented diet and exercise plan (Bhojpuri Xp 2016). As a result, her perceptible weight gain, which created quite a stir among Bhojpuri fans and media, and her ultimate decision to work hard for a leaner frame com-plicate the notions of fat acceptance in an industry that is not only relatively tolerant of fat bodies but also culturally inclined toward them. On at least a couple of occasions, Amrapali has revealed to the media and her viewers that she was either deeply hurt whenever somebody pointed out her fatness (she said she almost felt as if broken shards of glass had been forcefully inserted in her ears so that they would start bleeding soon enough) (Next9Political Byte 2018) or was greatly committed to lose weight for the sake of her fans (by proving how she was not irresponsible and was at least making sincere efforts in that direction) (Bindaas Bhojpuriya 2017).[6] These shifting positions only make sense when one realizes that even in the world of Bhojpuri music videos, there are arbitrary gradations of fatness that sooner or later converge and crystallize around the notions of what can be understood as the *cute and chubby* aspect of corpulence and what is regularly construed as *distasteful/ repulsive fat*. In other words, acceptable stoutness that is often deemed plea-surable for male viewers soon elicits an oppositional response of disap-proval and repudiation the moment it slides into the excessive and the su-perabundant.

This point can be further illustrated through another example that also underscores the dichotomous gendered paradigms of Bhojpuri cinema. Rani Chatterjee, yet another Bhojpuri actress who has a well-rounded physique, is an extremely successful figure in the industry. At times, her films, such as *Durga* (Narayan and Sanu 2015), *Real Indian Mother* (Chauhan 2016), and *Sanwariya Mohe Rang De* (My love, color me happy) (Gulati 2017), boast of a strong female lead whose narrative centrality positions the male hero in a relatively inconsequential role. Her fight sequences within the diegetic spac-es of some of these films rely heavily on the idea of packaging fatness as a spectacle. Having been accepted, valued, and recognized in the vernacular circuit, Rani recently lost eighteen kilos as part of her preparation for *Fear Factor: Khatron Ke Khiladi* (Players of danger) (Mukherjee et al. 2008–), an

Indian stunt reality television show largely inspired by the American series *Fear Factor*. Her bodily transformation, radically different from Amrapali's so-called offensive weight gain, should logically have been either frowned upon by vernacular audiences or treasured by those who largely subscribe to Western yardsticks of slenderness. But, as in Amrapali's case, here too random evaluative parameters of body sizes have proved to be an infuriating source of unpleasant experiences for Rani. A peculiar mix of fat prejudice and online bullying has made sure she has to not only battle depression but also overcome the suicidal thoughts engendered because of this (Keshri 2020). On a related note, the alarming levels of intimidation and death threats that Akshara Singh received from Pawan Singh owing to the fact that she decided to end her friendship with him after he got married in March 2018 indicate a much larger discourse of gender violence that undergirds the male-dominated world of this vernacular cinema (*Hindustan Times* 2019).

What must also be emphasized here is that even the cute and chubby image (that is ideally privileged by the Bhojpuri film industry) is not simply constructed through limited corpulence but also by taking recourse to the fair-complexioned female celebrity. This is because dark-skinned women are conspicuous by their very absence in Bhojpuri cinema and music videos. The fact that many dark-complexioned boys and girls are increasingly finding themselves spurned and unsuitable for marriage in the Bhojpuri-speaking regions of Bihar bears testimony to this (*Hindustan Times* 2007). As Avijit Ghosh perceptively points out, girls who are not fair faced often become "victims of taunts and abuses within the family and grow up with an inferiority complex, on account of society's preference for light skinned women" (2012, 79). This also relates to the critique of fat studies that some scholars have begun to identify and foreground because it lacks intersectional research (Pausé 2014; Williams 2017). Thus, in the ultimate analysis, even though it appears as if the Bhojpuri entertainment industry is much more capacious and receptive vis-à-vis fat bodies as compared to Hindi cinema, this vernacular idiosyncrasy, in itself, gets circumscribed by the elements of fetishism, scopophilia, and the voyeuristic gaze of the male spectators who otherwise lust after these corpulent actresses, but only when they are fair and not too fat to handle.

ACKNOWLEDGMENTS

The author is grateful to Yuvaan, Santosh, and Pooja for their comments on earlier versions of this chapter. The author is also thankful to the editors and reviewers of this volume for their suggestions. A special thanks to Aditi, Ashima, Naqiya, and Saumya for engaging with successive versions. The responsibility for any error, however, remains entirely with the author. This chapter is humbly dedicated to the author's late parents.

NOTES

1. The spelling of the word *ghaghari* in the title of the song is a dialectal variety and therefore should not be misconstrued as or confused with the Hindi word *gagri*, which usually refers to a small, earthen, globular water pot.

2. In Haryana, a widow was often forced to marry her younger brother-in-law. See Chowdhry (1994). Besides, Tupur Chatterjee also draws attention to the fact that one of the most common search terms in India, as far as pornography is concerned, was "'Indian *bhabhi*' (sister-in-law), a reference to the infamous pornographic comic strip—Savita bhabhi—chronicling the escapades of a married Hindu housewife named Savita, with an insatiable appetite for sex" (2017, 53).

3. The blatantly outrageous nature of this comparison can only be better understood by taking into account the kind of widespread protest, furor, debate, and controversy that surrounded Casey Affleck's Oscar win in 2017. Amanda White, one of the two women who had worked with Casey on the mockumentary *I'm Still Here* (2010), had filed a sexual harassment lawsuit against him, according to which one of the charges leveled against the actor was his repeated reference to women as "cows" (McNamara and Ceron 2017).

4. On a related note, while writing about the *devar-bhabhi* songs, Madhusri Shrivastava astutely observes that "the underlying message is unequivocal: the bhabhi may feign anger and exasperation, but she is secretly flattered, and more than willing" (2014, 6).

5. He further comments, "Be it the figure of the street urchin, the *ganwaar* (rural person), or the public woman (prostitute), the films repeatedly allow them a space to launch themselves discursively, to not only attack the arrogance of the privileged but also render a moral surplus to the underprivileged in terms of a carefully adhered-to value-system" (Kumar 2014, 197).

6. Some of the viewer comments on this video also corroborate this sentiment of disapproval that gained momentum around her so-called excessive fat.

REFERENCES

Bhojpuri Xp. 2016. "Amrapali Dubey Actress Fit to Fat." November 2, 2016. YouTube video. Available at https://www.youtube.com/watch?v=B4fKwIef2mQ.

Bindaas Bhojpuriya. 2017. "Amrapali Dubey to Lose Weight." January 9, 2017. YouTube video. Available at https://www.youtube.com/watch?v=e5RwOJRVux8.

Bipl. 2021. "Holi Mein Chuve Lagal Gagri." March 20, 2021. YouTube video. Available at https://www.youtube.com/watch?v=NGJAkNKlM3E.

Bordo, Susan. 1993. *Unbearable Weight: Feminism, Western Culture, and the Body*. Berkeley: University of California Press.

Braziel, Jana Evans. 2001. "Sex and Fat Chics: Deterritorializing the Fat Female Body." In *Bodies out of Bounds: Fatness and Transgression*, edited by Jana Evans Braziel and Kathleen LeBesco, 231–254. Berkeley: University of California Press.

Butler, Judith. 1990. *Gender Trouble*. New York: Taylor and Francis.

Chatterjee, Tupur. 2017. "'I Am a Porn Star!' Sex and Sunny Leone Unlimited in Bollywood." *Porn Studies* 4 (1): 50–66.

Chauhan, Bhishma, dir. 2016. *Real Indian Mother*. Mumbai: Arise Films.

Chowdhry, Prem. 1994. *The Veiled Women: Shifting Gender Equations in Rural Haryana 1880–1990*. Delhi: Oxford University Press.

Derné, Steve. 2008. *Globalization on the Ground: New Media and the Transformation of Culture, Class, and Gender in India*. New Delhi: Sage.

Doane, Mary Anne. 1982. "Film and the Masquerade: Theorising the Female Spectator." *Screen* 23 (3/4): 74–87.

Dwyer, Rachel. 2000. "The Erotics of the Wet Sari in Hindi Films." *South Asia: Journal of South Asian Studies* 28 (1): 143–160.

Fredrickson, Barbara L., and Tomi-Ann Roberts. 1997. "Objectification Theory: Toward Understanding Women's Lived Experiences and Mental Health Risks." *Psychology of Women Quarterly* 21 (2): 173–206.

Gamman, Lorraine. 1988. "Watching the Detectives: The Enigma of the Female Gaze." In *The Female Gaze: Women as Viewers of Popular Culture*, edited by Lorraine Gamman and Margaret Marshment, 8–26. London: Women's Press.

Ghosh, Avijit. 2012. "Bhojpuri Cinema: Between Yesterday and Tomorrow." *South Asian History and Culture* 3 (1): 70–80.

Gulati, Dilip, dir. 2017. *Sanwariya Mohe Rang De*. Mumbai: Sushila Bhatia Productions.

Gupta, Charu. 2001. *Sexuality, Obscenity, Community: Women, Muslims, and the Hindu Public in Colonial India*. Delhi: Permanent Black.

Hardy, Kathryn C. 2010. "Mediating *Bhojpuriya*: Migration, Circulation, and Bhojpuri Cinema." *South Asian Popular Culture* 8 (3): 231–244.

Hindustan Times. 2007. "Fair Is Lovely in Bihar's Heart of Darkness." May 17, 2007. Available at https://www.hindustantimes.com/india/fair-is-lovely-in-bihar-s-heart-of-darkness/story-aqIiTGDvs4uCGsgsImHx6N.html.

———. 2019. "Bhojpuri Actor Akshara Singh Files FIR against Singer Pawan Singh, Alleges He Threatened to Kill Her." August 4, 2019. Available at https://www.hindustantimes.com/regional-movies/bhojpuri-actor-akshara-singh-files-fir-against-singer-pawan-singh-alleges-he-threatened-to-kill-her/story-YR6jgotqs43pG9d9UYGGfN.html.

Hines, Sally. 2018. *Is Gender Fluid? A Primer for the 21st Century*. London: Thames and Hudson.

Hollinger, Karen. 1998. "Theorizing Mainstream Female Spectatorship: The Case of the Popular Lesbian Film." *Cinema Journal* 37 (2): 3–17.

Holtzman, Linda. 2000. *Media Messages*. Armonk, NY: M. E. Sharpe.

hooks, bell. 2003. "The Oppositional Gaze: Black Female Spectator." In *The Feminism and Visual Cultural Reader*, edited by Amelia Jones, 94–105. New York: Routledge.

Hussain, Nazir, dir. 1965. *Hamaar Sansaar*. Mumbai: Nazir Hussain Productions.

Husselbee, Rebecca. 2023. "Pool Day: Big Boss Star Monalisa, 40, Stuns in Bikini on 'Rest Day' from Filming after Incredible Weight Loss." *The Sun*, September 17, 2023. Available at https://www.the-sun.com/entertainment/9109859/bigg-boss-star-monalisa-bikini-weight-loss/.

Jain, Satish, dir. 2014. *Nirahua Hindustani*. Mumbai: Nirahua Entertainment and Rahul Khan Production.

———, dir. 2015. *Nirahua Rickshawala 2*. Mumbai: Rahul Khan Production.

Jones, Angela. 2019. "The Pleasures of Fetishization: BBW Erotic Webcam Performers, Empowerment, and Pleasure." *Fat Studies* 8 (3): 279–298.

Kaur, Raminder, and Saif Eqbal. 2015. "Gendering Graphics in Indian Superhero Comic Books and Some Notes for Provincializing Cultural Studies." *Communication and Critical/Cultural Studies* 12 (4): 367–396.

Keshri, Shweta. 2020. "Bhojpuri Actress Rani Chatterjee Alleges Harassment: 'Will Kill Myself, I Can't Take it Anymore.'" *India Today*, July 2, 2020. Available at https://www.indiatoday.in/movies/regional-cinema/story/bhojpuri-actress-rani-chatterjee-alleges-harassment-will-kill-myself-i-can-t-take-it-anymore-1696187-2020-07-02.

Khan, Ummni. 2017. "Fetishizing Music as Rape Culture." *Studies in Gender and Sexuality* 18 (1): 19–30.

Khushboo. 2019. "Khesari Lal Yadav Chalengey Salman Khan Ki Raah, Karengey Ye Bada Kaam" [Khesari will follow in Salman's footsteps, will do this major thing]. *Live Hindustan*, April 28, 2019. Available at https://www.livehindustan.com/entertainment/story-bhojpuri-actor-khesari-lal-yadav-new-project-will-do-as-same-as-salman-khan-photo-viral-2506489.html.

Kishwar, Madhu. 1995. "When India 'Missed' the Universe." *Manushi* 88:9–19.

Kumar, Akshaya. 2014. "The Aesthetics of Pirate Modernities: Bhojpuri Cinema and the Under Classes." In *Arts and Aesthetics in a Globalising World*, edited by Raminder Kaur and Parul Dave-Mukherji, 185–203. Oxford: Berg.

———. 2016a. "Bhojpuri Cinema and the 'Rearguard': Gendered Leisure, Gendered Promises." *Quarterly Review of Film and Video* 33 (2): 151–175.

———. 2016b. "Bhojpuri Consolidations in the Hindi Territory: Infrastructure, Aesthetics, and Competing Masculinities in North India." *BioScope: South Asian Screen Studies* 7 (2): 189–206.

Kumar, Kundan, dir. 1962. *Ganga Maiyya Tohe Piyari Chadhaibo*. Patna: B. P. Shahabadi Productions.

Kumar, Pawan, dir. 2009–2010. *Rehna Hai Teri Palkon Ki Chhaon Mein*. Mumbai: Rashmi Sharma Telefilms Limited. Aired on NDTV Imagine.

Lorber, Judith. 1994. *Paradoxes of Gender*. New Haven, CT: Yale University Press.

Malhan, Mritunjaya. 2019. "Why Is the Bhojpuri Heroine So Fat?" Quora. November 9, 2019. Available at https://www.quora.com/Why-is-the-Bhojpuri-heroine-so-fat.

Manuel, Peter. 2014. "The Regional North Indian Popular Music Industry in 2014: From Cassette Culture to Cyberculture." *Popular Music* 33 (3): 389–412.

McNamara, Brittney, and Ella Ceron. 2017. "Why Casey Affleck's Oscars 2017 Win Made People Mad." *Teen Vogue*, February 27, 2017. Available at https://www.teenvogue.com/story/why-casey-affleck-oscars-2017-win-made-people-mad.

Mukherjee, Aritra, Nishant Nayak, Udit Singh, and Taranjiet Singh Namdhari, dir. 2008. *Fear Factor: Khatron Ke Khiladi*. Mumbai: Sphere Origins and Endemol Shine India. Aired on Colors TV.

Mulvey, Laura. 1987. "Changes: Thoughts on Myth, Narrative, and Historical Experience." *History Workshop Journal* 23 (1): 3–19.

———. 1988. "Visual Pleasure and Narrative Cinema." In *Feminism and Film Theory*, edited by Constance Penley, 57–68. New York: Routledge.

Murray, Samantha. 2004. "Locating Aesthetics: Sexing the Fat Woman." *Social Semiotics* 14 (3): 237–247.

Narayan, Manoj, and Sanu, dir. 2015. *Durga*. Varanasi: Sunil Kumar Productions.

Neale, Steve. 1983. "Masculinity as Spectacle." *Screen* 24 (6): 2–17.

Next9Political Byte. 2018. "Amrapali Weight Loss." December 31, 2018. YouTube video. Available at https://www.youtube.com/watch?v=JkW1JWH-6Oc.

Nirahua Music World. 2014a. "Naee Jhulani Ke Chhaiyan." July 4, 2014. YouTube video. Available at https://www.youtube.com/watch?v=V7-5-Waswlk.

———. 2014b. "Ud Jaibu Ye Maina." July 5, 2014. YouTube video. Available at https://www.youtube.com/watch?v=fkYI8t3kPCI.

Parameswaran, Radhika. 2004. "Global Queens, National Celebrities: Tales of Feminine Triumph in Post-Liberalization India." *Critical Studies in Media Communication* 21 (4): 346–370.

Pausé, Cat. 2014. "X-Static Processes: Intersectionality within the Field of Fat Studies." *Fat Studies: An Interdisciplinary Journal of Body Weight and Society* 3 (2): 80–85.

People Biography. 2019. "Khesari Lal Ko Lekar Naya Vivaad, Phone Kar Chhakka Bol Rahe Hai Khesari Ke Dushman?" September 14, 2019. YouTube video. Available at https://www.youtube.com/watch?v=bqQTaj3uFm8.

Puhl, Rebecca, and Kelly D. Brownell. 2004. "Bias, Prejudice, Discrimination, and Obesity." In *Handbook of Obesity: Clinical Applications*, edited by George A. Bray and Claude Bouchard, 69–74. New York: Marcel Dekker.

Rawat, Chitra. 2020. "Launda Naach: Men Dress as Women and Dance in Front of Sexually Hungry Men in Bihar." *ED Times*, May 16, 2020. Available at https://edtimes.in/launda-naach-men-dressing-as-women-dancing-in-front-of-sexually-hungry-men-in-bihar/.

Rodowick, David Norman. 1991. *The Difficulty of Difference: Psychoanalysis, Sexual Difference and Film Theory*. New York: Routledge.

Sarang, Rakesh, and Rajan Shahi, dir. 2005–2009. *Saat Phere: Saloni Ka Safar*. Mumbai: Sphere Origins. Aired on Zee TV.

Sharma, Saurabh. 2017. "How Bhojpuri Cinema Went from 'Family Friendly' to 'Soft Porn.'" *Youth ki Aawaz*, April 5, 2017. Available at https://www.youthkiawaaz.com/2017/04/evolution-of-bhojpuri-cinema/.

Shrivastava, Madhusri. 2014. "Music for the Migrant's Soul: Blending the Traditional with the Topical." *Networking Knowledge* 8 (1): 1–12.

———. 2015. "The 'Bhojpuriya' Mumbaikar: Straddling Two Worlds." *Contributions to Indian Sociology* 49 (1): 77–101.

Singh, Premanshu, dir. 2016. *Sajan Chale Sasural 2*. Mumbai: Alok Kumar Productions.

Sinha, Ajay, dir. 2004. *Sasura Bada Paisawala*. Mumbai: Balaji Cine-Vision.

Srivastava, Sanjay. 2013. "Thrilling Affects: Sexuality, Masculinity, the City and 'Indian Traditions' in the Contemporary Hindi 'Detective' Novel." *Interventions: International Journal of Postcolonial Studies* 15 (4): 567–585.

Thomas, Pattie, and Carl Wilkerson. 2005. *Taking Up Space: How Eating Well and Exercising Regularly Changed My Life*. Nashville, TN: Pearlsong Press.

Times of India. 2014. "Think Bhojpuri Films, You Think of Soft Porn." April 23, 2014. Available at https://timesofindia.indiatimes.com/entertainment/hindi/bollywood/news/Think-Bhojpuri-films-you-think-of-soft-porn-Neetu-Chandra/articleshow/28593061.cms.

Tripathy, Ratnakar. 2007. "Bhojpuri Cinema: Regional Resonances in the Hindi Heartland." *South Asian Popular Culture* 5 (2): 145–165.

T-Series Hamaar Bhojpuri. 2012. "Lehnga Utha Deb Rimot Se." November 8, 2012. YouTube video. Available at https://www.youtube.com/watch?v=9PXjfREgyrI.

Wave Music. 2015. "Lollypop Lagelu." April 2, 2015. YouTube video. Available at https://www.youtube.com/watch?v=Gr8G_ldltDE.

———. 2016. "Bhouji Ko Dudh Nahi Hota He." February 25, 2016. YouTube video. Available at https://www.youtube.com/watch?v=l82Hn_jmYyY.

———. 2017. "Bhar Jata Dhodi." October 30, 2017. YouTube video. Available at https://www.youtube.com/watch?v=j-2JqDJk0cE.

West, Candace, and Don Zimmerman. 1987. "Doing Gender." *Gender and Society* 1 (2): 125–151.

Williams, Apryl. 2017. "Fat People of Color: Emergent Intersectional Discourse Online." *Social Sciences* 6 (15): 1–16.

Williams, Linda. 2004. *Porn Studies*. Durham, NC: Duke University Press.

Wolf, Naomi. 2002. *The Beauty Myth: How Images of Beauty Are Used Against Women*. New York: Harper Perennial.

Worldwide Records Bhojpuri. 2016a. "Chhalakata Hamro Jawaniya." May 9, 2016. YouTube video. Available at https://www.youtube.com/watch?v=c4JD7rEtIj8.

———. 2016b. "Sakhi Salai Rinch Se Kholela." July 8, 2016. YouTube video. Available at https://www.youtube.com/watch?v=sUvNezbh3Cw.

———. 2017. "Tohar Dhodi Ba Phulaha Katori Niyan." February 28, 2017. YouTube video. Available at https://www.youtube.com/watch?v=qjkZFQrM14U.

———. 2020. "Meri Jawani Hai Made in Bihar." January 17, 2020. YouTube video. Available at https://www.youtube.com/watch?v=P6lbrwGPNkI.

V

Neoliberal Cultures and Female Body Image in Indian Advertisements and Popular Media

10

Gender, Body Image, and the Aspirational Middle-Class Imaginary of Indian Advertising

Kavita Daiya, Sukshma Vedere, and Turni Chakrabarti

Introduction

This chapter analyzes Indian discourses on body image and identity in contemporary Indian advertising from 2010 to 2020 through a focus on three types of commercials: skin-care product ads, matrimonial ads, and jewelry ads. Each of these genres, we argue, proffers a prescriptive and heteronormative idea about female body image such that this idealized image is intimately tied to prevailing hierarchies of power in neoliberal and globalized India. Engaging millennial and postmillennial feminist and queer theories, we ask these questions: How do contemporary advertisements represent the ideal female body? How do they address and emblematize a neoliberal rhetoric about women's empowerment and heteronormativity? What modes of resistance and critique, individual and collective, challenge this rhetoric about normative body image?

Several scholars have analyzed the relation between body image and women's ideas of self-worth in contemporary India. As Meenakshi Menon and Preeti Pant observe, "In urban Indian women, there has been an increasing concern with one's physical appearance and body dissatisfaction (Goswami et al. 2012) that may be attributed to the influence of the media (Kapadia 2009)."[1] In dialogue with contemporary feminist scholarship on media representations, this chapter analyzes colorism and body shaming embedded in skin-care product, jewelry, and matrimonial advertising in Hindi and English, as well as feminist activism that challenges these body and skin color norms.

Through a discursive analysis that attends to the audioscapes and visualscapes of particular commercials, as they appear across television and YouTube, we track how contemporary commercials mobilize new ideas of women's empowerment and gender equality to sell old products like skin-lightening creams and gold jewelry. Further, we demonstrate that these commercials often reproduce heteronormative conventions of intimacy that, in South Asia, are also linked to racism, caste, and class discrimination. Finally, we identify modes of feminist activism that challenge these body norms propagated across media and point to new strategies and arenas for creating change. Through Indian commercials in contemporary Hindi and English media, we examine how mass media functions as a space for the reinforcement as well as renegotiation of body normativity in the context of India's aspirational middle-class imaginary. In sum, we map the appearance of colorism, heteronormativity, and patriarchal joint family values to unveil the interplay of capital, female empowerment, and heteronormative intimacies in media discourses about modern Indian women's embodiment.

Colorism and the Politics of Women's Empowerment in Skin-Care Advertising

In her anthropological study titled *Living Color*, Nina Jablonski demonstrates that the skin color differences now central to the modern definition of sociocultural identity emerge from the work of Immanuel Kant, "one of the most influential racists of all time."[2] She reveals that Kant insisted, in his influential philosophical writings, that "skin color denote[s] qualities of personality and morality."[3] His misguided insistence that skin color (or differences in skin pigmentation) was tied to hierarchical differences of nature and character eventually became one of the foundational myths for the systematic and stereotypical ideas about racial differences that persist even today in societies across the world. One of the most visible ways that this colorism, or the privileging of less-pigmented skin, appears in India's consumer culture is through commercials that market cosmetics and beauty products.

Much feminist scholarship has shown that Indian media, while drawing upon Western beauty ideals, propagates thinness as a body norm. Itisha Nagar and Rukshana Virk demonstrate that an increase in exposure to the thin ideal in media images leads to internalization and body dissatisfaction, which in turn lowers women's self-esteem.[4] Relatedly, Indian discourses about women's beauty in the twentieth and twenty-first centuries have valorized less-pigmented skin. In periodicals like *Sound, Filmindia*, and *Star & Style* from the 1930s and 1940s, British companies regularly advertised women's face creams, like Afghan Snow, that claimed to increase the skin's fairness, light, and glow. This has changed little since India gained independence in 1947: markets for skin-lightening creams have only multiplied. The skin-lightening cream named Fair & Lovely, first launched by Hindustan Lever in 1975, quickly became the preeminent fairness cream in India. After economic liberalization in the 1990s opened up Indian consumer markets to multinational companies, a plethora of companies invented fairness creams, including multinationals like L'Oreal, Garnier, and Revlon. The development of newer creams like Fair and Handsome, targeting male consumers, also suggests that skin color norms that privilege less-pigmented skin have intensified under globalization. Researchers estimate that the fairness industry in India "currently represents 50% of India's entire skincare market, with estimates of its worth varying between $US 450–535 million."[5] Across the Asia-Pacific region, this market is estimated to be approximately $13 billion. As Sonali Johnson argues, "India's historical preoccupation with fair skin is in fact racism and sexism expressed through various cultural and historical mediums and reinforced by the contemporary beauty industry."[6]

Beauty product advertising propagates skin color norms integral to ideas of body image and body normativity. At least 50 percent of the beauty product industry in India revolves around skin-lightening products, which range from face creams to soaps and products for genitalia. The privileging of less-pigmented skin as being part of an idealized body image for women is most evident in commercials that market cosmetics and skin products for skin-lightening. This colorism, we suggest, is racialized, as well as marked by other axes of power relations in South Asia like caste, class, and sexuality, among others. We map how colorism is integrated into, and reinforced by, body normativity in Indian commercials because, as Radhika Parameswaran and Kavitha Cardoza note, "these commercially sponsored texts execute the pedagogic task of reminding India's expanding female consumer markets to imagine that it is their bodies' excess production of melanin, not historical and institutional structures of power, that retards their social mobility . . . (Reddy, 2006, p. 124)."[7] How is this reflected in the narrative arc and visual representations of earlier commercials in comparison with later commercials? In many ads from the mid-twentieth and late twentieth century, the narrative arc is structured around a before-and-after transformation, producing a discourse around these products that instigates anxiety about one's skin. This discourse promises to empower the female consumer psychically and materially. The transformed, less-pigmented consumer, usually female, is also transformed psychically and socioeconomically: she becomes more confident in the job interview and the arranged marriage interview and successfully acquires both capital and love. In response to public outcry over the racism embedded in these commercials' discourse, companies have recently shifted to a strategy that posits that using skin-lightening creams is a feminist act of self-empowerment.

As problematic as this shift sounds, many contemporary commercials for skin-lightening products often suggest that using their merchandise protects the consumer's skin from the sun, thus inviting the female consumer to choose self-care and unrestricted mobility. For example, in a 2009 commercial for Neutrogena's Fine Fairness Cream, the Hindi film actor Deepika Padukone asserts, "Skin experts say that one hour in the sun can set your fairness back by eight weeks. Does this mean we shouldn't step out into the sun?"[8] The camera then follows her as she boldly steps out onto the balcony of her posh, modern home. Padukone turns to the viewer and triumphantly declares, "Of course not." A voiceover then introduces us to the Fine Fairness Cream, which, we are told, includes, among its ingredients, "Healthy White complex," which, the voiceover promises, will lighten skin tone "from the inside." It also includes "150% sunscreen protection," we are informed. The commercial opens with a series of wide shots of Padukone's slim body, and it concludes with a series of successive close-up shots of her face, ostensibly lightened. We address this commercial because of its regressive representation of less-pigmented skin as desirable, complete with pseudoscientific racialized language about its ingredients ("Healthy White complex"), which is representative of how multinational and national cosmetic companies now market face creams in India. In 2014, after considerable public debate and outcry over the regressive and demeaning representations in such ads, the advertising industry watchdog, Advertising Standards of India (ASCI), issued new guidelines that tackled the before-and-after narrative structure that was a staple in these ads. According to these guidelines, companies need to ensure that their ads "do not depict people with dark skin as somehow inferior to those who are fairer."[9] ASCI mandates that ads should not associate less-pigmented skin with any socioeconomic, psychological, or professional disadvantage or with a particular caste, class, or religious background. The guidelines state, "These ads should not reinforce negative social stereotyping on the basis of skin colour. Specifically, advertising should not directly or implicitly show people with darker skin, in a way which is widely seen as, unattractive, unhappy, depressed, or concerned."[10]

If this mandate forces the abandonment of explicitly racist and demeaning representations that negate most Indian skin tones, it nonetheless leaves untouched the related issue of body image and normative conceptions of ideal skin in many, if not all, ads. Indeed, capital morphs in the pursuit of profit, and these beauty products have adapted to the market by renaming their creams, using synonyms that largely leave unchanged the privileging of less-pigmented skin and thinness in these commercials. For example, a

2018 ad for Garnier's skin-lightening cream calls it "Garnier Light Complete Serum Cream."[11] In the audioscape of the ad, we are promised that the product will "brighten" skin, remove "dark spots" caused by the sun, and make one's skin "spotless and bright." The female actors in the ad, with the lead played by Hindi film actor Alia Bhatt, only reinforce hegemonic body image norms: they are conventionally thin with less-pigmented skin. These new commercials now abandon the before-and-after narrative logic of earlier commercials (especially of the Fair & Lovely brand), which suggested that those who use these products will get a desirable job or get married to that eligible bachelor. Instead, they reframe the use of these products as a sign of female independence, self-care, and self-protection that enables women's mobility beyond the home.[12]

In this context, it is important to note how feminist voices and activists have challenged and resisted ideals of desirable skin tone and body norms. Given this complex commercial mobilization of middle-class feminist rhetoric of empowerment toward problematic body image norms, resistance to colorist body images has come from several quarters. From successful protests organized by the All India Democratic Women's Association (AIDWA) to media campaigns like Kavitha Immanuel's Dark Is Beautiful in 2009, feminist resistance has illuminated the sociocultural and economic violence engendered by these commercials. In 2002, AIDWA campaigned against corporate giant Hindustan Lever's offensive fairness ad campaign—this was debated in the Indian Parliament, and the ad was eventually withdrawn due to state pressure, which became a successful moment of women's organized resistance. Likewise, in 2009, Kavitha Immanuel, founder of Women of Worth (WOW), launched the Dark Is Beautiful campaign to combat the lived experience of colorism in India. Further, in 2013, celebrity actor and film director Nandita Das joined this campaign to disrupt the racialized rhetoric about less-pigmented skin and to disseminate messages on body positivity. WOW's advocacy actions included organizing workshops, as well as developing print and TV ad campaigns that sought to create a public conversation about colorism and its dehumanizing effects. In Das's powerful PSA video about this issue, she asked Indians to "stay dark, stay beautiful." In 2019, Das renamed this campaign India's Got Color, and she has gone on record to argue that "while we must combat the various forms of discrimination based on caste, religion, gender and sexual preference, the least we can do is to end the bias based on skin colour."[13] As part of this campaign, Das created a two-minute music-based ad campaign in Hindi that identifies how racism based on skin color permeates social life in India and then goes on to challenge it. Through this counterdiscourse, the actor hopes to inspire Indian youth to "change the public discourse around this issue" and enact "a more holistic celebration of diversity"; as she asserts, "after all, we are more than 1.3 billion people and have that many shades of skin tones."[14] This ad's message thus challenges the capitalist exploitation of colorism evident in Indian media: it instigates a public conversation about skin color norms that disrupts the privileging of less-pigmented skin while celebrating skin color diversity.

Further, Parameswaran and Cardoza identify several media sites where one can discern a critique of colorism and Indian women's social experiences, from several Hindi and English-language films made in India and the diaspora to television series like *Saat Phere* and debates in India's popular women's magazine *Femina*.[15] If some celebrities have been brand ambassadors for skin-lightening products (Priyanka Chopra, for example, was for Garnier's cream), other Bollywood celebrities, like Taapsee Pannu and Abhay Deol, have criticized the racism and harm such endorsements bring.

Corporate India has responded to this growing shift in public perception and public critique of racialized skin and body norms in two ways: first, linguistically, corporations have shifted their tone to avoid words like "fair" and "whitening," and second, visually, they have erased from the narrative the eligible male potential partner (often lurking in the background)—instead, they position the use of these beauty products as instances of feminist individualism and as acts of self-empowerment, self-care, and self-assertion in a patriarchal society. Hindustan Unilever in 2020, for example, rebranded its flagship Fair & Lovely cream to what is now called Glow & Lovely. Has this shift to a new linguistic economy countered the privileging of less-pigmented skin? We argue otherwise. Indeed, its tacky name change plays into how synonyms like "bright" and "glow" have replaced words like "light," "fair," "lightening," and "whitening." This, however, does nothing to negate colorism and racism. The new visual ad for the face cream named Glow attempts to co-opt the language of feminist self-empowerment in multiple ways. First, it appears to celebrate body diversity, insofar as it includes multiple female models of different ages, body types, and skin tones with different levels of pigmentation, instead of the conventionally thin, less-pigmented model. The repetition of the refrain "Don't stop my glow" is positioned as a message of feminist self-assertion to Indian society. Yet, ultimately, the commercial's fetishization of the thin central female figure, "Dee," as the assertive self-empowered DJ who uses this product to *glow* reiterates the undesirable body image tropes of earlier ads.[16]

While it is beyond the scope of this chapter to consider Pakistani advertising, further attention is warranted for an ad that Hindustan Lever created for Glow & Lovely's Pakistani market. This ad, "Mitti Ke Sau Rung" (A Hundred Shades of Earth), articulates a more complex relationship to the South Asian female body in ways that reject colorism.[17] It opens with this line: "Glow and Lovely celebrates the diverse and glowing faces of Pakistan." The entire commercial features a fast-paced montage of video clips in which different women are filmed in action as they work in different professions, from sports to music, construction, entertainment, and the arts. The lyrics and the refrain of the background score assert a message of body diversity that centers anticolorism: "There are a hundred shades of earth; one is mine; another is yours." The cinematography notably includes several montages of low-angle shots of the different models, as they look straight at the camera with powerful expressions of confidence, strength, and defiance. By featuring each model in several action shots—playing soccer, supervising a construction site, playing the *tabla*, jogging in the streets, fighting in the boxing ring, and so on—the visualscape articulates along with the soundscape of the song, which exhorts the female viewer that "hardships will come, but you will fight them," and "in each color, you are complete, in each color you have a distinct existence." While none of the models featured reflect diversity in terms of age or weight, this commercial most explicitly (when compared to its counterparts in India) positions its skin-care product as affirming skin color diversity. Ads like this exemplify the capitalist appropriation of discourses of feminist empowerment through their individualist representation of aspirational middle-class female subjectivity in South Asia.

Adorning the Ideal Body in Tanishq's Wedding Jewelry Commercials

Contemporary Indian advertising has played no small part in proliferating colorism, ableism, and fatphobia arising from thin-ideal messaging. Madhusmita Das and Sangeeta Sharma note that by constantly "associating fairness and beauty with increased marriage eligibility, career achievement, and other positive outcomes," Indian television ads have caused "women and adolescent girls" to become "increasingly concerned about their appearance."[18] Their study reveals that women who are greatly affected by such negative messaging are "at greater risk to develop extreme preoccupation with weight and appearance, and are also more likely to display disordered eating patterns and/or clinical eating disorders."[19] In this section, we examine how wedding jewelry ads for the Indian brand Tanishq contribute to these harmful discourses and how feminist activism can challenge the normative and prescriptive ideals propagated by such jewelry commercials.

In the last two decades, Indian jewelry commercials have moved away from an explicit focus on familial wealth and prosperity toward the portrayal of the "new" Indian woman. Meenakshi Thapan defines this new Indian woman as "an ambivalent entity shaped by the social and public domain which simultaneously portrays her as glamorous, independent, conscious of her embodiment and of the many forms of adornment and self-presentation available to her, and yet enshrined in the world of tradition through her adherence to family and national values."[20] The ideal new Indian woman is also the ideal customer because she shows her connection to both tradition and modernity through consumption. Recent jewelry ads have appropriated this narrative by making the claim that the modern Indian woman can proudly proclaim her independence and individuality through her choice of jewelry. In these new ads, the bride is no longer shy, silent, and inconsolable at the thought of leaving her parents. Rather, she is someone with a distinct personality that she draws attention to through her choice of jewelry. Even as these ads attempt to tell individualized stories marked by ostensibly progressive values and ideals, they cannot seem to escape the limitations imposed by conventional beauty standards. Much like the magazine spreads Thapan analyzes in her work, these ads have absolutely no space for "the ageing, disabled, obese or out-of-shape body, which deviates from the perfect embodied state."[21] The casting of actresses whose bodies meet normative ideals is crucial to conserving, maintaining, and reproducing practices and norms that punish unconventional and unruly bodies.

Wedding jewelry ads that clearly value a specific skin color and body type over others send the message that the promise of heteronormative reproductive futurity (through marriage) is accessible only to those who fit conventional standards of beauty. Mallika Das, in her analysis of the portrayal of gender roles in Indian television ads, has also written about the concept of the modern "New Indian Woman" trapped in the limbo between modernity and tradition.[22] By using this trope of the new Indian woman, especially in the context of bridal jewelry, brands like Tanishq have appropriated the language of empowerment and diversity while continuing to showcase models and actresses who fit normative ideas of beauty. Launched in 2017, the ad campaign for Tanishq's Rivaah collection focuses on brides from different Indian states. During the launch, the company claimed that their wedding-centered collection aimed to "cater to 13 bridal communities across India and celebrate their culture."[23] The collection has grown since the initial launch, and the Tanishq website has a separate page dedicated to each "Rivaah Bride."[24] The page titled "The Bengali Bride," for example, has pictures and descriptions of traditional Bengali jewelry, such as the *paati haar* and *shaakha pola*.[25] The campaign claims to support and celebrate India's cultural diversity. The website describes their ideal bride with these words: "As varied as the communities she hails from, the Indian bride looks absolutely resplendent in her wedding finery."[26]

While each bride is supposed to be "as varied as the communities she hails from," what is perhaps most striking about the print campaign is the absolute lack of variation in the models' body types. Each category has a different model, but the uniformity of their physical features reveals that while the jewelry itself may vary, the idealized body image does not. Further, their to-kenistic inclusion of Muslim brides, delinked from any regional variations, only serves to highlight the overwhelmingly Hindu framework of the wedding collection. Unsurprisingly, the Rivaah ads, both print and for television, feature young, able-bodied, conventionally attractive models with less-pigmented skin as brides.[27] This collection, while explicitly claiming to celebrate cultural variations and diversity in India, ends up reproducing and propagating body normativity. Here, the dangerously depoliticized and idealized category of the new Indian woman allows them to do so.

Rivaah's ad campaign became the subject of a petition begun by Muna Beatty, an Indian anticolorism advocate. Beatty addressed the petition to Tanishq, criticizing the lack of models with more pigmented skin in the Rivaah campaign. A part of Beatty's #ColourMeRight campaign, the petition begins by acknowledging the impact made by an earlier Tanishq wedding ad that had featured a bride with more pigmented skin.[28] The 2013 ad begins with the bride (the actress Priyanka Bose) putting on her Tanishq jewelry. A girl, who calls her Mama, walks in, and they share a brief emotional moment together before the ceremony begins. After the wedding, the child asks the groom if she can finally call him Daddy. Created by Lowe Lintas India and shot by filmmaker Gauri Shinde, this ad received a lot of attention when it first came out. In an interview that year, Deepika Tewari, who was then vice president of marketing for Titan's (Tanishq's parent company) jewelry division, when asked about this particular ad, proudly claimed, "Tanishq has always represented progressive thinking and we have only mirrored reality. Marriage is a big decision and our latest wedding collection is for every new-age bride who is confident and believes in herself."[29] Arun Iyer, the national creative director of Lowe Lintas, said that they took pains to cast the actors, as "it had to look like a marriage of equals, not something that was done out of pity."[30] The ad has over 1,950,000 views on YouTube, and viewers' comments are overwhelmingly positive.

Beatty, who uploaded the petition with the username Dark Brown Woman, writes appreciatively about the Priyanka Bose ad and criticizes the ads for Tanishq's Rivaah wedding collection. Beatty's primary focus in her petition is colorism. It is interesting to note how Beatty uses recognizable tropes about womanhood—tropes that Tanishq uses for advertising—to argue for better representation. She establishes herself as a woman who knows her own mind, as well as a mother who is worried about her daughter's future. Beatty also goes on to write about her own self-esteem issues and how such biased advertising might affect her daughter: "My daughter has the same complexion as me. I wonder at times how it will be for her."[31] She ends her petition by asking Tanishq to "publicly commit to representing Indian women of all skin tones in all future ad campaigns" and reasserting the importance of swift action.[32] Beatty's petition received more than a thousand signatures in a short period of time and garnered a positive response from Tewari, who released a statement claiming to be committed to diversity: "Tanishq has always stood for diversity and we have consistently made efforts to ensure inclusivity is a cornerstone in all our advertisement work. . . . We will continue to create commercials that reflect the truly diverse nature of the country."[33] Beatty's success with Tanishq led her to start another petition on Change.org, this time demanding that Lakme, an Indian cosmetics brand, feature models with more pigmented skin in their ads. After Tanishq released its statement, Beatty exhorted the petition's signatories to continue to support such feminist activism. In her follow-up, titled "The Colour of Victory," Beatty writes how such an outcome has led her to hope that such a change "in our time [augurs] a better tomorrow for our children."[34] Thus, feminist activists have engendered change by holding corporations that claim to be committed to inclusivity and diversity accountable; their activism signals the urgent need to change normative visual narratives that perpetuate harmful ethnoracial and gendered stereotypes.

Fair and Normal: Skin Color, Able-bodiedness, and Capital in India's Digital Matrimonial Advertisements

We now turn to contemporary matrimonial advertisements in Indian digital media to explore how these ads reproduce or challenge conventional, patriarchal, and caste-ist ideas about colorism and body image for prospective brides and grooms. South Asian feminist scholars such as Rochona Majumdar, Sonora Jha, Jyotsna Vaid, and Neha Mishra have mapped how colonial and patriarchal ideological discourses have been recast in modern arranged marriages. Showing how market-related forces have influenced Indian marriages, these scholars underscore how the modern nuclear family reproduces patriarchal values. In what follows, we contend that modern Indian wedding advertisements center on and celebrate the joint family, reinforcing patriarchal body norms for women through a rhetoric of female empowerment.

Rochona Majumdar analyzes how the idea of the arranged marriage was reconstituted and rearranged in colonial India.[35] She argues that there remains "an unresolved tension at the heart of modernity" with the growth of Western education and the ideal of the bourgeois couple on the one hand and the normative construction of the joint family on the other.[36] The centrality of the couple is always subordinated to the ideal of the joint family founded on patriarchal values, such that the family, rather than the couple, is central in an arranged marriage; to explain this, Majumdar claims that "behind the celebration of the couple form was a commitment and concern about the longevity of the family."[37] Majumdar establishes the modernity of the Indian arranged marriage by demonstrating how a primarily urban, print-based arranged marriage market emerged in colonial Bengal; this marriage market reconceptualized marriage practices in response to changes in colonial laws, education, and power relations, while simultaneously reinforcing patriarchal ideas about gender and family. Relatedly, Sonora Jha notes how the marriage market in postcolonial India has been influenced by beauty and "fairness" ideals and skin tone has become "a visual agent" in placing individuals in "a local social hierarchy."[38] Jha traces the rise of the modern "super-bride," who emerged as the epitome of physical perfection in the 1990s. As Jha notes, with the advent of the Internet, patriarchal notions of colorism and sexism got reproduced by matrimonial websites; although online matchmaking enables an electronic interaction that bypasses face-to-face communication, it does not bypass skin color bias.[39] We argue that disguised under the garb of modernity, virtual matchmaking reinforces the hegemony of colorism.

This becomes evident across several online Indian matrimonial sites such as Shaadi.com, Bharatmatrimony.com, and Jeevansathi.com, which have been steadily growing in popularity. Since the ASCI released guidelines targeting tropes of fairness in advertising in 2014, matrimonial websites have removed the "complexion" and "body type" categories on their pages. In this context, we turn to two digital texts—a matrimonial video by Mainduck (2012)[40] on YouTube and a matrimonial advertisement on the website iMilap .com (2020)—to underscore how bias against more pigmented skin supersedes body image prejudice in the online matchmaking world. The matrimonial video was published before the ASCI guidelines, while the iMilap matrimonial profile was posted six years after the guidelines were issued. Although they are eight years apart, in both examples, colorism and body image bias are central to their vision of heteronormative intimacy.

Indian matrimonial websites require all prospective brides and grooms to submit a "biodata" to facilitate the search. The Indian marriage biodata is a document that details the age, date of birth, religion, education, caste, profession, salary, hobbies, and expectations of the alliance seeker, along with the names and professions of the candidate's parents. Since the biodata necessarily fails to capture the personality of the seeker, online matrimonial profiles can often include accompanying short YouTube videos created by prospective brides and grooms. One matrimonial video, called "Sahi Rishta Matrimonial: Naik # 7892" and posted through the YouTube channel Mainduck, ridicules the gendered expectations underlying Indian matchmaking and critiques middle-class sexism.[41] The matrimonial ad is produced by a company that makes comedic shows online. While sometimes funny and somewhat exaggerated, it reflects actual matrimonial videos that are produced today.[42] In "Sahi Rishta Matrimonial: Naik # 7892," the mother of the prospective groom (an art-of-living or spiritual/self-help teacher living in the United States) directs the search for her son's spouse and shares her criteria for the ideal daughter-in-law: "a tall, pretty, clear-minded, and dynamic girl who honors all relationships" is what she wants. Following this, the mother asserts, "but most important, girl should be fair." The mother underscores that "wheatish" and "dark-skinned" brides are "not very much preferred." She adds that there is "no country bar or caste bar," but "Hindu parentage is preferred." In contrast, the viewer knows very little about her expatriate son except that he is an Art of Living teacher and awaiting his green card. The mother claims that he is "handsome," "athletic," and "caring," with "no health issues." There is no mention of the son's skin color, body type, or interests; instead, the text's focus on the mother's colorist demands exemplifies dominant sexist and racist discourses that privilege less-pigmented skin. It also represents, as Majumdar has argued, the hetero-patriarchal reconstitution of the institution of marriage today such that the joint family continues to reign supreme.

History tells us that India's deep-rooted bias against more-pigmented skin, though predating the arrival of British colonizers, was reaffirmed by the racialized hierarchies of colonialism that privileged less pigmented skin. Engaging an intersectional lens with this phenomenon, we suggest that feminist scholarship can expand our understanding of how colorism in India is imbricated with caste and class. Neha Mishra notes that conventional Indian matrimonial searches often expect that the married couple will share both caste and religion and privilege less-pigmented women over more pigmented women.[43] Skin color can be overlooked only if the bride's family is wealthier than the groom's family. Jyotsna Vaid illuminates how "fairness" functions as a "bargaining chip" in Indian marriage negotiations such that less-pigmented skin is often used to compensate for status inconsistencies in cross-caste marriage, inadequate dowry, lack of education, or unemployment.[44] Vaid contends that Indian matrimonial ads promote "ascribed characteristics," such as family status, caste, region, and language, over "achieved characteristics," such as educational accomplishment, occupation, and personality traits.[45] In the case of the Naiks, the mother's assertion on "no country bar or caste bar" is tied to the intersections of both class and caste privilege—this privilege determines access to emigration. It also implies that less-pigmented skin is the bargaining chip to negotiate the inconsistencies in caste and citizenship/residency. Contemporary Indian matrimonial advertisements are thus replete with neoliberal jargon that strives toward but fails to disguise the deep-rooted and dispossessing biases defining the nation's culture.

Body image norms and colorism intersect in specific ways in matrimonial advertising for differently abled subjects in India. iMilap is a matrimonial website that describes itself as a platform for people who are *divyang*,[46] deaf, or physically challenged. It illuminates how people with disabilities are also often prejudiced against more pigmented skin such that many prioritize less pigmented skin over able-bodiedness when considering potential partners. iMilap allows members to categorize their complexion as "unspecified," "fair," "brown," "dark," or "very dark." It also classifies disability as follows: blindness, deafness, deafness and muteness, muteness, mental illness, physically challenged, polio, and accidental mental injury. Since self-identifying information in both categories is optional, some candidates describe their complexion as "fair" and "brown" but eschew noting anything in the disability section. Most profiles that mention disability are those of men. Further, it is noteworthy that the profiles of most women with disabilities are created by a parent or relative, implying that women with disabilities need to be protected and assisted by family members to make decisions on their behalf, while men with disabilities are independently capable of managing their online presence.

This speaks to how the marginalization of women of color who have disabilities is intertwined with colorism. Often, more pigmented women with disabilities list themselves as "fair" on this platform.[47] Ranjita Dawn argues that women with disabilities have consistently been denied traditional roles and access to heteronormative structures of intimacy like marriage. Either they are assumed to be incapable of fulfilling family responsibilities, or they are seen as asexual.[48] That the emancipatory possibilities of the digital media discussed above are complex and limited should be amply evident in how biases about religion, caste, skin color, and class status, among others, permeate the social organization of intimacy in this medium. One matrimonial profile posted in 2020 by a Kashmiri Hindu man with a disability states that he is looking for a "fair, beautiful, and loving professional woman" with a master's degree. He details that he has a slightly raised right foot but that he is entirely independent and mobile. He confirms that he is open to marrying a woman with a disability.[49] Such ads demonstrate that even while attempting to disrupt the privileging of able-bodiedness, their heteronormative rhetoric reproduces other conventional colorist biases about lesser-pigmented skin. They also suggestively evince how capital (professional earning capacities) and education come into play as markers of value in evaluating life partners.

Conclusion

Our analysis in the present study is not exhaustive, but we hope that it instigates further dialogue about how race is central to colorist body image norms propagated in modern India for the Indian female subject and how caste, class, able-bodiedness, and heteronormativity structure these hegemonic norms. A truly effective feminist critique of colorism, then, must be intersectional:

it must uncover how colorism is imbricated with caste, class, regional, sexual, gender, and religious differences and stereotypes; it must also confront these imbrications across and through media forms that purport to offer new emancipatory visions of empowerment. Such an intersectional feminist critique can deconstruct the harmful relation between body normativity and capitalist consumer culture in the ecosystem of India's media cultures. Our admittedly eclectic archive of commercials that target, frame, and invent the ideal female body and the ideal Indian female subject exemplifies how capital, technology, and gender oppression are intertwined in new ways today. Our task, then, is to continue to grow feminist voices and feminist activism, which, as we have demonstrated, can mobilize media forms as well as policy changes to challenge colorism and body normativity in contemporary India.

NOTES

1. Menon and Pant, "Are Contingencies of Self-Worth," 129.
2. Jablonski, *Living Color*, 127.
3. Jablonski, 127.
4. Nagar and Virk, "The Struggle."
5. Shroff, Diedrichs, and Craddock, "Skin Color, Cultural Capital."
6. Johnson, "The Pot Calling the Kettle," 215.
7. Parameswaran and Cardoza, "Melanin on the Margins."
8. Medi Tree India, "Deepika Padukone."
9. *Economic Times*, "ASCI Releases Guidelines."
10. *NBC News*, "New Ad Guidelines."
11. Garnier India, "Garnier Light."
12. See Bharpilania, "Sorry 'Indian Matchmaking.'"
13. Basu, "India's Got Colour."
14. *Hindustan Times*, "Nandita Das."
15. Parameswaran and Cardoza, "Melanin on the Margins."
16. Glow and Lovely India, "GLOW KO NA ROKO."
17. Glow and Lovely, "Glow & Lovely."
18. Das and Sharma, "Fetishizing Women," 120.
19. Das and Sharma, 123.
20. Thapan, "Embodiment and Identity," 415–416.
21. Thapan, 441.
22. Das, "Gender Role Portrayals," 209.
23. ETRetail.com, "Tanishq Launches New Sub Brand."
24. Tanishq, "Rivaah Brides."
25. Tanishq, "The Bengali Bride."
26. Tanishq (@TanishqJewelry), "As varied as the communities she hails from, the Indian bride looks absolutely resplendent in her wedding finery. #RivaahBridesByTanishq," Twitter, February 17, 2017, 1:17 P.M. Available at https://twitter.com/tanishqjewelry/status/832667734219427843.
27. TanishqJewellery, "Tanishq—Rivaah."
28. TanishqJewellery, "Tanishq Wedding Film."
29. Twishy, "Tanishq's Progressive Thinking."

30. Shah, "New Tanishq Ads."
31. Beatty, "Tanishq—We Can Do Better!."
32. Beatty.
33. *Business Standard*, "Tanishq Commercials."
34. Beatty, "Petition Update."
35. Majumdar, *Marriage and Modernity*, 2.
36. Majumdar, 13.
37. Majumdar, 241.
38. Jha, "Looking for Love," 68.
39. Jha, 71.
40. Mainduck, "Sahi Rishta."
41. Mainduck.
42. The Society for Anthropology in Community Colleges, "Annotated List."
43. Mishra, "India and Colorism."
44. Vaid, "Fair Enough?" 152.
45. Vaid, 153.
46. *Divyang*, meaning "divine body," was introduced as a new term by the Bharatiya Janata Party Prime Minister, Narendra Modi, in 2015, as a positive substitute for *viklang*, or "disabled." However, this term became controversial as people with disabilities and disability activists claimed that the term deified their impediments and overlooked their reality. See Karmakar, "'Divyangajan' Is a Controversial Word."
47. Their more pigmented skin was obvious in the profile pictures.
48. Dawn, "Our Lives, Our Identity."
49. iMilap.com.

BIBLIOGRAPHY

Basu, Nilanjana. "India's Got Colour: Nandita Das 'Reinvents' Her 'Dark Is Beautiful' Campaign." *NDTV*, updated September 30, 2019. Available at https://www.ndtv.com/entertainment/indias-got-colour-nandita-das-reinvents-her-dark-is-beautiful-campaign-2109680.

Beatty, Muna. "Petition Update: The Colour of Victory." Change.org. July 17, 2018. Available at https://www.change.org/p/tanishq-we-can-do-better-dark-skinned-women-matter-too-colourmeright/u/23018872.

———. "Tanishq—We Can Do Better! Dark Skinned Women Matter Too! #ColourMe Right." Change.org. May 30, 2018. Available at https://www.change.org/p/tanishq-we-can-do-better-dark-skinned-women-matter-too-colourmeright.

Bharpilania, Sumedha. "Sorry 'Indian Matchmaking' but 'Sahi Rishta' Convinced People to Never Get Married Before You Did." Buzzfeed. July 23, 2020. Available at https://www.buzzfeed.com/sumedha_bharpilania/hilarious-sahi-rishta-matrimonial-videos.

Business Standard. "Tanishq Commercials Will Reflect Diversity, Says Titan after '#Colourmeright Campaign.'" July 10, 2018. Available at https://www.business-standard.com/article/pti-stories/tanishq-commercials-will-reflect-diversity-says-titan-after-colourmeright-campaign-118071001094_1.html.

Das, Madhusmita, and Sangeeta Sharma. "Fetishizing Women: Advertising in Indian Television and Its Effects on Target Audiences." *Journal of International Women's Studies* 18, no. 1 (2016): 114–132. Available at http://vc.bridgew.edu/jiws/vol18/iss1/9.

Das, Mallika. "Gender Role Portrayals in Indian Television Ads." *Sex Roles* 64 (2011): 208–222. Available at https://doi.org/10.1007/s11199-010-9750-1.

Dawn, Ranjita. "Our Lives, Our Identity: Women with Disabilities in India." *Disability and Rehabilitation* 36, no. 21 (2014): 1768–1773. Available at https://doi.org/10.3109/09 638288.2013.870237.

Economic Times. "ASCI Releases Guidelines for Advertising of Fairness Products." Updated August 19, 2014. Available at https://economictimes.indiatimes.com/industry /services/advertising/asci-releases-guidelines-for-advertising-of-fairness-products/ar ticleshow/40405288.cms?from=mdr.

ETRetail.com. "Tanishq Launches New Sub Brand 'Rivaah' for Wedding Jewellery." March 16, 2017. Available at https://retail.economictimes.indiatimes.com/news/apparel-fash ion/jewellery/tanishq-launches-new-sub-brand-rivaah-for-wedding-jewellery/576 65014.

Garnier India. "Garnier Light Complete Serum Cream." July 7, 2018. YouTube video. Available at https://www.youtube.com/watch?v=wF-QNeMJ_bs.

Glow and Lovely. "Glow & Lovely | Mitti Ke Sau Rung." October 25, 2020. YouTube video. Available at https://www.youtube.com/watch?v=3srlHVba7LY.

Glow and Lovely India. "GLOW KO NA ROKO feat. DeeMC x Glow & Lovely." October 11, 2020. YouTube video. Available at https://www.youtube.com/watch?v=xRe-gUU Ly04&feature=emb_logo.

Hindustan Times. "Nandita Das Releases India's Got Colour Campaign, Radhika Apte, Ali Fazal, Swara Bhaskar Join Her." Updated September 30, 2019. Available at https:// widgets.hindustantimes.com/bollywood/nandita-das-releases-india-s-got-colour-cam paign-radhika-apte-ali-fazal-swara-bhaskar-join-her-watch/story-Hb11lRz2Bt31GjL 9R5ugVL.html.

Jablonski, Nina. *Living Color: The Biological and Social Meaning of Skin Color*. Berkeley: University of California Press, 2012.

Jha, Sonora. "Looking for Love in All the White Places: A Study of Skin Color Preferences on Indian Matrimonial and Mate-Seeking Websites." *Studies in South Asian Film and Media* 1, no. 1 (2009): 65–83.

Johnson, Sonali Elizabeth. "The Pot Calling the Kettle Black? Gender-Specific Health Dimensions of Colour Prejudice in India." *Journal of Health Management* 4, no. 2 (2002): 215–227.

Karmakar, Rahul. "'Divyangajan' Is a Controversial Word Similar to 'Mentally Ill', Says U.N. Body." *The Hindu*, September 25, 2019. Available at https://www.thehindu.com /news/national/other-states/divyangjan-is-a-controversial-word-similar-to-mentally -ill-says-un-body/article29508027.ece.

Mainduck. "Sahi Rishta Matrimonial: Naik # 7892." July 13, 2012. YouTube video. Available at https://www.youtube.com/watch?v=7JNHqKV68EI.

Majumdar, Rochona. *Marriage and Modernity*. Durham, NC: Duke University Press, 2009.

Medi Tree India. "Deepika Padukone Neutrogena Fine Fairness Cream." January 12, 2016. YouTube video. Available at https://www.youtube.com/watch?v=skJTp3VMIyg.

Menon, Meenakshi, and Preeti Pant. "Are Contingencies of Self-Worth Associated with Body Image in Indian and British Women?" *Psychological Studies* 60 (2015): 129–137. Available at https://doi.org/10.1007/s12646-014-0296-0.

Mishra, Neha. "India and Colorism: The Finer Nuances." *Washington University Global Studies Law Review* 14, no. 4 (2015): 725–750.

Nagar, Itisha, and Rukhsana Virk. "The Struggle between the Real and Ideal: Impact of Acute Media Exposure on Body Image of Young Indian Women." *Sage Open* 7, no. 1 (2017). Available at https://doi.org/10.1177/2158244017691327.

NBC News. "New Ad Guidelines Take On India's Skin Whitening Industry." September 4, 2014. Available at https://www.nbcnews.com/news/asian-america/new-ad-guidelines-take-indias-skin-whitening-industry-n194551.

Parameswaran, Radhika, and Kavitha Cardoza. "Melanin on the Margins: Advertising and the Cultural Politics of Fair/Light/White Beauty in India." *Journalism and Communication Monographs* 11, no. 3 (2009): 213–274. Available at https://doi.org/10.1177/152263790901100302.

Shah, Gouri. "New Tanishq Ads Received Bouquets and Brickbats." Livemint. October 29, 2013. Available at https://www.livemint.com/Consumer/3KipzmBH06Qqv2NDsSqy2K/New-Tanishq-ad-receives-bouquets-and-brickbats.html.

Shroff, Hemal, Phillippa C. Diedrichs, and Nadia Craddock. "Skin Color, Cultural Capital, and Beauty Products: An Investigation of the Use of Skin Fairness Products in Mumbai, India." *Frontiers in Public Health* 5, no. 365 (2017): 1–9. Available at https://doi.org/10.3389/fpubh.2017.00365.

The Society for Anthropology in Community Colleges. "Annotated List of Links to Supplementary Online Material—You Tube." Accessed August 10, 2023. Available at https://sacc.americananthro.org/wp-content/uploads/Annotated-list-of-links1.pdf.

Tanishq. "The Bengali Bride." Accessed November 4, 2023. Available at https://www.tanishq.co.in/rivaah/bengali.

———. "Rivaah Brides." Accessed November 4, 2023. Available at https://www.tanishq.co.in/rivaah.

TanishqJewellery. "Tanishq—Rivaah by Tanishq TVC." February 15, 2017. YouTube video. Available at https://www.youtube.com/watch?v=lmI-jd0X04Y. Accessed 10 August 2023.

———. "Tanishq Wedding Film (2013)." October 24, 2013. YouTube video. Available at https://www.youtube.com/watch?v=P76E6b7SQs8.

Thapan, Meenakshi. "Embodiment and Identity in Contemporary Society: Femina and the 'New' Indian Woman." *Contributions to Indian Sociology* 38, no. 3 (2004): 411–444. Available at https://doi.org/10.1177/006996670403800305.

Twishy. "Tanishq's Progressive Thinking Has Only Mirrored Reality." Exchange4Media. November 7, 2013. Available at https://www.exchange4media.com/marketing-news/tanishq's-progressive-thinking-has-only-mirrored-reality-53370.html.

Vaid, Jyotsna. "Fair Enough? Color and the Commodification of Self in Indian Matrimonials." In *Shades of Difference: Why Skin Color Matters*, edited by Evelyn Nakano Glenn, 148–165. Stanford, CA: Stanford University Press, 2009.

11

Unpacking Compliances and Resistances in the Indian Yummy Mummy

SUCHARITA SARKAR

Introduction

In the introduction to her memoir, *My Yummy Mummy Guide: From Getting Pregnant to Being a Successful Working Mother and Beyond,* actor Karisma Kapoor writes, "The path from being a svelte Bollywood actress to a pregnant woman who had put on 24 kilos during her pregnancy and coming back to the thin me was more challenging than the role in *Zubeidaa*! I wanted to reveal my secrets to everyone."[1] Kapoor's confession that her "challenging" journey to becoming a *yummy mummy* is an achievement that she heroizes above her National Award–winning performance as an actor opens up two significant suggestions. First, it indicates how deeply women often internalize the patriarchal essentialization of motherhood: that maternity is the basis and culmination of female identity. Second, it reveals how body image—here manifested in the titular yummy mummy of Kapoor's memoir-cum-guidebook—has become predominant in neoliberal maternal narratives of resilience. In this chapter, I aim to investigate the problematic body image of the yummy mummy in the context of contemporary Indian mothers, motherhood, and mothering. My theorizing is grounded in the central distinction proposed by motherhood studies: the distinction between motherhood as an oppressive institution and mothering as a choice and an experience that can be empowering and even feminist. This distinction can be deployed transculturally to examine the regulation and subjugation of mothers in patriarchal systems because the disciplinary strategies in Western and non-Western cultures often share multiple commonalities (as well as differences). Adrienne Rich distinguished between "two meanings of motherhood, one superimposed on the other: the *potential relationship* of any woman to her powers of reproduction and to children; and the *institution*, which aims at ensuring that that potential—and all women—shall remain under male control."[2] Andrea O'Reilly further clarified this distinction by stating that "the term motherhood refers to the patriarchal institution of motherhood that is male-defined and controlled and is deeply oppressive to women, while the word mothering refers to women's experiences of mothering that are female-defined and centered and potentially empowering to women."[3] Likewise viewing motherhood as a feminist issue, Indian scholars like Maithreyi Krishnaraj have analyzed how the "social construction"—the "meaning attached to the idea of motherhood, and the terms and conditions under which it is allowed to express itself"—makes mothers "vulnerable," and not the "mere fact of motherhood/mothering."[4]

In unpacking the meanings attached to the social construction of the yummy mummy—as evidenced in the opening quote from Kapoor—this concept can be read both as a neoliberal extension of patriarchal motherhood as well as a potentially empowering mothering choice. Significantly, in the traditional Indian imagination, the ideal mother is predominantly epitomized as self-sacrificing, sari clad, and sexless. During the nationalistic struggle, and especially in the postindependence period, such maternal constructs were disseminated through "popular cultural archives such as cinema, television, radio, spectacles, and the print medium," and these coalesced to produce the "docile and homely figure of the idealized *Bharatiya nari* (traditional Indian woman)."[5] Against this historical and cultural context, the regimes of self-care that becoming the yummy mummy necessitates may be considered as individualized resistances to Indian patriarchal motherhood, although in limited ways. I, however, argue that the borrowed and globalized construct of the yummy mummy coerces mothers—through a strategic marketized mix of celebrity endorsement and popular cultural enforcement—to discipline their bodies to conform to normative beauty and body standards. To explicate my contention, I study two sets of cultural and popular texts. First, I briefly look at cinematic and commercial representations of the patriarchal *good* mother. Second, I analyze visual and textual representations of the yummy mummy in the Indian context. Through the lens of motherhood studies, I also locate the complicated imbrications of compliance and resistance in the selected maternal images and narratives of being/becoming a yummy mummy. I conclude by indicating alternate possibilities of resistances to the stereotyping of the maternal body: possibilities that reject both the self-abnegating model of patriarchal motherhood as well as the self-disciplining and obedient model of the yummy mummy.

Iterations of the Good Mother in Popular Indian Imagination

The most common pre-neoliberal visual representation of the good Indian mother is the Hindi filmic mother: devoted, sari clad, and usually plump, or at least unconcerned about her appearance. For instance, the maternal roles enacted by Nargis in *Mother India* (1957), by Nirupa Roy in numerous films like *Deewar* (1975) and *Amar Akbar Anthony* (1977), and by Rakhee in *Ram Lakhan* (1989) all perpetuate a maternal body image subliminally associated with selflessness and sexlessness.[6] This popular stereotypical filmic/cultural maternal identity is deeply embedded in the notion of self-sacrifice, which, in turn, is integral to conventional Indian imagination. As film historian Jai Arjun Singh comments, "For much of her history, the Hindi-film mother has been a cipher—someone with no real personality of her own, existing mainly as the prism through which we view the male lead."[7] This code of self-sacrifice can be traced even in apparently self-caring traditional postpartum customs where new mothers stay in their natal homes after childbirth and where they are given an "unusually nutritious and fattening diet, and the compulsory rest for at least five weeks."[8] Such practices are partially intended to ensure an adequate supply of breastmilk for the child. The focal shift from matri-centric to child-centric practices builds familial and cultural expectations wherein the maternal body is primarily a vehicle for the sustenance of the child. This process concomitantly desexualizes the mother's body, and such images have been visibilized and perpetuated through filmic maternal figures.

Over time, this filmic good mother spilled over into other areas of popular culture like advertisements. In the 1980s and early 1990s, one of the most popular mothers in television commercials was the matronly, prudent, sari-clad Lalitaji, featuring in a series of advertisements for Surf detergent. Although she appeared more assertive than the stereotypical filmic mother, she nonetheless embodied the self-discipline associated with the maternal figure. Another more domesticated maternal representation was found in the advertisements for Everest Spices that had the tagline "Taste *mein* best, Mummy *aur* Everest" (The best taste in food comes when it is cooked by mother, and with Everest; translation mine). The mothers in these advertisements mimicked the template of decorum and devotion expected from the good Indian mother, and they wore identifiably "Indian" clothes like the sari or *salwar kameez*. The sari, especially, has an "ancient heritage associated with tradition and so-called feminine virtues like shame, introversion, decorum and respectability,"[9] and the Indian mom of the 1990s donned this garment in all its conventionality.

These visible markers of Indian-ness have constructed the Indian mother in conformity with a sanitized but oppressive Hindu patriarchal ideology of good motherhood. Historically, this docile, desexualized ideal of good motherhood can be traced to the religious culture of worshipping domesticated, nurturing, consort mother-goddesses like Lakshmi and Annapurna. A psychological reading of such images, however, reveals the repressed male desire for fetishizing the maternal body. Sudhir Kakar considers "Devi, the great goddess," to be "the hegemonic narrative of Hindu culture," especially in her "manifold expressions as mother in the inner world of the Hindu son," and he discusses case histories that are "repeated again and again" to explain how Indian men "maintain an idealized relationship with the maternal body."[10] In alignment with Kakar's psychoanalysis, it is expected that the good Indian mother will be self-sacrificing and will also sacrifice any desire to be visually or sexually attractive. Disobedient mothers who do not conform are usually blamed and shamed. The traditionalist discourse of the Hindu Right—for instance, *Nari Ank* and other enduringly popular publications from Gita Press—dissuaded women/mothers "from wearing Western clothes or using too much jewellery" and labeled those who dressed to "show-off in public" as displaying "corrupting characteristics."[11] Strikingly, if such deglamorized and earthy traits have traditionally defined embodiment in Indian mothers, glamor and normative beauty are increasingly becoming traits that the nation's neoliberal climate demands of its mommies.

Motherhood in Neoliberal India: Representations of the Yummy Mummy

The cover of Kapoor's *My Yummy Mummy Guide* visibly defies the prescriptions of the ethnically marked, modest, good mother circulated by traditionalist publications and older popular media. The yummy mummy image is seemingly replacing the earlier icons of maternal decorum with one of maternal desirability, substituting the ideal of self-sacrifice with that of self-care. It is in the context of the earlier homogenized cultural expectation of maternal self-denial and the pervasive maternal body imagery reinforcing this prescriptive ideal of good motherhood that the neoliberal construct of the yummy mummy—with its imbricated potentials for deviance and compliance—needs to be located. The yummy mummy project promises the rewards of self-validation and approval from others. The rejection of the traditional model of plump, sari-clad motherhood by the yummy mummy opens up a potential space for valorizing maternal sexuality and self-making. Indeed, the subtitle of Kapoor's book, *From Getting Pregnant to Being a Successful Working Mom and Beyond*, suggests such a celebratory arc of maternal empowerment.

The apparent choice to embrace maternal sexuality and focus on "me time" is, at one level, a defiance of traditional motherhood roles, and, expectedly, the yummy mummy has sometimes been the target of maternal shaming. While the infotainment industry usually glamorizes the yummy mummy, some traditionalist media reports accuse the yummy mummy of prioritizing "gyms, slimming centres, liposuction options" and neglecting "her children's whereabouts, her husband's work," and her caregiving duties toward the older family members, and she is often compared unfavorably with good mothers who do not "wear sleeveless clothes" but perform their maternal duties devotedly.[12] Yet the overall reception of the yummy mummy image is not just accusatory and derogatory. The multiplying saturation of images and narratives indicates how the yummy mummy embodies and generates complex responses. To unpack the matrix of deviance and compliance, we need to interrogate the product and process of becoming a yummy mummy.

The cover of Kapoor's book has a large color photograph of a slim, smiling Kapoor in a red, sleeveless Western dress without any visible sign of motherhood (for instance, she is not carrying a child). Superimposed on the glossy photograph are white, chalklike outline drawings of objects associated with childcare: a feeding bottle, a rattle, a pair of booties, a pacifier, and a teddy bear. The cover image subliminally conveys the message of the book: if the right prescription is obediently followed, then motherhood is a manageable performance that allows a (privileged) mother ample opportunity—and time—to look like a celebrity yummy mummy. According to Western feminist scholars, neoliberal capitalism made new "technologies" of "postfeminist femininity" available to women: these technologies appear to grant capacity and freedom of choice even as they lock women into "new constraining forms of gender power."[13] Angela McRobbie lists some of these technologies, like "the glamorous working mother, the so-called yummy mummy, the city high-flyer who is also a mother," referring to the allied construct of the "supermom" who seemingly balances work and home and looking good with ease.[14] Whereas the term "yummy mummy" is restricted to postpartum maternal bodies, feminist critic Imogen Tyler uses the broader phrase "pregnant beauty" to designate various representations of the commodified maternal body, from the pregnant to postpartum to lactating stages. Tyler analyzes "pregnant beauty" as a "particular neoliberal amalgam of maternity and femininity" that is "highly spectacular and contradictory," combining "signifiers of (sexual) freedom, consumption, choice, agency and futurity in a powerful and seductive post-feminist cultural ideal."[15] Pregnant beauty or yummy mummy makeovers are constituted of multiple and continuing consumer practices—like fitness and diet regimens, beauty-care routines, photo shoots (or selfie taking), and clothing and accessory upgrades—that are channeled into the aspirational narrative of self-transformation. These consumer practices offer sites of choice and agency while controlling women through strictly regulated and gendered norms. Originating in the Euro-American celebrity culture of the 1990s, hypermediated pregnant beauty and yummy mummy icons deny the lived realities and fluid boundaries of the maternal body.

An analysis of the media-circulated representations and narratives of celebrity actor-mothers like Shilpa Shetty, Aishwarya Rai, and Karisma Kapoor (along with others like Karisma's sister, Kareena Kapoor, and their friend Malaika Arora, who are not discussed in this chapter) reveals how Indian celebrity culture endorses and enforces the yummy mummy construct upon noncelebrity mother consumers while simultaneously enforcing a pervasive and public scrutiny of these celebrity mothers. Predictably, the yummy mummy cult is coded in the language of self-care and resilience. Actor Shilpa Shetty was featured in the January 2014 issue of *HiBlitz*—a fashion/celebrity magazine—which described her as "completely mommylicious." The maternal body is refigured here—in its yummy mummy iconicity—as an object of aspirational consumption. According to Shetty, the process of becoming "mommylicious" is "very difficult," but the rewards it offers are "more than just looking good"; she claims that it also allows mothers to feel good about themselves.[16] Similarly, Kapoor's motivational language focuses on individual agency, authority, and empowerment. Kapoor urges the individual reader to dress and stay fit for self-motivation: "I won't be frumpy—I'll be fabulous. . . . I will take time out to fix myself for myself."[17] Arguably, such "discourses of choice, freedom and empowerment . . . are complicit with, rather than critical of, postfeminism and neoliberalism."[18]

Diane Negra notes that "one of the most distinctive features of the postfeminist era has been the spectacular emergence of the underfed, over-exercised female body" and that these "contemporary beautification discourses place strong stress on the achieved self."[19] For Kapoor, it is not enough to reduce the postnatal maternal body from size extra-large (XL) to "a medium size"; yummy mummies must "never give up" until they go back to size small (S)[20] Kapoor uses the term "boot camp" to designate periods of rigorous exercise when "regular exercise fails" to transform mothers into yummy mummies, exposing the punishing regimen that the pursuit of the yummy mummy body entails.[21] She projects the reward of becoming a yummy mummy as worth the relentless labor and claims: "I will not give up when I'm almost at the end. My mom hasn't given me the genes to be fat. . . . I choose to maintain my ideal weight. I will feel so much better when I succeed."[22] Although Kapoor reiteratively projects the yummy mummy pursuit as primarily motivated by self-satisfaction, it is ironic that the prescribed yummy mummy contours and issues of ideal weight are mostly dictated by marketized standards of the ideal female body size and shape. Amid this, there is predictably an implied disapproval of nonnormative mothers through the repeated use of derogatory terms like "frumpy" and "fat." The prescriptive yummy mummy standards stigmatize and exclude all noncompliant mothers—for instance, those who are genetically obese or even those who are "medium size." When Kapoor affirms that "I will experiment till I get it right. I will be confident of who I am, irrespective of how people see me," there is an underlying contradiction.[23] If the *right* or *fabulous* body is only dependent on each mother's own sense of self-worth and not on "how people see" them, then why does Kapoor insist on and manipulate mothers to labor for a standardized size S body?[24] Her heroic narrative of self-achievement and self-transformation into the yummy mummy conceals how agency of the maternal body is circumscribed and how it reinforces media-distributed normative images of feminine desirability that are constructed through—and dependent upon—a hegemonic social gaze.

The yummy mummy body—in fact, any maternal body—is subjected to relentless and often invasive public scrutiny. Unlike Kapoor, when other celebrity mothers refuse to conform to dominant prescriptions of the perfect postpartum body, they are ridiculed, censured, and ultimately pressurized to conform. For instance, actor Aishwarya Rai's "shocking weight gain" when she appeared at the Cannes Film Festival after her daughter's birth was intensely policed on social media: videos body-shaming and lampooning her, "complete with elephant sound effects," have been repeatedly viewed and circulated.[25] In an interview, Rai makes her personal choice political: "I didn't set out on any mission except being myself. . . . In the mirror . . . I could see the weight gain. And I still chose to come out like this. And I am seeing all around, and even in showbiz, it has brought about a lot of change and I am glad."[26] Rai inserts her fat maternal body as a point of resistance in the regulatory yummy mummy discourse and exposes the pressure celebrity mothers are subjected to. This pressure coerces such women to conform to the new mother image that is institutionalized through cultures of mediatization. Significantly, in spite of her initial insubordination, Rai later conforms to the demands of celebrity maternal perfection: her most recent visits to Cannes showcase her as the ideal, glamorous yummy mummy, accompanied by her young daughter in color-coordinated outfits. The arc of Rai's yummy mummy story—from resistance to compliance—indicates how deeply pressurizing neoliberal constructs of embodiment are for mothers.

The scrutiny-driven pressures and self-focused discipline integral to the process of becoming a yummy mummy are further complicated by obsessive anxiety, self-surveillance, and even body dysmorphia. For Shilpa Shetty, the state of being "mommylicious" is marked by a strong revulsion for and denial of the earlier pregnant/fat self. Shetty reveals, "I was as fat as a cow. I was a size 14 for the first time in my life! It made me feel strange because it didn't feel like me—and I just wanted to be me."[27] Diane Negra defines the postfeminist woman or mother as "a self-surveilling subject whose concepts of body and behavior are driven by status anxiety."[28] This perpetual status anxiety is evidenced in a secret that Kapoor shares with her readers, which, according to her, is "the most important tip to lose weight," and she writes, "take a photo of yourself at the beginning of every month after delivery along with a record of your measurements and weight. . . . Look at it when you go out to eat, look at it when you're tempted to bunk your workout. . . . Before-and-after pictures of yourself will inspire you."[29] This reveals an obsessive self-scrutiny and a pathologizing of one's past non–yummy mummy body. Here, not only does the yummy mummy stigmatize other nonconforming mater-nal bodies, she also otherizes and disowns her own past self as monstrous. Further, the desire to lose weight is impelled by a dysmorphic self-hate. Ka-poor prescribes a month-by-month documentation of, and dissatisfaction with, one's own body: this foregrounds the inherent precarity and body dys-morphic disorder of the yummy mummy project. By continuously looking at before-and-after self-images, mothers harshly partition their own lives and bodies into an undesirable past and a yet-to-be-achieved future, with the present body always in an unstable stage that requires further disciplining and correction. Shetty's interview emphasizes the continuous effort required in this project: one has to "keep at it" to obtain and maintain the yummy mummy body.[30] Becoming yummy mummy necessitates an endless amount of body work, "continuous aesthetic labour to produce 'perfect' selves."[31] The yummy mummy is, thus, a corrective, self-fragmenting project of becoming rather than being, where any satisfaction is always undercut by anxiety and guilt.

Neoliberal Anxieties and the Mommy Beautiful

Clearly, celebrity yummy mummy narratives underplay the constant anxiety, extreme labor, and underlying self-revulsion and instead highlight a trium-phalist narrative that superficially conflates the reshaping of the maternal body with maternal self-making. This actually signals the "deeper commod-ification of maternity under neoliberalism."[32] Fitness is allied to a culture of consumerism through a sustained endorsement of the fashion-and-beauty complex. Even while working out, it is deemed necessary to be fashionable. Kapoor shares her "workout secrets" and claims, "I bought bright workout gear and wore that for my walks. You don't need to look cool for anyone else—you just need to feel slightly stylish for yourself, to keep yourself motivated."[33] In such cases, bodily fitness by itself is a necessary but not sufficient goal: the perfect yummy mummy body should be commodified and exhibited through stylish apparel and accessories. Feeling motivated and good about oneself is predicated upon looking cool. Acquisition of fashion and beauty commod-ities is an anodyne for the anxieties of becoming yummy mummy. Strikingly, in this project the conversion of emotional, internal values into purchasable, external capital is a key feature of neoliberalism that is governed by the strategies of market exchange. The deep commodification of all values and expe-riences under neoliberalism—that is visible in yummy mummy narratives—is accompanied by "a mobile, calculated technology for governing subjects who are constituted as self-managing, autonomous and enterprising."[34] The projection of the yummy mummy as autonomous and enterprising misdi-rects the extent to which she is dependent on externals—commodities or the gaze of others—for self-validation. Using the neoliberal trope of individual self-improvement, the yummy mummy construct fetishizes the female body, excludes a range of nonnormative maternal bodies, and becomes a compli-ant tool for capitalist market regimes.

Another misdirection that Kapoor's book and other yummy mummy narratives reinforce is the false equivalence of maternal beauty with mater-nal health. Although Kapoor writes of "fitness after pregnancy," she charts a plan for size and weight reduction from size XL to size S.[35] The integrated combination of physical and emotional maternal health—which is necessary to undertake the challenges of maternal work and selfhood—is shifted to the outermost boundaries of the maternal body. A few decades back, Naomi Wolf critiqued the cosmetic surgery industry for "manipulating ideas of health and sickness" and overturning "the feminist redefinition of health as beauty" into the perverted "notion of beauty as health."[36] The yummy mummy construct is complicit with this pernicious and disabling agenda. The slippages of sig-nification in Kapoor's text (fitness being equated with size) erase those moth-ers who are physically and emotionally healthy but not slim (size S) or nor-matively beautiful. Thus, the construct of the yummy mummy or pregnant beauty offers women a plastic and manufactured figuration of maternity that is "abstracted from the turbulent and messy realities," the "radical bodily changes" and "extraordinary emotional physical demands that accompany" lived experiences of mothering.[37] As indicated by the cover page and the sub-sequent narrative, Kapoor's yummy mummy guide is based on a promise that the visible signs of maternal experience can be erased from the maternal body and that this erasure is not only achievable but also desirable because it is (falsely) equated to maternal health.

The increasing circulation of celebrity yummy mummy spectacles pres-surizes other mothers to conformity and/or anxiety. In digitized economies, this circulation occurs through intermeshed networks connecting print media, audiovisual media, social media, and individual consumers. The con-sumption of celebrity yummy mummy images by noncelebrity mothers, for instance, is often via the conduit of social networking sites, like mom blogs. Mom-blogger Mansi Zaveri of *Kids Stop Press* includes Karisma Kapoor in her list of "Supermoms of Bollywood," applauding her for achieving "the per-fect work-life balance and [making] it even look easy."[38] In a blog post on "16 Fittest Moms of Bollywood," another popular mom blogger, Sangeetha Menon, celebrates the "dedication and hard work" of Bollywood yummy mummies, eulogizing Karisma Kapoor as "a fit celebrity mom" who "looks beautiful."[39] These representative blog posts insist that the journey or goal of becoming a yummy mummy is a liberating choice for mothers that ensures maternal self-care, fitness, health, and beauty. Yet, if we unpack the endorsement, we can find evidence of the scrutiny and mimicry that the cult of celebrity yummy mummy generates, both in mainstream as well as in social media.

Sangeetha Menon herself emulates the celebrity yummy mummy narrative of resilience and transformation that she disseminates through her blog. Like other yummy mummy narratives, Menon's embodied self-project is also fraught with self-shaming and body image anxiety. In a blog post about her "tummy story post-baby," Menon remembers how she had a "feel of consciousness and shame" when her manager intrusively body-shamed her by saying that her "tummy has bulged out" after her Caesarean delivery.[40] Menon narrates her "weight loss journey" in one of her most popular blog posts, which has over thirty comments by mothers requesting weight-loss advice, indicating a pervasive and widespread anxiety in mothers about their bodies: Menon both fuels this anxiety and promises a solution by posting before and after (pre- and post-weight-loss) photographs of herself.[41] In the way she has been inspired by celebrity yummy mummies, Menon hopes that her "weight loss journey inspires one mom or two."[42] By focusing only on the process of physical transformation, by invisibilizing those mothers who bodies defy regulatory yummy mummy standards, and by refusing to address the systemic causes that make mothers body-shame themselves (for instance, the male gaze and public scrutiny of female bodies that is evident in her own manager), Menon is complicit with—as well as victimized by—the neoliberal construct of the yummy mummy. As evident in the narratives of Kapoor, Shetty, and Menon—all labeling themselves as working mothers—the yummy mummy is constructed as an obedient mother-worker, a biological *reproducer* as well as an economic *producer* necessary for the functioning of both the patriarchal family and the neoliberal economy.

Menon, in spite of her overt aspiration of becoming a yummy mummy, is careful to situate herself within a framework of Indian values and visuals. From the initial introductory blog post itself, she strategically projects herself as a successful working professional with a manifest Indian identity. In this introductory post, Menon inserts two photographs of herself: one with her newborn daughter, where she is traditionally dressed in a sari with a garland in her hair, and the other a solo photograph where she is in Western attire sitting at a computer terminal.[43] These contrasting photographs visually reinforce a hybridized identity of a traditionally rooted mother who is also a technology-enabled professional. Kapoor, like Menon, also seemingly endorses a traditional Indian ethics of prudence, common sense, and frugal-ity. While advocating pregnancy fashion, Kapoor is careful to emphasize that there is no "need to overspend to get stylish pregnancy clothes"; she also shares tips on mixing, matching, and re-tailoring "maternity wear into reg-ular wear."[44] Even for achieving yummy mummy body dimensions, Kapoor suggests that mothers who cannot "head to the gym or get a personal trainer" do not "need any of that as long as you have determination."[45] Shetty has writ-ten a dietary and weight-loss guidebook titled *The Great Indian Diet*, where-in she urges the mother-reader to adopt an ethnically marked diet as well as "techniques and tips" like yoga and meditation, which are "part of Indian history."[46]

It is worth noting here that India's neoliberal economy is characterized by this confusion of Indian/traditional and global/modern value systems, in-cluding the clashing coexistence of consumerism and frugality. Contextual-ized thus, it is clear how the Indian neoliberal yummy mummy combines the glamor of the Western yummy mummy with a rootedness in Indian ethics and, sometimes, aesthetics. Rupal Oza's critique of neoliberalism in India ex-plicates how "the Indian woman was carefully crafted within public cultural discourses to be modern, representing globalizing India, yet 'Indian' by be-ing anchored in 'core' values."[47] In their careful and sustained imbrication of traditional Indian motherhood and modern neoliberal professionalism, embedded within the marketized, triumphalist construct of the yummy mum-my, Kapoor, Shetty, and Menon reproduce this dominant discourse of the ideal Indian neoliberal female/maternal subject. They reveal the anxieties gen-erated by the conflict of Indian and Western values but gloss over the con-tradictions instead of interrogating or critiquing them.

This narrative of ideal neoliberal motherhood—visibilized in the glam-orized but restrained Indian yummy mummy icon—also permeates the con-sumerist domain of advertisements in magazines and on television. Oza's study of several Indian television and print commercials reveals how wom-en in advertisements are "represented as modern, yet aware of their intrinsic roles as mother and wife."[48] The new Indian woman—a wider category that includes the Indian yummy mummy—cannot be unruly or challenging, de-spite her exposure to modernity and Western culture. Obedience to patri-archal norms continues to be a marker of the good Indian mother, and this obedience is imposed insidiously through circulated mass media like films, television serials, and advertisements. Further, in spite of some emerging, mod-ern, transgressive maternal representations, mainstream Hindi films continue to depict the "highly-valued ideal of the self-sacrificing mother," who obedi-ently performs the role of the "perfect home builder and the perfect nurturer," although she may appear in "updated" yummy mummy avatars.[49] Despite the *yummy* quotient that resexualizes the Indian mother, the essentializing *mummy* role ensures that the practices of cosmetic self-care and financial self-sufficiency do not subvert the core ideology of obedient, devoted, and patriarchal good motherhood.

It is also this core of obedience and the observed boundaries of Indian ethics/aesthetics that lock the Indian yummy mummy within a framework of male approval and within new forms of gendered power inequities. Because it is depoliticized, the constrained resexualization and self-care regimes of the Indian yummy mummy—in fact, of all yummy mummy embodiments—never become challenging enough to insist on structural changes in Indian patriarchal systems. The Indian yummy mummy thus embodies a "cultural politics of disarticulation" that is typical of postfeminism.[50] McRobbie explains postfeminism as a "double movement" of "disarticulation and displacement, accompanied by replacement and substitution," that operates through "a wide range of social and cultural spaces," generates the assumption that feminist action is no longer needed, and typecasts feminists as unfeminine and hostile to men.[51] In a neoliberal, postfeminist society, feminist ideology is disarticulated by patriarchal institutions of the state, the media, and the market, which offer substitutes through individualized discourse of choice and achievement—like the project of becoming a yummy mummy—while invalidating any collective or radical feminist agenda of self-making or social change.

Conclusion: Need for Alternative Maternal Body Images

To contest this invalidation, I finally look at other possibilities of resistances to the stereotyping of the maternal body: possibilities that reject both the self-abnegating model of patriarchal motherhood and the self-punishing model of the yummy mummy. In her interview, Aishwarya Rai emphasizes the significance of the concept of *being myself*: this may be contrasted with Shilpa Shetty's and Karisma Kapoor's project of *fixing myself*. Notably, this difference between being myself and fixing myself indicates a space for alternative possibilities for mothering and self-care, although these are difficult choices for mothers in a terrain saturated with disciplinary yummy mummy images and expectations. One choice may be to embody a more deviant, more overtly desiring and desirable, and more Western Indian yummy mummy—like actor Neena Gupta, for instance, who had her daughter out of wedlock—although this can perhaps escalate moral panic. Including such rebellious yummy mummies, however, can pluralize the predominantly heteronormative domain where most Indian yummy mummies locate themselves. Another option can be to reject the rushed demands to become yummy mummy after delivery. Rai—initially at least—chooses to love herself as she is, resisting the pressures of public gaze and market expectations. Mothers can choose to have confidence and pleasure in their as-is maternal body and reshape their body at a self-selected pace like Rai, and to self-selected fitness standards, rather than immersing themselves in a panic-driven pursuit of perfect yummy mummy beauty dimensions.

Structural resistances to coercive maternal body images are only possible through radical and/or collective feminist action. Although lack of space disallows a discussion here on collective maternal action, one form of individual action is to engage in *feminist mothering*, which enables mothers to have agency over their bodies and to create a feminist maternal legacy of empowered and informed body choices for their daughters. Feminist mothering is "constructed as a negation of patriarchal motherhood. . . . It may refer to any practice of mothering that seeks to challenge and change various aspects of patriarchal motherhood that cause mothering to be limiting or oppressive to women."[52] Choosing feminist mothering would equip mothers to dismantle and contest seductive yet coercive stereotypes like the yummy mummy.

Indian academics like Shilpa Phadke have recently engaged with the risks and rewards of feminist mothering in India, especially in the practice of mothering daughters in the context of societal expectations and moral panic about women's sexuality. Considering feminist mothering as a commitment to the "larger women's movement," Phadke offers no easy solutions.[53] Instead, she and the feminist mothers she interviews focus on practicing and passing on a mothering politics wherein they and their daughters would be comfortable in their nonconformity. Caught as we are between subjugating constructs of self-sacrificing motherhood and self-disciplining yummy mummy—a predicament deepened by pervasive saturation of these images and invasive scrutiny of all maternal bodies—the commitment to not become a yummy mummy is perhaps the most radical self-validation women can perform, as mothers and daughters, individually and collectively. By unpacking and refusing the yummy mummy—and by raising feminist consciousness in our daughters to enable them to critically understand such spectacular images and pernicious ideologies—we perform a feminist mothering that interrupts hegemonic motherhood discourses and supports maternal choices and bodies who choose to not conform.

NOTES

1. Kapoor, *Yummy Mummy*. Kapoor is an Indian actor and celebrity who has acted in several popular Hindi films and has won several acting awards, including a National Film award. She is also a mother of two.

2. Rich, *Of Woman Born*, 13, emphasis in original.

3. O'Reilly, *Feminist Mothering*, 3.

4. Krishnaraj, "Motherhood," 22.

5. Oza, *Making of Neoliberal India*, 22.

6. Khan, *Mother India*; Chopra, *Deewar*; Desai, *Amar Akbar Anthony*; Ghai, *Ram Lakhan*.

7. Singh, "Milky Ways," 37.

8. Kosambi, *Crossing Thresholds*, 135.

9. Sarkar, "Cultural Construction," 278.

10. Kakar, *Intimate Relations*, 131–134.

11. Mukul, *Gita Press*, 381.

12. *India TV News*, "How Relevant Is Yummy Mummy."

13. McRobbie, *The Aftermath*, 1, 7.

14. McRobbie, 80.

15. Tyler, "Pregnant Beauty," 22–23.

16. Dadyburjor, "Lights," 77.

17. Kapoor, *Yummy Mummy*, 132.

18. Gill and Scharff, *New Femininities*, 7.

19. Negra, *What a Girl*, 119.

20. Kapoor, *Yummy Mummy*, 95.

21. Kapoor, 107.

22. Kapoor, 119.

23. Kapoor, 143.

24. Kapoor, 143.

25. Manzoor, "Aishwarya Rai's Post-Baby Body."

26. Chopra, "The Front Row."

27. Dadyburjor, "Lights," 77.

28. Negra, *What a Girl*, 153.

29. Kapoor, *Yummy Mummy*, 102.

30. Dadyburjor, "Lights," 77.

31. Phadke, "How to Do Feminist Mothering," 251.

32. Tyler, "Pregnant Beauty," 23.

33. Kapoor, *Yummy Mummy*, 89.

34. Gill and Scharff, *New Femininities*, 5.

35. Kapoor, *Yummy Mummy*, 94.

36. Wolf, *The Beauty Myth*, 220–224.

37. Tyler, "Pregnant Beauty," 30.

38. Zaveri, "The Supermoms of Bollywood," para. 8.

39. Menon, "16 Fittest Moms," paras. 1, 17.

40. Menon, "15 Amazing Ways," para. 3.

41. Menon, "From Flab to Fab."

42. Menon, para. 8.

43. Menon, "About Me."

44. Kapoor, *Yummy Mummy*, 127, 131.

45. Kapoor, 118.

46. Kundra and Coutinho, *Great Indian Diet*, 169.

47. Oza, *Making of Neoliberal India*, 22.

48. Oza, 35.

49. Riaz, "Selfless to Selfish," 173.

50. McRobbie, *The Aftermath*, 35.

51. McRobbie, 26.

52. O'Reilly, *Feminist Mothering*, 4.
53. Phadke, "How to Do Feminist Mothering," 260.

BIBLIOGRAPHY

Chopra, Anupama. "The Front Row: Aishwarya Rai Bachchan." *India Real Time Blog. Wall Street Journal*, January 4, 2013. Available at http://blogs.wsj.com/indiarealtime/2013/01/04/the-front-row-aishwarya-rai-bachchan/.

Chopra, Yash, dir. *Deewar*. 1975, Trimurti Films; Mumbai: Eros Entertainment, 2007. DVD.

Dadyburjor, Farhad J. "Lights . . . Camera . . . Motherhood." *HiBlitz*, January 2014.

Desai, Manmohan, dir. *Amar Akbar Anthony*. 1977, MKD Films; Mumbai: Shemaroo Entertainment, 2009. DVD.

Ghai, Subhash, dir. *Ram Lakhan*. 1989, Suneha Arts; Mumbai: Eros Entertainment, 2005. DVD.

Gill, Rosalind, and Christina Scharff, eds. *New Femininities: Postfeminism, Neoliberalism and Subjectivity*. London: Palgrave McMillan, 2011.

India TV News. "How Relevant Is Yummy Mummy Title for Young Indian Moms?" May 11, 2014. Available at http://www.indiatvnews.com/lifestyle/news/are-young-indian-moms-are-yummy-mummy-2557.html.

Kakar, Sudhir. *Intimate Relations: Exploring Indian Sexuality*. New Delhi: Penguin, 1989.

Kapoor, Karisma. *My Yummy Mummy Guide: From Getting Pregnant to Being a Successful Working Mother and Beyond*. New Delhi: Penguin, 2013.

Khan, Mehboob, dir. *Mother India*. 1957, Mehboob Productions; Mumbai: Eros Entertainment, 2003. DVD.

Kosambi, Meera. *Crossing Thresholds: Feminist Essays in Social History*. Ranikhet: Permanent Black, 2007.

Krishnaraj, Maithreyi. "Motherhood, Mothers, Mothering: A Multi-Dimensional Perspective." In *Motherhood in India: Glorification without Empowerment?*, edited by Maithreyi Krishnaraj, 9–43. New Delhi: Routledge, 2010.

Kundra, Shilpa Shetty, and Luke Coutinho. *The Great Indian Diet: Busting the Fat Myth*. New Delhi: Random House India, 2015.

Manzoor, Sarfraz. "Aishwarya Rai's Post-Baby Body Forces India to Confront Its Attitude towards Women." *The Guardian*, May 15, 2012. Available at http://www.theguardian.com/world/2012/may/15/aishwarya-rai-body-india-women.

McRobbie, Angela. *The Aftermath of Feminism: Gender, Culture and Social Change*. London: Sage, 2009.

Menon, Sangeetha. "About Me." *Bumps n Baby* (blog). Accessed April 15, 2017. Available at http://www.bumpsnbaby.com/about-me/.

———. "15 Amazing Ways to Lose Tummy Fat Post Baby." *Bumps n Baby* (blog). October 9, 2013. http://www.bumpsnbaby.com/15-amazing-ways-lose-tummy-fat-post-baby/.

———. "From Flab to Fab—My Weight Loss Journey, Diet & Exercise Regime." *Bumps n Baby* (blog). August 15, 2013. http://www.bumpsnbaby.com/from-flab-to-fab-my-weight-loss-journey-diet-exercise-regime/.

———. "16 Fittest Moms of Bollywood." *Bumps n Baby* (blog). December 19, 2013. http://www.bumpsnbaby.com/16-fittest-moms-bollywood/.

Mukul, Akshaya. *Gita Press and the Making of Hindu India*. Noida: HarperCollins, 2015.

Negra, Diane. *What a Girl Wants? Fantasizing the Reclamation of Self in Postfeminism*. London: Routledge, 2009.

O'Reilly, Andrea, ed. *Feminist Mothering*. Albany: State University of New York Press, 2008.

Oza, Rupal. *The Making of Neoliberal India: Nationalism, Gender and the Paradoxes of Globalization*. London: Routledge, 2006.

Phadke, Shilpa. "How to Do Feminist Mothering in Urban India? Some Reflections on the Politics of Beauty and Body Shapes." In *Aesthetic Labour: Rethinking Beauty Politics in Neoliberalism*, edited by Rosalind Gill, Christina Scharff, and Ana Sofia Elias, 247–261. London: Palgrave Macmillan, 2017.

Riaz, Amber Fatima. "Selfless to Selfish: Trajectory of 'Mother' from Bollywood's *Mother India* to *Pyar Mein Twist*." In *South Asian Mothering: Negotiating Culture, Family and Selfhood*, edited by Jasjit K. Sangha and Tahira Gonsalves, 165–175. Bradford, ON: Demeter Press, 2013.

Rich, Adrienne. *Of Woman Born: Motherhood as Experience and Institution*. New York: W. W. Norton, 1995.

Sarkar, Mahua. "Cultural Construction of Gender in Colonial Bengal: The 'Sari' and the Bengali 'Nari': A Dress Code." In *Gender and Modernity*, edited by Amitava Chatterjee, 273–292. Calcutta: Setu Prakashani, 2015.

Singh, Jai Arjun. "Milky Ways: A Contemplation of the Hindi-Movie Maa." In *Of Mothers and Others*, edited by Jaishree Mishra, 32–53. New Delhi: Zubaan, 2013.

Tyler, Imogen. "Pregnant Beauty: Maternal Femininities under Neoliberalism." In *New Femininities: Postfeminism, Neoliberalism and Subjectivity*, edited by Rosalind Gill and Christina Scharff, 21–36. London: Palgrave McMillan, 2011.

Wolf, Naomi. *The Beauty Myth: How Images of Beauty Are Used against Women*. New York: Harper Perennial, 2002.

Zaveri, Mansi. "The Supermoms of Bollywood." *Kids Stop Press* (blog). September 4, 2013. Available at https://kidsstoppress.com/the-supermoms-of-bollywood/.

12

"Hey! She's a Bro!"

Tomboys, Body Image, and Desire in India

KETAKI CHOWKHANI

GEORGE: I hate being a girl. I won't be. I don't like doing the things that girls do. I like doing the things that boys do. . . . I never do cry, you know, because boys don't and I like to be like a boy.

—ENID BLYTON, *FIVE ON A TREASURE ISLAND*

ANJALI: Hey! Don't call me a girl.
RAHUL: Actually you are right, you are not a girl. . . . I am less handsome than you, you have a bigger moustache. . . . If I don't find any girl, I'll marry you. Anyway no one will marry you.

—KARAN JOHAR, *KUCH KUCH HOTA HAI*

LUCKY: My girlfriend will be the world's most beautiful woman. Not a plain Jane like Sanju.
SANJU/SANJANA: I have tried to be my father's son since childhood. Look, I have succeeded. No one even remembers I am a girl.

—FARAH KHAN, *MAIN HOON NA*

Introduction

Tomboys present to us a particular deviation from the ideal of the heteronormative female body. Not only do they challenge gender norms, but they also, and more importantly, upset normative female body image. As the aforementioned epigraphs suggest, tomboys do not want to be girls, be called girls, or even do things that girls conventionally do. At the same time, if they are heterosexual female protagonists like Anjali from *Kuch Kuch Hota Hai* (Johar 1998) and Sanju from *Main Hoon Na* (Khan 2004)—two popular Hindi films produced by neoliberal India—they are not considered desirable or attractive by men they are friends with.[1] Lookism in relation to tomboys has deep effects on their romantic and sexual desirability as well as their self-identity. Unlike other forms of lookism, being a tomboy puts into question the femininity of women themselves, existing within that grey area among woman, trans man, and man. While Judith Halberstam (1998), in her foundational study of female masculinity, notes the futility of the tomboy narrative (8) and concentrates on "queer female masculinity almost to the exclusion of heterosexual female masculinity," since the latter "represents an acceptable degree of female masculinity as compared to the excessive masculinity of the dyke" (28), I argue that the category of the tomboy—and especially that of the *heterosexual* tomboy—is productive since it troubles our ideas of femininity, body image, desire, gender relations, and heteronormativity. My chapter weaves autoethnography, narratives from tomboys, and analysis of Hindi cinema to uncover how the cultural construct of the tomboy affects body image, self-identity, desire, and gender relations in India. The chapter is divided into two sections. The first section examines some of the complexities of self-identity and body image experienced by tomboys, and the second section unpacks the question of desire among tomboys. While many tomboys experience tomboyism as pleasurable, the discrimination and pain that tomboys face in their deviance from heteronormative feminine ideals becomes most apparent in their search and desire for male partners. Simply put, I point out how, in an appearance-conscious society, romantic desire sharply brings to the fore their failure to perform ideal femininity, especially with relation to their bodies.

There is little research on embodiment issues among tomboys in the Indian context. I specifically examine heterosexual tomboys since studies of female masculinity (Halberstam 1998) or female-to-male (FTM) persons in India (Shah et al. 2015) locate the masculinity of women and girls within queer identities, leaving heterosexuality and cis-gendered personhood underexplored. As the narratives of the tomboys in the following sections demonstrate, it is easier for society to deal with the gender transgressions of tomboys by locating them within lesbianism and transgenderism rather than accepting their transgressions as a challenge or an alternative to heterosexual femininity. In part, I borrow from Emma Renold (2008) in understanding tomboyism as a form of girlhood and femininity rather than as a form of transgenderism or female masculinity.

Significantly, tied to this exploration of the tomboy is the question of female body image and lookism. Lookism is "a form of discrimination based on an individual's physical appearance" (Granleese 2016, 1) and has been primarily studied in the context of discrimination in the workplace (Minerva 2017, 3). While it might be common knowledge that lookism affects one's romantic life (3), it has not been studied in the Indian context or examined for its effects on the self-identity and femininity of women. Trying to understand the lookism faced by tomboys in India helps us understand the complexities of body image that girls and women face outside the limited and limiting binary of female attractiveness/unattractiveness. To this effect, I seek to ask the following questions: What are the issues of body image that tomboys face? What does being a tomboy do to desire and gender relations in the family and in school? What are the messages of masculinity and femininity that tomboys receive from the family? Is tomboy an aspirational category or an aspiration for girls to have access to the freedoms enjoyed by boys?

My chapter draws on the narratives of six middle-class, heterosexual women between the ages of twenty-three and thirty-nine, reflecting on their childhood, adolescence, and adulthood to talk about their experiences of being a tomboy. One of these is an autoethnographic narrative. For most of these women, the discrimination they faced for being a tomboy was neither uniform nor homogenous. Instead, their experiences are based on various factors related to their departure from heteronormative feminine ideals, which include Indian culture's associations with colorism (Parameswaran 2011), "unfeminine" clothes, "boy-cut" hair, "masculine" gait, and the absence of prominent breasts. The women appearing in this chapter belong to different religious and linguistic communities and live in Chennai, Hyderabad, Pondicherry, Dehradun, Mumbai, and Manipal. Their backgrounds are similar: educated, English speaking, middle-class, and urban. And they are all in so-called respectable professions. This, however, is not a representative sample, and the group of interviewees is purposefully small because the attempt is to open up the question of tomboyism, body image, and desire to closer examination for future studies. The chapter's scope is also limited because it specifically examines a homogenous group of women who are middle-class and English educated.[2] Apart from fieldwork, the chapter also draws on Hindi cinema over the last few decades to build a cultural context and to substantiate narratives from the women participants. Specifically, this chapter draws upon *Kuch Kuch Hota Hai* and *Main Hoon Na*,[3] each of which have a tomboy character. They are important to analyze here since they are popular cultural representations of the discrimination that many of tomboys in my study face, such as lack of desire from men for being tomboyish, social ridicule for not being heteronormatively attractive, and the pain and unspeakability of failed desire.

Tomboys, Gender Identity, and Bodily Freedoms

In this section I examine how the participants in my study identified as tomboys, how they were perceived by others as tomboys, and how this affected their body image. All participants self-identified as tomboys up to and into their early adulthood. Only thirty-year-old Ray, who is married to a man, still continues to identify as a tomboy today. Echoing the quote from Enid Blyton's book at the beginning of the chapter, most of the participants maintain that they do not want to be a girl or be identified as one and would prefer to be called a boy or be a boy. Another participant, twenty-three-year-old Alice, opened our conversation by revealing, "For the longest time as a child I didn't want to be a girl, I was very uncomfortable being one. I thought it was very freeing [being a tomboy], I thought the more feminine I was the more restricted [it was]." This presents tomboyism as an aspirational category that allows a girl like Alice to access the freedoms of being a boy. But as covered later, this is not the only reason Alice gives for being a tomboy. Similarly, another participant, Sivagami, expresses that she was "comfortable with [being a] boy" and that she "used to act like a boy." While she stopped being a tomboy in her early twenties, the reasons for which are explored in the next section, Sivagami explained how much she enjoyed being a tomboy. "I really, really enjoyed it. It was no pressure, so comfortable. I saved a lot of time, without having to spend time on being a girl, dressing up like a girl, walking like a girl, run anywhere, it was comfortable and I am so happy. I think I liked being myself as a tomboy better than what I am now," she claims. Like Alice, Sivagami experienced the freedoms and joys of being a tomboy since she was not restricted by strict codes of femininity. She also describes it nostalgically as her most preferred mode of being.

Thirty-five-year-old Mira, another of my other participants, also speaks about the pleasures of being a tomboy. She notes, "My greatest joy and pleasure lay in being identified as a boy. When I was thirteen, I visited Mumbai for the first time. As I stood in a queue at Essel World, a couple of girls behind me exclaimed *boy* upon seeing me. I still remember the thrill and pleasure I felt back then. I loved to perform a *boyish masculinity*. It was fun and desirable to be one of the boys, it was fun to be like the boys." Unlike Alice and Sivagami, Mira did not deploy tomboyism as a means to gain access to male privilege. Nevertheless, she describes it as a pleasurable and desirable experience. While Mira experiences tomboyism as a thrilling experience, George's aspirations are associated with a wayward and partly hegemonic masculinity. George, yet another of my participants, claims, "When I was little I was asked what I want to be, I used to say I want to be a boy, ride a bike . . . like a *mohalla lafanga* [neighborhood rowdy]." While George does not explicitly mention the privileges of being like a boy, she does aspire to be carefree and fearless like a rowdy man. Tomboyism for her is an adolescent as well as an adult dream. George also mentions that she first came across the word *tomboy* while reading Enid Blyton. She notes, "That was the first time that I saw a representation of myself over there. This is a girl, who looks like a boy, who wants to be a boy, she just wants to run wild, that's it. She just wants to be herself. Those were things that I also felt. This is exactly me." George here explains the importance of a text like *Famous Five* and the role it plays in representing scores of tomboys like her. She notes that if we today were to completely disengage with Enid Blyton for her racist and patriarchal content, we would lose this important source of representation for young tomboys. Similarly, Tara, another participant in my study, spoke about the influence of Enid Blyton's *Famous Five* series on her life. She mentions how her cousins and friends, growing up in the 1990s, were reading Enid Blyton's detective novels and often said to her, "You are like George." In these narratives, we see the important role children's literature, especially Enid Blyton's books, plays in constructing childhood and adolescent gender identities among many Indian children.

Tied to the pleasures of being a boy is the centrality of sports. Ray, Alice, George, and Sivagami mention that they grew up around boys who were cousins, brothers, friends, and neighbors and that this influenced and shaped their tomboyism. They all loved playing sports with these boys. George recounts that she played cricket with her male cousins, much to her mother's chagrin. Ray narrates that she played sports in college and was part of the gang of sporty girls, as opposed to being part of the girly girl, nerdy girl, or teacher's pet gang. She did roller-skating and was often out on the streets playing with her brother and other boys. Alice gleefully notes that she used to wrestle with her male cousins and brother and found it odd that the girls in her school were not interested in wrestling. Her relatives and neighbors were simultaneously shocked and annoyed by her unfeminine behavior and body language. Sivagami says that she would be running everywhere, instead of walking like a "proper" girl. This trope of the sporty tomboy is well represented in *Kuch Kuch Hota Hai*, where the tomboy protagonist, Anjali, is shown playing basketball skillfully and inevitably defeating the hero.

Along with their love for sports, tomboys are also more comfortable around boys than girls. Alice notes that she could not comprehend the conversations girls in her school had and preferred to not befriend them. She was not particularly fond of them and felt that she was not only different but more competent than the other girls. In fact, Alice's position resonates with Anjali's tomboy character from *Kuch Kuch Hota Hai*, who also distances herself from other girls because she is not like the girls that her best friend, Rahul, flirts with. This, of course, is before Anjali's transformation into a feminine woman, which gets her the affection and attention of Rahul. On similar lines, the real-life George mentions feeling superior to the girls she grew up with since she was a tomboy and hence better than them in many activities. In this context, Sivagami and Ray also mention how some girls thought that they were rowdy. Sivagami especially got along better with the rowdy back-bencher boys than the studious ones of the front benches. She did have girlfriends, but she was far more comfortable with the boys. This notion of being more competent or superior to girls because of being like the boys is present in the tomboys' narratives as well as the cinematic representations of tomboys. While some of this stems from the patriarchal idea of the superiority of masculinity over femininity, the tomboys' experiences also suggest a challenge to emphasized femininity and a conscious distancing from it. As covered later, this distancing from other girls is also a result of being shamed for being boyish, as well as an inability to genuinely connect with feminine activities.

Tomboys, Femininity, and Experiences of Lookism

Lookism, as my study demonstrates, plays a large part in the dynamics between the tomboys and other girls. It is also intimately connected to tomboys' experiences of their bodies. Alice mentioned being teased at her all-girls school for being too fat, and Sivagami and Ray spoke about being told at work and school that they were flat chested. Notably, tomboys' body image is a careful performance with clothes and hair. Mira mentions that she had "boy-cut hair (short hair)—partly during my childhood but mostly during my adolescent years. I was underweight, thin and tall and often wore pants, shorts or even skirts." Everyone except Ray had boy-cut hair while growing up, and Sivagami gleefully mentions that she even got herself tonsured on one occasion. Ray laments not being allowed to cut her hair since she learned Bharatnatyam, a classical Indian dance form. George mentions how she was often forced to wear a frock, but she resisted. She mentions that she would follow butch fashion,[4] which she thought was smart and sophisticated rather than associated with queerness. She bought loose clothes that were too large for her so that her breasts were not visible or accentuated. George distinguishes between her tomboyism and transgenderism by explaining that she did not bind her chest. Rather, she wanted to inhabit an androgynous body and compared her bodily image with George's from Blyton's *Famous Five*. Sivagami likewise recounts how she always wore shorts, T-shirts, and "normal Bata flip-flops" and tore her jeans at the feet so that it did not look girly. She felt that the tomboy look was more about hair than clothes. She also discusses how her male cousin's masculine clothes were passed on to her, allowing her to have nice boy clothes. Interestingly, until she was ten, Sivagami would run around topless at home, and her parents were thankful when she wore clothes outside. She describes instances when she was asked to wear girls' clothes and she obliged since these were rare occasions.

Not all my participants, however, enjoyed wearing feminine clothes even if it was a one-off occasion. George recounts how she resisted when her mother insisted she wear frocks. Alice narrates how she used to buy clothes from the men's section and kept her look simple with plain black shirts and jeans. She mentions that "it was just easier to wear masculine clothes, because it was difficult to find clothes that I thought looked flattering on me as a woman." Similarly, Ray recounts that she hated wearing frocks and always chose to wear pants. She preferred loose and baggy clothes and felt uncomfortable in tight clothes. Tara describes herself as an eleven-year-old who wore *kajal*,[5] eyeliner, shorts, and boots; she had very short hair and would go out with a large, ferocious dog on a chain. Tara describes this scene as tomboy/butch. One can see how her embodied experience of being a tomboy involves makeup, too, and upsets a stereotypical understanding of tomboys as not interested in any form of makeup or jewelry. While some tomboys enjoy wearing lose clothes to hide signs of their feminine physique, others wear makeup, indicating the heterogeneity of tomboy existence—and in the process challenging all existing notions of femininity and lookism.

The other trope of tomboy identity that I came across in the narratives is being tough, not crying, and not being afraid. Mira reveals that she enjoyed being "tough and to be never seen crying in public." But she claims that she "never had enough physical strength. The 'feminine' girls were often physically stronger than me and I felt like the lack of physical strength was a failure to perform a certain masculinity." George, on the other hand, never experienced the weakness of a girl and went out of her way to prove her lack of fear. She repeatedly mentions that her risk-taking behavior was due to her desire to prove herself to others, rather than an innate sense of bravery or fearlessness. Mira's tomboyism was not restricted to clothes since she even wore skirts, but her tomboyism included the performances of normative boys—not crying, being tough, and playing with the boys. For Mira, tomboyism is experienced both as a source of pleasure and as a sense of failure to perform a kind of hegemonic masculinity. Strikingly, such narratives open to us ways in which tomboys can or cannot perform masculinity. They complicate the idea that tomboyism is necessarily about agential transgressions and breaking of gender binaries. Feminist theorists like Bordo (1993, 57) have examined how negative body image, and the resultant lack of self-worth and confidence, is an inherent part of being a woman today. I extend this to think about performances not just of femininity among women but also of masculinity. Mira's embodied experiences of being a tomboy point to the sense of failure in not being able to conform to either emphasized femininity or hegemonic masculinity.

Clearly, tomboys share a complicated relationship to their bodies. Mira and Sivagami mention being very thin and lean. While Mira is tall, Sivagami barely reaches five feet. She shared that part of her parents' acceptance of her tomboyism had to do with her being so skinny, flat chested, and tiny that it erased many signs of femininity. The other reason for their acceptance was that her family wanted a boy. Since her older sister was socialized as a girl, it was easier for them to accept Sivagami as a tomboy.[6] Mary John (2014) mentions that son preference in India is less about desiring only sons and more to do with having at least one son. Even though Sivagami plays the role of a son, she still had to grow up and marry a man and perform the duties of a wife and mother. But while she was growing up, her family's son preference allowed her the space to explore tomboyism. Unlike Sivagami, Ray and George have a different relationship with their families and relatives. Ray discusses how, on a number of occasions, she was suspected of being a lesbian, and George mentions how her mother tried to scare her into femininity by telling her about the painful process of sex reassignment surgery. As mentioned earlier, this shows how easy it to socially locate tomboyism within lesbianism and transgenderism rather than use tomboyism to destabilize heterosexuality and normative assumptions about femininity.

If this is true, it is also true that there are overlaps between tomboyism and transgenderism. Alice and George both mention how they were shocked and hated getting their periods; they were waiting to achieve menopause. This is similar to FTM and trans men's experiences of periods and their sense of betrayal and hate at menstruating (Shah et al. 2015). But the disavowal of menstruation is not the only body image/gendered issue that tomboys experience. In fact, a participant like Alice has a complex relationship with her body and tomboyism. She recounts:

> I wasn't very comfortable with myself also I had a lot of body issues. Being unfeminine was the way to escape from that. After I went to college, I became a little more woke, then became more comfortable with who I am and I actually made friends of all genders . . . I didn't feel the need to escape so much . . . being a heavy kid and boyish there was a lot of . . . remarks made in school about it by my classmates and my friends. I wanted to be separate from them. I was quite fat for a long time. It is not that I had an eating problem. I just liked to sit in one corner and just read for a very long time. . . . In that sense my parents were worried about me. I don't think they approached it very well.

Alice's escape from femininity and her tomboyism appear to be a complex mixture of her body image issues, her weight, her comfort with boys, her love of sports, and her desire to escape the patriarchal restrictions placed on girls. This points to how, while tomboys might aspire to enjoy the privileges of being a boy, it is not their only reason. It also demonstrates the reason why tomboys have difficult relationships with girls or why they consider themselves superior to them. In the same vein, Ray also discusses at length her body image issues and how she was shamed for her looks and clothes by those in school, those in the neighborhood, and her relatives:

> In the North [of India] there were comments on how I was dusky . . . I thought I had ugly feet because they are too broad and manly and other girls had dainty feet. Mom said I had the feet of a runner. . . . It wasn't a very nice time post thirteen years of age. My looks get commented on a lot. I was told I got a moustache like a man. I was like "so what, it is ok." I was comfortable being a tomboy and on the other hand I was made to feel uncomfortable being a tomboy. . . . My cousin told me to improve the way I dress. [She said,] "We need to do something about the clothes you wear. If you dress like that you will never get a boy in your life." . . . Things got better in college. [I] got better acceptance.

Here it is clear how Ray was consistently made to feel uncomfortable being a tomboy. While she was shamed for her body and the clothes she wore, she internalized certain notions of feminine beauty and started hating parts of her own body. Like Alice, Ray gained acceptance only in college. She also mentions that during her master's degree, she did a course on body image, which helped her be comfortable with her own body and accept herself. In both Ray's and Alice's narratives, the migration for higher education is a catalyst for them to come to terms with themselves and their bodies.

The transition toward becoming increasingly comfortable in their female bodies through early adulthood is common across all narratives of tomboys in my study. Tara mentions that she was a tomboy between the ages of eleven and fourteen and describes it as a "phase." She recounts how she went from performing a tomboy identity to a more feminine one and then going back to performing a tomboy identity again in her early twenties. She characterizes these as "phases of experimentation" that were intimately tied to her intercity migrations for work and education. The spaces she occupied during her growing-up years deeply influenced the ways she experienced these phases. Similarly, Alice became more feminine and learned to take care of her skin and deal with her body image issues in college and in her early twenties. Ray first wore a skirt only in her early twenties, and Sivagami wore heels and feminine clothes only when she stayed in a hostel in her early adulthood. She saw the other girls dressing up and wanted to try it out. She explicitly mentions that she stopped being a tomboy at the age of twenty-five because her family was looking to arrange her marriage. For Sivagami, her transition from tomboy to woman was primarily because of her family's hunt for a groom and their injunctions for her to look feminine. She mentions how she has never seen a tomboyish married woman. As mentioned earlier, Sivagami does state that she enjoyed being a tomboy the most, though she still maintains short hair and even got tonsured once as a married woman.

In all these narratives, we see how the performance of tomboyism may or may not be linked to wearing shorts and boys' clothes or performing hegemonic masculinity. These narratives also point to the heterogeneity of the tomboy experience and the role that peers and family play in identity formation. Mira, Tara, Alice, Sivagami, Ray, and George, while not entirely embodying a girly-girl existence as adult women, also do not identify as trans men or transgender. They clearly state that they identify as adult women. Their body image issues as tomboys are linked to lookism and, as covered in the next section, to heterosexual desire and romantic relationships.

Tomboys, Body Image, and Heterosexual Desire

While it is well established that lookism is central to romantic relationships (Minerva 2017, 3), there remains a dearth of literature on how lookism among tomboys is different from issues of lookism for those deemed unattractive or not conforming to the prescribed social measures of beauty. I argue in this section that the lookism faced by tomboys questions their womanhood itself. Two of my participants, Tara and Mira, speak of the "costs" of being a tomboy and desiring to be a boy. Mira describes how her "image and personality" did not make her attractive enough to boys. This made her unhappy, and while she did try to prettify herself up a bit, she did not succeed at it since it did not come from within. Mira felt sad that she did not have a boyfriend and could not be like others. Likewise, while growing up Tara constantly questioned herself:

> Why does everyone want to be my friend but not a potential romantic partner? Should I feminize myself more, be like other girls who don't talk, who don't fight? I had arbitrary crushes, imaginary crushes, on the boy next door, on film stars, on cricketers. I had imaginary partners with whom I was highly sexual in my dreams. My parents would tell me that I moaned in my dreams.

Tara goes on to disclose that by the time she first started dating a boy at the end of the tenth standard, she had already "feminized" herself a great deal. Tara also discusses how she desired both boys and girls when she was growing up but did not speak about any same-sex relationships or the complexities of such relationships while growing up. Similarly, Ray, who also spoke about having a crush on a girl but eventually married a man, revealed how she met her first boyfriend in the twelfth standard:

He preferred girly girls. He gave comments about the way I looked and dressed. He would pit me against another girl who was, according to him, more attractive because she was more girly, who put [on] makeup. I didn't use makeup. My self-confidence and self-esteem was affected. He broke up with me. I wanted to be the girl he wanted me to be, so I put in effort. I wasn't comfortable [with] the way I looked.

In Ray's earlier narrative, she was shamed for her looks and clothes by some peers and relatives. Here, she is also shamed by her boyfriend, which deeply affects her self-esteem and her understanding of her own desirability. Like her earlier quote, she was made to feel uncomfortable in her own body, and she tried to change herself. Similarly, Alice, who explicitly mentions not being attracted to women but only men, talks about how she also tried to change herself: "At that time I remember thinking that maybe I should change myself because I wasn't sure if the person I was then or the way I acted was conducive to getting someone to like me back. It was for the longest time till I managed to get some confidence in myself." The pressure of heteronormative coupledom is what leads Alice and Ray to try to bodily change themselves. Familial pressure or shaming at school did not have the same impact on their body image and self-esteem. They were able to resist familial pressure to conform but succumbed to the heteronormative pressures of coupledom.

Hence, one could read the efforts of Ray, Alice, and Tara to feminize themselves as a form of hetero-patriarchal pressure on concepts of desirability where a tomboy eventually grows up to be a pretty, feminine, and heteronormative woman, forgetting her tomboy past. This is a common trope in the cinematic narratives of *Kuch Kuch Hota Hai* and *Main Hoon Na*, where the female protagonists start off as tomboys, experience rejection from the male hero, and months or years later feminize themselves to finally get the attention and romantic love of the hero. While Anjali in *Kuch Kuch Hota Hai* and Sanju in *Main Hoon Na* are able to become feminine, heteronormative women, Alice, Ray, and Tara, despite all their efforts, fail to do so. Their failure to entirely feminize themselves points out how the narrative of hetero-patriarchal pressure to conform is flawed and that there might be tomboys who, despite themselves, fail to become entirely feminine. Ray's boyfriend's body shaming and Alice's and Tara's internalized notions of sexual desirability do not succeed in entirely feminizing them even though their self-esteem and confidence are deeply affected for a while. It may then be argued that lookism among tomboys not only tries to feminize them but also points to the impossibility of the presence of sexual desire in their lives as heterosexual tomboys.

This failure to find sexual desirability, which, in turn, profoundly affects their body image, leaves many tomboys deeply distraught. Mira and Sivagami, for instance, speak up about this problem in their poignant narratives. Mira notes:

> I loved boys—right from the age of eight or nine. In my mind, I liked to be called a boy, be like them, and love them too; all the while inhabiting a girl's body. But maybe the boys I knew were all conforming to strict gender roles. They seemed to only love girls who performed the role of a girl. And suddenly, the tomboy *seemed* undesirable. Maybe I didn't try hard enough. But my adolescent self never experienced any gaze of attraction or desire from boys. Why would a boy like another boy in a heteronormative world? This challenge and question structured most of my interactions with boys and men for most of my growing-up and adult life. This was encapsulated by a comment a male friend made to me a few years back: "you were a tomboy; how can you have a boyfriend?"

Mira's narrative challenges heteronormativity—not from the perspective of queerness, but from within heterosexuality itself. She is a heterosexual girl who enjoys being like a boy but feels comfortable in a girl's natural body. Desire in a heteronormative world is meant to exist only between women and men, and Mira challenges this heterosexual womanhood itself. She does not want lesbian love or gay love, and she does not want to change her body to become a man. Rather, her tomboyism challenges femininity itself, and hence heterosexual desire. Similarly, Sivagami speaks about the pain of not being desired and of being "friend zoned" by men:

> But they would not look at me as a girl. They would look at me only as a friend whom they can talk about other girls, their crushes. *It is so painful.* And they assumed that you are strong because you are tomboy, a strong person to handle all the pain and emotions; and I would always tell my friend, maybe if I was *girly* they would have thought before hurting me, rejecting me. If I was a girly girl, they wouldn't have bluntly said no. I still have a friend, I was interested in him, he used to tell me everything, we used to talk a lot, but he said I can only look at you as a friend. I can tell you anything and everything. That time I used to think, and I used to try to dress up but then I cannot put in so much effort, one day itself is too much, I cannot go through this exercise every single day. It takes time to dress up, to select jewelry, to look like that, I don't think I want to spend my time on those.

Sivagami's narrative adds another layer to this challenge to heterosexual desire and norms of female body image. Heterosexual boys are more likely to be *best friends* with tomboys but cannot experience heterosexual desire for them. This is represented in *Kuch Kuch Hota Hai* and *Main Hoon Na*, where the tomboy and the male hero are best friends but the male hero refuses to see the tomboy as romantically or sexually desirable. The tomboy, representing a form of marginalized femininity, is accorded the space of the friend, the confidante, and the bro. Currently, social media is also invested in understanding tomboys and the tomboy best friend trope. Scoopwhoop (2014) lists "20 signs that you were once a tomboy," among which the nineteenth point claims, "But life isn't easy for a Tomboy. We have lost many of our crushes to Overly Womanly Women or have been friend zoned by them because 'Hey! She's a bro!'" It is also worth noting that the term "friend zoned," which is mostly used for men, is used here for tomboys, too.

Predictably, the most painful part in Sivagami's and Mira's narratives is the pain of rejection and the impossibility of being ever desired by boys/men. *Kuch Kuch Hota Hai* and *Main Hoon Na* represent the pain that Sivagami and Mira experience. Anjali in *Kuch Kuch Hota Hai* is deeply hurt when she is rejected by Rahul, as is Sanju in *Main Hoon Na* when she is ignored by Lucky. Apart from being impossible, this desire also seems unspeakable. It is for this reason that Anjali in *Kuch Kuch Hota Hai* chimes, "Tujhe yaad na meri aye kisi se ab kya kehna" (You don't remember me, what is the point of speaking about it to anyone) (Johar 1998). Such pain of rejection is also not restricted to adolescence but spills over into adulthood, as seen in Mira's narrative as well as in the two films discussed here. But *Kuch Kuch Hota Hai* and *Main Hoon Na* imagine that the resolution to this impossibility of desire lies in transforming the tomboy into a heteronormative feminine or purportedly beautiful woman: a resolution that both Sivagami and Mira resist and often fail to perform. While Sivagami is expected as a tomboy to fail in her wifely and motherly roles, she lives up to the challenge. But that does not feminize her entirely given that her bodily appearance continues to display short hair and she refuses to spend time dressing up. Evidently, then, lookism in relation to tomboys means not just a pressure to become more feminine but also the utter impossibility of finding or experiencing heterosexual male desire itself.

Concluding Remarks

Judith Halberstam (1998), while discussing tomboyism, states that "tomboyism is punished . . . when it threatens to extend beyond childhood into adolescence" (6) and that "it is in the context of female adolescence that the tomboy instincts of millions of girls are remodeled into compliant forms of femininity" (6). Furthering Halberstam's assertions, in this chapter I have tried to establish how tomboyism does extend into adulthood without really obvious threats and that the tomboy instinct need not always be remodeled into "compliant forms of femininity." My ethnographic data demonstrates how the experiences of tomboys are far more complex than simple formulas of external punishment or compliance. Failure also emerges as a common trope throughout the chapter: the failure of performing emphasized femininity or hegemonic masculinity, and the failure of attaining heterosexual desirability. Lookism therefore intersects with tomboyism to show us how it affects body image while also creating the impossibility for tomboys to attain heterosexual romantic desire.

NOTES

1. Heteronormative desire is based on women, as well as men, performing strict gender roles. As this chapter discusses later, women's failure to perform normative femininity marks a failure of heteronormative desire as well.

2. Because of COVID-19 and restrictions on travel, the interviews were conducted in English through phone calls and video calls, and some interviews were audio or video recorded with the consent of the participant. Consent forms were obtained from the participants where they have given me written consent to use their quotes in my chapter. The participants—all of them self-identified tomboys—were selected through snowballing, especially through trusted networks, online and offline. Names have been changed to protect their identities, especially in the case of women. In this chapter, they are called Mira, Tara, Alice, George (in this case, the participant preferred to be called George after the character of George/Georgina in Enid Blyton's *Famous Five* series), Sivagami, and Ray. The reason for selecting English-educated, middle-class participants was the ease of access to them, especially during the pandemic. This choice, however, does not reflect on the relationship between being middle-class and English educated and being affected by negative body image.

3. *Kuch Kuch Hota Hai* is a wildly popular and iconic film directed by Karan Johar. Anjali and Rahul are best friends in college. Anjali has short hair, wears boyish clothes, does not apply makeup, and spends a large part of her time playing basketball with boys. Rahul and Anjali's friendship is threatened when Tina, a feminine and sexually attractive young woman sporting long hair, short dresses, and full makeup, joins their college. Rahul and Tina fall in love with each other, making Anjali realize that she actually loves Rahul, who only considers her a friend since she is unattractive and tomboyish. Years pass, and Tina dies after giving birth to a baby girl, also named Anjali. In her posthumous letters to her daughter, Tina urges the little Anjali to reunite her father, Rahul, with the adult Anjali. The latter is no longer a tomboy and is seen wearing chiffon saris and sporting long hair and makeup. The little Anjali, with the aid of her grandmother, successfully plots to get her father to fall in love with the adult Anjali. Unlike in their college days, this is not hard for Rahul, since Anjali has now become feminine and attractive. This film has been critiqued for showing that a woman is attractive only if she has long hair and wears feminine clothes, exposing the inherent imbalanced gender dynamics in society (Pathiyath, 2013). Eighteen years after the making of the film, Karan Johar publicly apologized for the transformation of Anjali from a tomboy to a feminine woman in *Kuch Kuch Hota Hai* (The News Minute 2016).

The film *Main Hoon Na*, directed by Farah Khan, depicts a similar transformation in the college-going tomboy, Sanjana, and how her best friend, Lucky, falls in love with her only when she transforms herself into a feminine woman. Unlike *Kuch Kuch Hota Hai*, this transformation is not central to the plot of the film, which revolves around an undercover commando, Major Ramprasad Sharma, posing as a college student to protect Sanjana and Lucky, his half-brother. We also notice how Sanjana actively takes a part in her transformation, approaching the feminine and attractive teacher, Miss Chandni, who turns her overnight from a girl wearing torn jeans and a cap into a girl wearing flowing chiffon tunics, with her silky hair flying in the air. This transformation is also reflected in her name. She is earlier referred to as Sanju, and after the transformation, her birth name is reinstated as she apparently becomes whole again to be called Sanjana.

4. George does not seem to make a distinction between butch and tomboy fashion and uses the terms interchangeably. Yet, while growing up, she did not seem to consider butch fashion queer.

5. *Kajal* is also called *kohl*, which is a black eye cosmetic worn on the upper and lower waterline of the eyelids.

6. The film *Qissa* (2013) is a similar and yet drastically different example of a family fulfilling their desire for a son by having their daughter grow up as a boy.

REFERENCES

Blyton, Enid. 1942. *Five on a Treasure Island*. London: Hodder and Stoughton.

Bordo, Susan. 1993. *Unbearable Weight: Feminism, Western Culture, and the Body*. Berkeley: University of California Press.

Granleese, Jacqueline. 2016. "Lookism" *The Wiley Blackwell Encyclopedia of Gender and Sexuality Studies*, edited by Nancy A. Naples, 1–3. John Wiley & Sons. Available at https://doi.org/10.1002/9781118663219.wbegss055.

Halberstam, Judith. 1998. *Female Masculinity*. Durham, NC: Duke University Press.

Johar, Karan, dir. 1998. *Kuch Kuch Hota Hai*. Mumbai; Dharma Production.

John, Mary. 2014. *Sex Ratios and Gender Biased Sex Selection: History, Debates, and Future Directions*. New Delhi: UNFPA and UN Women.

Khan, Farah, dir. 2004. *Main Hoon Na*. Mumbai: Red Chillies Entertainment and Venus Movies.

Minerva, Francesca. 2017. "Lookism." *International Encyclopedia of Ethics*, edited by Hugh LaFollette, 1–7. New Jersey, John Wiley & Sons. Available at https://doi.org/10.1002/9781444367072.wbiee838.

The News Minute. 2016. "18 Years Later, Karan Johar Apologises for Ajali's Transformation in Kuch Kuch Hota Hai." December 5, 2016. Available at https://www.thenews minute.com/article/18-years-later-karan-johar-apologises-anjali-s-transformation-kuch -kuch-hota-hai-53880.

Parameswaran, Radhika. 2011. "E-Race-ing Color: Gender and Transnational Visual Economies of Beauty in India." In *Circuits of Visibility: Gender and Transnational Media Cultures*, edited by Radha Hegde, 68–89. New York: New York University Press.

Pathiyath, Anjali. 2013. "Revisiting Kuch Kuch Hota Hai." *Anveshi Broadsheet*. 2.2&3 (36). Hyderabad: Anveshi Research Centre for Women's Studies.

Renold, Emma. 2008. "Queering Masculinity: Re-Theorizing Contemporary Tomboyism in the Schizoid Space of Innocent/Heterosexualized Young Femininities." *Girlhood Studies* 1, no. 2 (Winter): 129–151.

Scoopwhoop. 2014. "20 Signs That You Were Once a Tomboy." July 18, 2014. Available at https://www.scoopwhoop.com/entertainment/signs-tomboy.

Shah, Chayanika, Raj Merchant, Shals Mahajan, and Smriti Nevatia. 2015. *No Outlaws in the Gender Galaxy*. New Delhi: Zubaan.

Singh, Anup, dir. 2013. *Qissa*. Koln, Harlem, Paris, Mumbai: Augustus Film, Ciné-Sud Promotion, National Film Development Corporation of India.

Conclusion

Womanhood and Body Positivity

Problems, Possibilities, and Promises

SHWETA RAO GARG

This edited volume is primarily a result of the editors' instinctive response to the tyranny of beauty. Growing up in India in the 1990s and responding to subliminal messages stemming from the nation's changing sociocultural forces deeply affected us as women. The conflict between the desire to fashion our bodies according to Western or globalized norms and our own inability—nay, genetic impossibility—informed our bodily choices, critical inquiries, and creative practices. As feminists and postcolonial scholars, we were later able to make connections between our lived experiences and the discourse of an ideal body image.

Like a majority of the women we know, we grew up being subjected to biases based on our looks—color, weight, age, sexuality, caste—and other aspects of appearance. We also witnessed women (and men) close to us being discriminated against because of their body types. We noted how comments disparaging a person based on appearance are routinely normalized in our culture. The discomfort we felt had been powerfully articulated by Western feminist scholars like Naomi Woolf, Laura Mulvey, and Susan Bordo, among others, who—as we encountered their works—gave us the initial vocabulary to examine the deep-rooted systemic problems of appearance bias, beauty politics, and an ideal body image. We also found that while a majority of contemporary Indian feminist scholarship deals with many urgent issues, beauty politics, body image, and body shaming have not been scrutinized enough. We, as editors, feel that these issues are deemed as relatively trivial even when they deeply affect women from all strata of Indian society. We are certain that the chapters in this collection have brought to fore the regulative tenacity of beauty norms and the oppression they cause in Indian women's lives.

The chapters in this volume have come from an affective place, too. These selected chapters examine how the body image of women in India has been shaped through forces of capitalism and patriarchy after the economic liberalization of India. This volume is cognizant of the fact that the category "women" in India is highly stratified and diverse. Class, caste, disability, sexual expression, sexual orientation and gender, and age play a huge part in defining and objectifying women's bodies. The role of popular culture in shaping these ideals has therefore been discussed in several chapters. Chapters that explore challenges faced by bodies that are alienated because of marginalized identities, alternate sexuality, or disability are covered in this volume. The beauty politics in popular Hindi and regional films has also been included in some chapters. Some chapters examine memoirs, advertisements, and media, magazines, or even blogs, all of which deal with complex discourses of female body image. While some scholars in the volume have laid bare the discriminations faced by nonnormative bodies, others have highlighted resistance against an oppressive ideal body image. In addition to the rich and diverse offerings in this volume, we would also like to briefly mention, in this conclusion, how the increasingly popular genre of Indian graphic narratives is presently delving into the problematic of gender, nationhood, and even body image. Furthermore, we note how many Indian social media influencers have been gradually but surely destigmatizing divergent bodies and creating online communities that foster body positivity. While outlining all of this, we conclude by looking at the possibilities and promises these resistive voices generate in deconstructing the beauty politics in India.

The timeline of this volume begins around the economic liberalization of India: 1991 was the year when India transformed its economic policies from the erstwhile License Raj, or the control economy. Crafted during the Second World War by the British colonial government, the control economy in India was dismantled because of the acute economic crises it engendered.[1] The Narasimha Rao government of the early 1990s, owing to some pressure from the International Monetary Fund, had to open up the economy at this point. Foreign direct investment brought new opportunities hitherto inaccessible to the people. It also flooded the market with consumer products never before available. This ushered in a new consumer culture by creating a financial surplus for some parts of the society. Since then, however, a vast section of the population has yet to benefit from these reforms. The economic inequality has only been exacerbated since.[2] Nonetheless, much has changed, too. Just a few decades ago, the government of India, to uphold austerity, used to look down upon and prevent manufacturing of "unnecessary luxury goods."[3] However, since 1991, a whole range of luxury goods have been made available in the Indian market. The cosmetics industry grew its consumer base, a trend that has only seen an upward trajectory ever since.[4] Not surprisingly, an acute awareness of body image maintenance has been perceptible since this time. Increasingly, women began to undergo beauty services in the newly expanding beauty parlors, which since the 1990s have become an aesthetic imperative for a large majority of middle- and upper-middle-class women in urban and semiurban India. These parlors are spaces that empower semiskilled women workers, who, in turn, bank on the aspirations for lighter skin and purportedly prettier faces and bodies through bleaches, facial massages, hair removals, and other techniques.

Like in most capitalist societies, the pattern in neoliberal India is quite clear—the beauty imperative is financially beneficial for the multinational cosmetic industries. Hindustan Unilever's (formerly Hindustan Lever) Fair & Lovely, for example, has been the most popular face cream in India since 1975. The company renamed and rebranded the product into Glow & Lovely in 2020.[5] Following the empowerment discourse, the online platform established by the company, Glow & Lovely Careers, enables women by vocationally training them free of cost. Ironically, their website echoes their advertisements: "We are changing with the times."[6] The company has established this center to show its commitment to change and to manage backlash against their promotion of colorism through blatant misogynist ads for years. Skin lightening, however, continues to be deeply associated with the brand. Despite the ad campaigns upholding narratives of how the face cream aids women's empowerment, "glow" seems to be a thinly disguised euphemism for "fair." It may take some more time for the brand's image to transform and be recognized for enhancing skin health and not lightening skin tone.

Another significant change since the 1990s has been the winners and runners-up in global beauty pageants. From Madhu Sapre to Priyanka Chopra, Indian "beauties" and India as a nation were touted as the "new bonafide beauty superpower."[7] These women, Radhika E. Parameshwaran points out, were seen as heroic figures, rising up against the challenges of social and global inequality—no doubt including beauty pageants, with their apparent misogyny fetish for certain kind of bodies. Such blatant objectification of women in neoliberal India, however, has been seen as empowering. And the body perfections championed by the beauty queens continue to bolster concepts of an ideal body image in contemporary India.

With liberalization, Indians also got access to cable television in addition to the state-sponsored Doordarshan channels. These new channels (Zee TV, Channel [V], and STAR, among others) brought with them a novel visual culture that was previously not available to the Indian audience. American TV series dubbed in Hindi were aired to an audience who would have found the entire set-up unfamiliar. Along with global narratives on other issues, images of Caucasian bodies were being transmitted, too, and this had a huge impact on India's beauty politics. It further reinforced the colonial legacy and the aspiration toward lighter skin and Caucasian body types. Global standards of beauty were now even easier for the audience to gaze at and desire. White, athletic, and nubile bodies were deemed as the epitome of beauty compared to brown, indigenous, earthier ones. Liberalization likewise brought a boom of ready-made retail clothes. A variety of Euro-American sartorial choices that were out of reach for urban middle-class Indians began to be available easily. This further created a pressure to regulate and fit the Indian female body into clothes created for very different body types. Thus, postliberalization, as the spending capacity of the middle-class increased, the pressure to live up to an imagined physical image also increased.

The late 1990s and early 2000s also saw the advent of the Internet and the rise of the information technology sector in India. Since then, the Internet has been a space for images of bodies to travel across borders. Interestingly, while it builds on the hegemonic and dominant notions of body ideals, the Internet also provides opportunities for these ideals to be subverted and undercut. The Web, with its predominance of the visual, gives currency to what is considered desirable and what is not. With an increasingly large number of users from Asia and Africa, there is indeed a growing diversity of representations. However, the bodies that align the most with Eurocentric beauty ideals are celebrated and circulated more. Any minor deviation from the picture-perfect image could trigger body shaming and slut shaming. Nishant Shah, through his study of shame and selfies, observes that slut shaming is not just about punishing female promiscuity, or any particular behavior, but is shaming for just appearing in public.[8] Bodies in the present cultural climate, then, are shamed for being natural bodies. This is perhaps why even the most well-known former beauty queen and Bollywood actor, Aishwarya Rai, was subjected to brutal trolling when she was unable to shed weight after giving birth to her daughter in 2011.[9] The very body that was put on a pedestal as the epitome of Indian beauty and a source of national pride had become a source of embarrassment for the actor and her sympathizers on the Internet. Rai was trolled as she resisted beauty labor immediately as soon as giving birth. Even her young daughter was the object of public scrutiny. Unfortunately, her daughter's age did not deter the commenters from applying the same standards of appearance bias that they did for her mother.[10] This episode reminds us that due to the participatory nature of platforms like Twitter, there can be multiplicity of voices, and the comments that shame certain celebrities also end up being critiqued. What remains fairly undiminished, however, is an all-pervasive beauty bias.

As empowering and informative as the World Wide Web has been, there are multiple studies that confirm the negative impact on young women from exposure to picture-perfect bodies on sites like the Instagram.[11] Indeed, some feminist content creators from South Asia have been intervening through body positive narratives on platforms such as these. And yet, despite creating content that is Instagram friendly, with filters and edits, they speak about many issues that stem from their own life experiences and their immediate surroundings. The curation of authenticity becomes their brand among their fans and followers. Many of these influencers create content, endorse products, and offer services to pander to different body types. A brief analysis of the Instagram accounts of some of these celebrities and influencers opens up interesting paradigms. One such influencer is Sameera Reddy. Though Reddy's older sisters were actors and models, she herself was always overweight. After working on her body to shed weight, she became a model and actress herself, but subsequently her weight increased during pregnancy due to a hormone imbalance. As a result, Reddy was fat-shamed and trolled both online and offline. Her gray hair also caused people to make ageist comments against her. Reddy struggled and overcame her depression because of her naturally transformed body. Finally, she kick-started the #ImperfectlyPerfect campaign on social media as a way of celebrating bodies that are changed through birthing and motherhood.[12] In one of her public talks, Reddy revealed how she underwent postpartum depression and self-loathing for gaining 105 kilos that she could not lose.[13] Reddy wanted to raise awareness about imperfect experiences during motherhood and about her own struggle with body image. Today Reddy shares her weight and calorie count regularly in an attempt to normalize the process of what she calls staying fit.

A second and significant example here is a less known celebrity named Falguni Vasavada, a professor of strategic marketing at MICA Ahmedabad, who creates content on fashion and raises awareness on body positivity. Vasavada usually endorses purportedly affordable products from lesser-known fashion houses and designers. With 110,000 followers,[14] she featured in Hershey's HERSHE campaign for the International Women's Day in 2021.[15] Her image on the chocolate wrapper is a validation of her growing presence and influence. Thankfully, Vasavada is by no means singular in her trajectory. There are a growing number of social media influencers whose content focuses on their own bodies and whose efforts are to destigmatize different types of nonnormative bodies. Another notable Instagram persona is Anwesa Chakraborty, the winner of Ms Plus Size India 2019. With 13,600 followers,[16] Chakraborty spreads messages not only about body positivity and fashion but also about overcoming the stigma of widowhood and remarriage in India. One of the most well-recognized body positivity activists currently, however, is Harnaam Kaur.[17] Born in England to a Punjabi family, Kaur suffered from polycystic ovaries and exhibited hirsutism. Tired of stigma, Kaur decided to embrace her condition and grow a beard. She is now an influencer, model, and even motivational speaker who talks about self-love in the face of depression, bullying, and body shaming.

It is worth noting here that most body positivity influencers interact with their followers. Occasionally, they also respond to messages that shame them in order to emphasize their own significance and justify the existence of their content. Many other online platforms, though not focused on body image exclusively, regularly raise awareness about it. Some of these are Feminism in India,[18] SheThePeople.tv,[19] and Agents of Ishq.[20] With increasing follower-ship, these platforms showcase stories about different bodies, desires, sexualities, and so on. Although there are no statistics about the viewership of these channels, from the comments on these sites, it appears that the majority are women.

It goes without saying that the life narratives of body positivity influencers are almost always inextricably linked to their bodies. With the focus on their bodies on Instagram, these influencers also try to situate themselves within the larger discussion on society, feminism, and the online community of women. On Instagram alone, there are more than ten million followers of #bodypositivity. Just after a cursory glance, however, it is clear that the bodies depicted there belong to "plus size" white women, mostly in beach wear. While the message on the dignity and acceptability of nonnormative bodies is clear, one does wonder if a globally growing body positive movement is yet another instance of how colluding forces of Eurocentrism, capitalism, and patriarchy elide India's feminist agenda on body inclusivity through blatant commodification.

While speaking of resistive voices against appearance discrimination, it is worth turning to the steadily growing popularity of graphic novels in India. As mentioned earlier, graphic novels complicate discourses on space, nation, identity, gender, sexuality, and body in many ways. One of the earliest Indian graphic novels published was *Kari* by Amruta Patil. It is the story of a young advertising professional who traverses life in Mumbai. The protagonist is homosexual and struggles with body dysmorphia. When a friend points out that she is "Chow Yun Fat with boobs," she is shocked and responds, "Sure enough, I'd grown boobs. I fought them all evening."[21] Earlier in the book, we are shown Kari and her female roommates enjoying a lunch together. We notice how these straight cis women with conventionally beautiful and feminine bodies make passes at Kari jokingly. We are told in confidence, "Make no mistake—there is nothing like a fully straight woman."[22] Just a page later, Kari is shown bare chested, staring into the mirror. She confesses that she does not hate mirrors but "just [does not] know what they are trying to tell

[her]."[23] She says that while her friends wonder why Kari does not wear kohl, she herself wonders "why I amn't [sic] looking like Sean Penn."[24] The contrast of Kari's body image versus the normative female body aligns with the images drawn by Amruta Patil in this graphic narrative. Despite Kari's struggles, we note how visual and textual images come together to construct a body that is beautiful and erotic despite not falling within the parameters of heteronormative appearance for an Indian woman in her twenties.

Zubaan, one of the oldest feminist presses in the country, published a series of graphical anthologies as a response to the Nirbhaya rape case in 2012.[25] One of these books is *Drawing the Line: Indian Women Fight Back*, and it has a number of narratives on the crisis of female body image. The book has illustrated stories born out of the lives of illustrators and story writers. It opens with Harini Kannan's graphical story, "That's Not Fair."[26] Kannan narrates the tale from the point of view of a female fetus, who responds to people expressing their desire for a light-skinned child to her dark-skinned mother. Deepani Seth's "The Walk"[27] is a narrative of a woman working in a beauty parlor in a small town in India. The story, more through images than through the text, creates the elusive, temporary intimacy between the beautician and her clients. Within the bubble that these spaces provide, women can come together away from the male gaze and yet are compelled to "beautify" themselves and others to be accepted and appreciated by the world at large.

Another story in this collection that brings colorism to the fore is "Melanin" by Bhavana Singh.[28] Singh anthropomorphizes the pigment melanin and draws various funny and absurd episodes around it. Singh also subverts the fourteen-day shade card popularized by Fair & Lovely, calling it a "scale" promoting "self-loathing," by creating images of Melanin in two weeks' time. It shows the character Melanin indulging in various outdoor activities for fourteen days and getting tonally darker. Melanin, in one of the Kafkaesque episodes, transforms into a bug in what is called "Melanin in Morphosis." Melanin also interacts with UV rays in "Supermel & Yooviji in Entitlement." In "Melanin in Skinteresting Facts," Singh gives us infographics taken from several sources. For instance, she quotes the *Economic Times* from April 14, 2014, to argue that the pigment Melanin is responsible for annually bringing a business of 3,000 crores to India. With this, Singh compellingly deconstructs the fetish for light skin in India, which for her evokes complete hopelessness and "bewilderment." Singh's narrative ends with a mandala-inspired drawing of Melanin in "Melanin in Infinite Wonder" where the pigment revels in almost goddess-like assurance, persisting despite all the skin-whitening and skin-bleaching products.

In yet another graphic novel, entitled *The Elephant in the Room: Women Draw Their World*, Priya Kuriyan's "Ebony and Ivory"[29] talks about the author's grandmother. In the course of the story, we are told that the grandmother was pained by the dark skin of one of her granddaughters. She gives some "pocket money" to the child's mother and asks her to buy some Fair & Lovely for the child. In this story, Kuriyan tries to understand the conditions that made her grandmother become the woman she was. For Kuriyan, her grandmother's blatant colorism was one of her flaws, as was her thrift. The grandmother, due to her own skin tone, is called "Ivory," and her grandfather, a seemingly flashy and likable person, is supposedly "Ebony." Strikingly, this contrast highlights the imbalance of power and acceptability where bodies and skin tones of Indian men and women are concerned. "My Secret Crop," by Kaveri Gopalakrishnan,[30] is another graphic short story in the collection, and it is her tribute to body hair. In an abstractionist style, Gopalkrishnan records the growth of hair, panel after panel. Interestingly, the correspond-ing speech bubbles have statements related to body shaming and body-hair shaming. The juxtaposition of hair patterns with disparaging comments is a subtle way to get across the message of body love. Beauty standards and conventions are not absolute. Women with body hair are deemed repulsive, but by aestheticizing hair mass in her drawings, Gopalkrishnan astutely sub-verts the hairless body imperative for women.

Significantly, some graphical works also try to bring about gender sen-sitivity and awareness of feminist issues among children and young adults. *Priya's Shakti*,[31] a comic and augmented reality venture by Ram Devineni and others, was a response to the Nirbhaya rape case, like *Drawing the Line: In-dian Women Fight Back*. The second installment, *Priya's Mirror*,[32] was co-written by Paromita Vohra (a filmmaker and the founder of Agents of Ishq) and Ram Devineni and illustrated by Dan Goldman. The story uses tropes from Indian mythology as an entry point into issues faced by survivors of acid attacks. An acid attack is a particular form of violence against women, especially in South Asia. It is usually perpetrated by a toxic man to punish a woman by destroying her face in the most violent way possible and render-ing her disfigured for life. In the comic, Priya, a superhero who is herself a gang-rape survivor, comes across a group of acid-attack survivors. The sur-vivors live an isolated life, away from society. Priya is gifted the mirror of love by the goddess to empower the survivors. She shows the mirror to the women, who initially react by calling Priya insensitive for showing a mirror to acid survivors. Priya persists, and one after another, the women begin to "see" themselves. The readers could have expected Priya's mirror to reflect the sur-vivors' faces completely healed, but the mirror only reflects their current faces, which remain disfigured because of acid and restorative surgeries. The mir-ror goes beyond that and makes them see their inner selves, leading them to accept their appearance. The realization that their bodily disfigurement has nothing to do with who they really are brings about their transformation and "frees" them. In the process, the narrative also engenders a powerful critique of India's toxic masculinity and patriarchy, which together violate and shame women's bodies at will.

On similar lines, Orijit Sen, the first graphic novelist from India, created *Comixense*, a collaborative comic quarterly for young adults. The recently launched magazine covers stories that build critical and analytical understanding in readers. One of the issues in this quarterly carried a story titled "The Tyranny of Beauty," written and illustrated by Priyanka Paul. In this story, Paul directly addresses the young readers and shares her thoughts about beauty.[33] "Sitara Devi,"[34] written by Rupleena Bose and illustrated by Nayna Yadav, is about a female star from West Bengal coming to terms with her aging body after living indoors for years. The back cover features a graphically illustrated picture of Harnaam Kaur, the body positive influencer discussed earlier. Clearly, the graphical works mentioned here are some attempts aimed at both young adult and other readers to make them understand that beauty is a social construct. These stories encourage them to question and dismantle the overarching power of heteronormative beauty and body ideals.

While body positive discourses are gaining ground in India, it is also true that mainstream television, Web series, and print media continue to air programs and advertisements that enhance body insecurities among women. Nonetheless, and in contrast, Instagram and Facebook are platforms where conscientious, small-scale, and exclusive companies advertise for an intimate audience base. Tailor & Circus is one among many such body-conscious brands. In addition to creating undergarments with a comfortable fit and soft fabric, they call themselves and their customer base a "body positivity circus."[35] Their advertisements feature models without makeup and with diverse skin tones and sizes, and they often display body hair, stretch marks, or vitiligo or other skin conditions. Some models flaunt their underwear from wheelchairs. They include people of all genders, too. We are aware of neither their profit and growth rate nor how their brand image helps them create their client base, but we know that Tailor & Circus resists using commodified, picture-perfect bodies and displays a genuine interest in practicing body positivity.

In the present day, the Internet is a space that arbitrates discourse on bodies. The inherent contradiction of this space is that while it can propagate the mainstream, patriarchal, and capitalist discourse, it also provides a platform for individuals and groups who want to critique these values. Amid this massive amalgamation of cultural and economic forces, it is clear that some accounts that initiate discussions on body positivity end up as neoliberal marketing ploys. Despite that, we conclude that visual practices on the Internet and elsewhere show that there are possibilities of resistance against a hegemonic and prescriptive body image and that the discursive nature of these platforms will enable the promises of inclusivity to be realized, at least to a certain extent. With changing discourses across India's cultural sectors, we hope to see more such possibilities and promises that accommodate women's embodiment in all its diversity in the future. It is with this hope that we conclude this project.

NOTES

1. Mohan in his introductory essay, "The Road to the 1991 Industrial Policy Reforms and Beyond: A Personalized Narrative from the Trenches," writes on this matter from the point of view of the policymaker.

2. Researchers have critiqued the role of economic liberalization in creating inequality in the country. See Jha, "Reducing Poverty," and Kannan and Raveendran, "Growth sans Employment."

3. Industrial Licensing Policy Inquiry Committee of 1969, quoted in Mohan, "The Road," 12.

4. See GlobeNewswire, "India Cosmetics Market Report 2021."

5. See Jain, Greenfield, and Cavale, "Unilever's 'Fair & Lovely.'"

6. Glow & Lovely, "About Glow & Lovely Careers."

7. Parameshwaran, "Global Beauty Queens," 347.

8. Shah, "The Selfie and the Slut," 91.

9. Manzoor, "Aishwarya Rai's Post-Baby Body."

10. Nijhara, "Aishwarya's Daughter."

11. See Brown and Tiggemann, "Attractive Celebrity." Also see Kleemans et al., "Picture Perfect," and Tiggemann and Anderberg, "Social Media Is Not Real."

12. TNN, "Sameera Reddy Speaks."

13. Reddy, "Embracing Originality."

14. See Vasavada's Instagram.

15. Rathod, "Hershey's HERSHE Bars."

16. See Chakraborty's Instagram.

17. To know more about Harnaam Kaur, see her website.

18. The *Feminism in India: Intersectional Feminism Desi Style* podcast, founded by Japleen Pasricha, is an online portal that creates popular, accessible content on Indian feminism.

19. SheThePeople.tv is an online channel that is committed to circulating positive stories of women from all walks of life.

20. Agents of Ishq is the first online resource of this kind and the brainchild of filmmaker Paromita Vohra. The website is a sex-positive portal focusing on "sex, love and desire in India."

21. Patil, *Kari*, 85.

22. Patil, 58.

23. Patil, 59.

24. Patil, 60.

25. The Nirbhaya case refers to a brutal gang rape of a twenty-three-year-old student in New Delhi in December 2012. The brutality of crime created uproar and widespread protests. It was instrumental in bringing some amendments in India's rape laws. For more, see McLoughlin, "India's Nirbhaya Movement."

26. Kannan, "That's Not Fair."

27. Seth, "The Walk."

28. Singh, "Melanin."

29. Kuriyan, "Ebony and Ivory."

30. Gopalakrishnan, "My Secret Crop."

31. *Priya's Shakti* is a story of a young woman who survives rape. The goddess empowers her to fight against her perpetrators and spread awareness about sexual violence. The comic book is also an augmented reality project. See Devineni, Goldman, and Menon, *Priya's Shakti*.

32. See Paromita, Devineni, and Goldman, *Priya's Mirror*.

33. Paul, "The Tyranny of Beauty," 14–16.

34. Bose and Yadav, "Sitara Devi."

35. See "Body Positive Circus."

BIBLIOGRAPHY

Agentsofishq. "We Give Sex a Good Name." Accessed May 10, 2022. Available at https://agentsofishq.com/.

"Body Positive Circus." Tailorandcircus.com. Accessed June 15, 2022. Available at https://www.tailorandcircus.com/circus.

Bose, Rupleena, and Nayna Yadav. "Sitara Devi." *Comixense* 1, no. 4 (2022): 17–22.

Brown, Zoe, and Marika Tiggemann. "Attractive Celebrity and Peer Images on Instagram: Effect on Women's Mood and Body Image." *Body Image* 19 (December 2016): 37–43. Available at https://doi.org/10.1016/j.bodyim.2016.08.007.

Chakraborty, Anwesa (@dah_boss.lady). Accessed May 22, 2022. Available at https://www.instagram.com/dah_boss.lady/.

Feminism in India: Intersectional Feminism Desi Style. Accessed April 15, 2022. Available at https://feminisminindia.com/.

Globenewswire.com. "India Cosmetics Market Report 2021: Analysis & Forecasts 2014–2026 by Body Care, Hair Care, Color Cosmetics, Men's Grooming, Fragrances, Others," January 25, 2021. Available at https://www.globenewswire.com/news-release/2021/01/25/2163224/28124/en/India-Cosmetics-Market-Report-2021-Analysis-Forecasts-2014-2026-by-Body-Care-Hair-Care-Color-Cosmetics-Men-s-Grooming-Fragrances-Others.html.

Glow & Lovely. "About Glow & Lovely Careers." Accessed May 22, 2022. Available at https://www.glowandlovelycareers.in/en/about-us.

Gopalakrishnan, Kaveri. "My Secret Crop." In *The Elephant in the Room: Women Draw Their World*, edited by Spring Collective, 115–126. New Delhi: Zubaan Books, 2018.

Jain, Rupam, Charlotte Greenfield, and Siddharth Cavale. "Unilever's 'Fair & Lovely' to Get Makeover After Backlash." *Reuters*, June 25, 2020. Available at https://www.reuters.com/article/unilever-whitening-southasia/unilever-rivals-mull-changes-amid-global-backlash-against-skin-lightening-products-idINKBN23W0XE?edition-redirect=in.

Jha, Raghbendra. "Reducing Poverty and Inequality in India: Has Liberalization Helped?" In *Inequality Growth and Poverty in an Era of Liberalization and Globalization*, edited by Giovanni Andrea Cornia, 297–326. WIDER Studies in Development Economics. Oxford, 2004 online edition. Available at https://doi.org/10.1093/0199271410.003.0012.

Kannan, Harini. "That's Not Fair." In *Drawing the Line: Indian Women Fight Back*, edited by Priya Kuriyan, Larissa Bertonasco, and Ludmilla Bartscht, 5–10. New Delhi: Zubaan Books, 2015.

Kannan, K. P., and Raveendran, G. "Growth Sans Employment: A Quarter Century of Jobless Growth in India's Organised Manufacturing." *Economic and Political Weekly* 44, no. 10 (2009): 80–91. Available at https://www.jstor.org/stable/40278784.

Kaur, Harnaam. Accessed May 22, 2022. Available at http://harnaamkaur.com/.

Kleemans, Mariska, Serena Daalmans, Ilana Carbaat, and Doeschka Anschütz. "Picture Perfect: The Direct Effect of Manipulated Instagram Photos on Body Image in Adolescent Girls." *Media Psychology* 22, no. 12 (2018): 93–110. Available at https://doi.org/10.1080/15213269.2016.1257392.

Kuriyan, Priya. "Ebony and Ivory." *The Elephant in the Room: Women Draw their World*, edited by Spring Collective, 199–220. New Delhi: Zubaan Books, 2018.

Manzoor, Sarfraz. "Aishwarya Rai's Post-Baby Body Forces India to Confront Its Attitude to Women." *The Guardian*, May 15, 2012. Available at https://www.theguardian.com/world/2012/may/15/aishwarya-rai-body-india-women.

McLoughlin, Susan. "India's 'Nirbhaya Movement': What Has Changed Since Then?" *Wiisglobal.org*, March 16, 2020. Available at https://wiisglobal.org/indias-nirbhaya-movement-what-has-changed-since-then/.

Mohan, Rakesh. "The Road to the 1991 Industrial Policy Reforms and Beyond: A Personalized Narrative from the Trenches." In *India Transformed: 25 Years of Economic Reforms*, edited by Rakesh Mohan, 3–45. Washington: Brookings Institution Press, 2018.

Nijhara, Apoorva. "Aishwarya's Daughter Aaradhya Trolled for Her Walk in this Video & It's Uncalled For." *mensxp.com*, November 24, 2021. Available at https://www.mensxp.com/entertainment/bollywood/96766-aishwarya-rai-bachchan-daughter-aaradhya-trolled.html.

Parameswaran, Radhika E. "Global Beauty Queens in Post-Liberalization India." *Peace Review: A Journal of Social Justice* 17, no. 4 (2005):419–426. Available at https://doi.org/10.1080/10402650500374702.

Patil, Amruta. *Kari*. New Delhi: Harper Collins, 2008.

Paul, Priyanka. "The Tyranny of Beauty." *Comixense* 1, no. 4 (2022): 14–16.

Ram, Devineni, Dan Goldman, and Vikas K. Menon. *Priya's Shakti*. 2014. Available at https://www.priyashakti.com/priyas-shakti.

Rathod, Kalwyna. "Hershey's HERSHE Bars are the Perfect Women's Day Tribute to These Sheroes." *Femina,* March 11, 2021. Available at https://www.femina.in/trending/in-the-news/hersheys-hershe-bars-are-the-perfect-womens-day-tribute-to-these-sheroes-188405.html.

Reddy, Sameera. "Embracing Originality." Filmed at Sri Sairam IT, India. TEDx talk. August 14, 2019. Available at https://www.youtube.com/watch?v=uDwR12fJbjI.

Seth, Deepani. "The Walk." In *Drawing the Line: Indian Women Fight Back*, edited by Priya Kuriyan, Larissa Bertonasco, and Ludmilla Bartscht, 77–94. New Delhi: Zubaan Books, 2015.

Shah, Nishant. "The Selfie and the Slut: Bodies, Technology and Public Shame." *Economic and Political Weekly* 50, no. 17 (2015): 86–93. Available at https://www.jstor.org/stable/24481830.

Shethepeople.tv. Accessed May 22, 2022. Available at https://www.shethepeople.tv.

Singh, Bhavna. "The Melanin." In *Drawing the Line: Indian Women Fight Back*, edited by Priya Kuriyan, Larissa Bertonasco, and Ludmilla Bartscht, 65–76. New Delhi: Zubaan Books, 2015.

Tiggerman, Marika, and Isabella Anderberg. "Social Media Is Not Real: The Effect of 'Instagram vs Reality' Images on Women's Social Comparison and Body Image." *New*

Media & Society 22, no. 12 (2020): 2183–2199. Available at https://doi.org/10.1177/1461 444819888720.

TNN. "Sameera Reddy Speaks about Postpartum Depression, Body Issues and Being Imperfectly Perfect." August 5, 2020. Available at https://timesofindia.indiatimes.com /entertainment/tamil/movies/news/sameera-reddy-speaks-about-postpartum-depres sion-body-issues-and-being-imperfectly-perfect/articleshow/77368119.cms.

Vasavada, Falguni (@falgunivasavada). Accessed May 22, 2022. Available at https://www .instagram.com/falgunivasavada/.

Vohra, Paromita, Ram Devineni, and Dan Goldman. *Priya's Mirror.* 2016. Accessed May 22, 2022. Available at https://www.priyashakti.com/priyas-mirror.

Further Reading

Agarwal, Navya. *Art of the Good Fight: Dissecting Indian Social Ills through Sun Tzu's Art of War*. Chennai: Notion Press, 2021.

Banfield, Sophie. S., and Marita P. McCabe. "An Evaluation of the Construct of Body Image." *Adolescence* 37, no. 146 (2002): 373–393.

Bannerji, Himani. "Textile Prison: Discourse on Shame (Lajja) in the Attire of the Gentlewoman (Bhadramahila) in Colonial Bengal." *Canadian Journal of Sociology* 9, no. 2 (1994): 169–93. Available at https://www.jstor.org/stable/3341343.

Barker, Clare, and Stuart Murray, eds. *The Cambridge Companion to Literature and Disability*. Cambridge: Cambridge University Press, 2017.

Barrera, Mario. *Race and Class in the Southwest*. Notre Dame: University of Notre Dame, 1979.

Bartky, Sandra. "Foucault, Femininity and the Modernization of Patriarchal Power." *Feminism and Foucault, Reflections on Resistance*, edited by Irene Diamond and Lee Quinby, 29–44. Boston: Northeastern University Press, 1988.

Basu, Soma. "How Nepali Women Are Forced to 'Sell' Their Skin to Make Rich Indians Beautiful." *Youth Ki Awaaz*. 2017. Accessed August 24, 2018. Available at https://www.youthkiawaaz.com/2017/03/how-women-from-nepal-are-trafficked-to-india-and-disfigured-to-make-rich-men-and-women-beautiful/

Berer, Marge. "Editorial: Cosmetic Surgery, Body Image and Sexuality." *Reproductive Health Matters* 18, no. 35 (May 2010): 4–10.

Beteille, Andre. "Race and Descent as Social Categories in India." In *Colour and Race*, edited by John Hope Franklin, 166–185. Boston: Houghton Mifflin, 1968.

Bhargava, Jyotsna Mohan. *Stoned, Shamed, Depressed: An Explosive Account of the Secret Lives of India's Teens*. New Delhi: HarperCollins, 2020.

Blackman, Lisa. *The Body: The Key Concepts*. London: Bloomsbury, 2008.

Blum, Virginia L. *Flesh Wounds: The Culture of Cosmetic Surgery*. Berkeley and Los Angeles: University of California Press, 2003.

Bordo, Susan. *The Male Body: A New Look at Men in Public and Private*. New York: Farrar, Straus and Giroux, 2000. Originally published 1999.

———. *Unbearable Weight: Feminism, Western Culture, and the Body*. Berkeley: University of California Press, 2003. Originally published 1993.

Brewis, Alexandra A., Amber Wutich, Ashlan Falletta-Cowden, and Isa Rodriguez-Soto. "Body Norms and Fat Stigma in Global Perspective." *Current Anthropology* 52, no. 2 (2011): 269–276.

Butler, Judith. *Bodies That Matter: On the Discursive Limits of 'Sex'*. New York: Routledge, 1993.

Cash, Thomas F., and Linda Smolak, eds. *Body Image: A Handbook of Science, Practice, and Prevention*. 2nd ed. New York: Guilford Press, 2012.

Cavale, Jaiyant, and Dweep Chand Singh. "Current Status of Body Image Research in India." *India Journal of Psychological Science* 5, no. 1 (July 2014): 124–131.

Chakravarty, Sumita S. "Reflections on the Body Beautiful in Indian Popular Culture." *Social Research* 78, no. 2 (Summer 2011): 395–416. Available at https://www.jstor.com/stable/23347183.

Chanana, Kuhu Sharma. *LGBTQ Identities in Select Modern Indian Literature*. New Delhi: D.K Printworld, 2015.

Chatterjee, Partha. "Colonialism, Nationalism, and Colonialized Women: The Contest in India." *American Ethnologist* 16, no. 4 (November 1989): 622–633. Available at https://www.jstor.org/stable/645113.

Chatterjee, Srirupa, and Shreya Rastogi. "The Changing Politics of Beauty Labour in Indian Cinema." *South Asian Popular Culture* 18, no. 3 (2020): 271–282.

———. "Television Culture and the Beauty Bias Problem: An Analysis of India's Postmillennial Television Serials." *Media Asia* 49, no. 3 (2022): 213–234.

Chopra, Shaili, and Megha Pant, eds. *Feminist Rani: India's Most Powerful Voices on Gender Equality*. New Delhi: Penguin Random House, 2018.

Connolly, Jess. *Breaking Free from Body Shame: Dare to Reclaim What God Has Named Good*. Grand Rapids: Zondervan, 2021.

Craig, Maxine Leeds. *The Routledge Companion to Beauty Politics*. London: Taylor and Francis, 2021.

Dehejia, Harsha V., and Makarand Paranjape, eds. *Saundarya, the Perception and Practice of Beauty in India*. New Delhi: Samvad India Foundation, 2003.

Dewey, Susan. *Making Miss India Miss World: Constructing Gender, Power, and the Nation in Postliberalization India*. Syracuse: Syracuse University Press, 2008.

Etcoff, Nancy. *Survival of the Prettiest: The Science of Beauty*. New York: Anchor Books, 2000. Originally published 1999.

Faludi, Susan. *Backlash: The Undeclared War against American Women*. New York: Crown Publishers, 1991.

Fanon, Frantz. *Black Skin, White Masks*. Pluto Press, 2008. Originally published 1952.

Forbes, Geraldine. "Small Acts of Rebellion: Women Tell Their Photographs." In *Behind the Veil*, edited by Anindita Ghosh, 58–82. Palgrave Macmillan, 2008.

Foucault, Michel. *The History of Sexuality*. Vol. 1. New York: Pantheon Books, 1978.

Ghosh, Nandini. *Interrogating Disability in India: Theory and Practice*. New Delhi: Springer, 2016.

Gilman, Sandra L. *Making the Body Beautiful: A Cultural History of Aesthetic Surgery*. Princeton: Princeton University Press, 2000.

Glenn, Evelyn Nakano. *Shades of Difference: Why Skin Color Matters*. Stanford: Stanford University Press, 2009.

Grogan, Sarah. *Body Image: Understanding Body Dissatisfaction in Men, Women, and Children*. London: Routledge, 2007.

Haraway, Donna. *A Cyborg Manifesto*. Minneapolis: University of Minnesota Press, 2016.

Hasan, Zoya, Martha Nussbaum, Vidhu Verma, and Aziz Huq, eds. *The Empire of Disgust: Prejudice, Discrimination, and Policy in India and the US*. New Delhi: Oxford University Press, 2018.

Heyes, Cressida J. *Cosmetic Surgery: A Feminist Primer*. London: Routledge, 2016.

Huberman, Warren L. *Through Thick and Thin: The Emotional Journey of Weight Loss Surgery*. New York: Graphite Press, 2012.

Hutson, David J. "Standing OUT/Fitting IN: Identity, Appearance, and Authenticity in Gay and Lesbian Communities." *Symbolic Interaction* 33, no. 2 (2010): 213–233.

Jethwaney, Jaishri. *The Beauty Paradigm: Gender Discourse in Indian Advertising*. New Delhi: Sage, 2021.

Jha, Meeta Rani. *The Global Beauty Industry: Colorism, Racism, and the National Body*. New York: Taylor and Francis, 2015.

Jha, Sonora, and Mara Adelman. "Looking for Love in All the White Places: A Study of Skin Color Preferences on Indian Matrimonial and Mate-Seeking Websites." *Studies in South Asian Film and Media* 1, no. 1 (January 2009): 65–83. Available at https://doi.org/10.1386/safm.1.1.65_1.

June, Pamela B. *The Fragmented Female Body and Identity*. New York: Peter Lang, 2010.

Kullrich, Nina. *Skin Colour Politics: Whiteness and Beauty in India*. Berlin and Heidelberg: Springer, 2022.

Kumar, Anuranjita. *Colour Matters? The Truth That No One Wants to See*. New Delhi: Bloomsbury, 2019.

Liebelt, Claudia, Sarah Böllinger, and Ulf Vierke, eds. *Beauty and the Norm: Debating Standardization in Bodily Appearance*. New York: Palgrave Macmillan, 2019.

Madhukar, Madu S. *Black Tea: The Story Is About India's Bias against Darker Skin Color, Particularly Pertaining to Women*. Bloomington: iUniverse, 2008.

McBride, Hillary L. *Mothers, Daughters, and Body Image: Learning to Love Ourselves as We Are*. Nashville: Post Hill Press, 2017.

McKittrick, Katherine. *Demonic Grounds: Black Women and the Cartographies of Struggle*. Minneapolis: University of Minnesota Press, 2006.

Merleau-Ponty, Maurice. *Phenomenology of Perception*. London: Routledge and K. Paul, Humanities Press, 1974.

———. *The Visible and the Invisible*. Translated by Alphonso Lingis. Evanston: Northwestern University Press, 1968.

Mitchell, Catriona, ed. *Walking toward Ourselves: Indian Women Tell Their Stories*. New Delhi: Harper Collins, 2016.

Mitra, Sreya. "Trolled, Body-Shamed and Slut-Shamed: The Desecration of the Contemporary Bollywood Female Star on Social Media." *Celebrity Studies* 11, no. 1 (2020): 101–115.

Nagar, Itisha. "The Unfair Selection: A Study on Skin-Color Bias in Arranged Indian Marriages." *Sage Open* 8, no. 2 (April–June 2018): 1–8. Available at https://doi.org/10.1177/2158244018773149.

Nario-Redmond, Michelle R. *Ableism: The Causes and Consequences of Disability Prejudice*. Hoboken: Wiley-Blackwell, 2019.

Nihalani, Shobha. *Reboot, Reflect, Revive: Self Esteem in a Selfie World*. New Delhi: Sage, 2021.

Pathak, Gauri. "'Presentable': The Body and Neoliberal Subjecthood in Contemporary India." *Social Identities: Journal for the Study of Race, Nation and Culture* 20, no. 4–5 (2014): 314–329.

Philips, Amali. "Gendering Colour: Identity, Femininity and Marriage in Kerala." *Anthropologica* 46, no. 2 (2004): 253–272. Available at https://doi.org/10.2307/25606198.

Pitts, Victoria. "Visibly Queer: Body Technologies and Sexual Politics." *Sociological Quarterly* 41, no. 3 (2000): 443–463.

Pompper, Donnalyn. *Rhetoric of Femininity: Female Body Image, Media, and Gender Role Stress/Conflict*. London: Rowman and Littlefield, 2016.

Puri, Jyoti. *Woman, Body, Desire in Post-Colonial India: Narratives of Gender and Sexuality*. New York: Routledge, 1999.

Ramasubramaniam, Srividya, and Parul Jain. "Gender Stereotypes and Normative Heterosexuality in Matrimonial Ads from Globalizing India." *Asian Journal of Communication* 19, no. 3 (September 2009): 253–269. Available at https://doi.org/10.1080/0129 2980903072831.

Reischer, Erica, and Kathryn S. Koo. "The Body Beautiful: Symbolism and Agency in the Social World." *Annual Review of Anthropology* 33 (2004): 297–317.

Rhode, Deborah L. *The Beauty Bias: The Injustice of Appearance in Life and Law*. New York: Oxford University Press, 2010.

Rice, Carla. *Becoming Women: The Embodied Self in Image Culture*. Toronto: University of Toronto Press, 2014.

Russell-Cole, Kathy, Midge Wilson, and Ronald E. Hall, eds. *The Color Complex: The Politics of Skin Color in a New Millennium*. New York: Anchor Books, 2013.

Sault, Nicole, ed. *Many Mirrors: Body Image and Social Relations*. New Brunswick: Rutgers University Press, 1994.

Taub, Diane E., Patricia L. Fanflik, and Penelope A. Mclorg. "Body Image among Women with Physical Disabilities: Internalization of Norms and Reactions to Nonconformity." *Sociological Focus* 36, no. 2 (May 2003): 159–176.

Utley, T. Jerome, and William Darity Jr. "India's Color Complex: One Day's Worth of Matrimonials." *Review of Black Political Economy* 43, no. 2 (2016): 129–138. Available at https://doi.org/10.1007/s12114-016-9233-x.

Contributors

Aratrika Bose (she/her pronouns) is a Ph.D. scholar in the Department of English and Cultural Studies, CHRIST University, India with her area of specialization being gender studies. Her current research is on the intersectionality of homosexuality and heteronormativity in modern India. She has published reviews and articles on Indian queer texts and visual media in journals such as *Monthly Review* and *QED*, as well as conference proceedings presented at international conferences that critically examine hegemonic femininity in female sexualities in India. Her other interests are feminist literature, queer literature, sexuality, and visual media studies.

Turni Chakrabarti is Assistant Professor of English at Jindal School of Languages and Literature at O. P. Jindal Global University in Sonipat, India. She received her Ph.D. in English from George Washington University in Washington, D.C., in May 2022. Her work has been published in peer-reviewed journals like *Verge: Studies in Global Asias, South Asian Review*, and *Portals: A Journal of Comparative Literature*, among others.

Anurima Chanda is Assistant Professor in the Department of English, Birsa Munda College, University of North Bengal, India. Previously, she has worked with the Centre for Writing and Communication, Ashoka University, where, among other things, she extensively worked with English as a second language (ESL) students and students with learning disabilities, trying to devise teaching modules according to individual needs. She completed her Ph.D. on Indian English children's literature from JNU. She was a predoctoral fellow at the University of Würzburg under the DAAD Programme "A New Passage to India," working under Isabel Karremann. She is also a literary translator and children's author (published with Scholastic and DK). Her latest work includes *How I Became a Writer: An Autobiography of a Dalit* (translation of the second volume of Manoranjan Byapari's *Itibrittye Chandal Jibon* from Bengali to English).

Srirupa Chatterjee is Associate Professor of English, Gender Studies, and Body Studies in the Department of Liberal Arts at the Indian Institute of Technology Hyderabad, India. She has published research papers in journals such as *Critique: Studies in Contemporary Fiction, South Asian Popular Culture, Papers on Language and Literature, LIT: Literature Interpretation Theory, English Studies, Women: A Cultural Review, Journal of Language, Literature and Culture, ANQ: A Quarterly Journal of Short Articles, South Central Review, Notes on Contemporary Literature*, and *The Explicator*. Her other works include an edited volume titled *Gendered Violence in Public Spaces: Women's Narratives of Travel in Neoliberal India* from Lexington Books and forthcoming monographs entitled *Body Image in Contemporary American Young Adult Literature* from Routledge and *Body Image: An Introduction* from Orient Blackswan.

Ketaki Chowkhani is Assistant Professor at Manipal Centre for Humanities, Manipal Academy of Higher Education, India, where she teaches India's first-ever course on singles studies. She is coeditor of *Singular Selves: An Introduction to Singles Studies* (Routledge 2023) and author of *The Limits of Sexuality Education: Love, Sex, and Adolescent Masculinities in Urban India* (Routledge 2023). Her other writing on gender, sexuality, and singlehood has appeared in the *Indian Journal of Medical Ethics*, the *Journal of Porn Studies*, the *New York Times, Square Peg*, and *The Hindu*, as well as in edited volumes published by Routledge and Cambridge University Press. Ketaki has a Ph.D. in women's studies from Tata Institute of Social Sciences, Mumbai.

Kavita Daiya is Professor of English and Women's, Gender, and Sexuality Studies and the former director (2018–2021) of the Women's, Gender, and Sexuality Studies Program at George Washington University in Washington, D.C. Her areas of expertise span South Asian and South Asian American cultural studies, transnational feminism, migration, and race and ethnic studies. She is the author of several articles and two books: *Violent Belongings: Partition, Gender, and National Culture in Postcolonial India* (Temple University Press, [2008] 2011; Yoda Press, 2013) and *Graphic Migrations: Precarity and Gender in India and the Diaspora* (Temple University Press, 2020; Yoda Press, 2021). Her interest in transmedia and public culture appears in her edited volume, *Graphic Narratives about South Asian and South Asian America: Aesthetics and Politics* (Routledge, 2019). She served on the Founding Board of Directors of a digital humanities initiative, the 1947Partition-Archive.org (2015–2021).

Shweta Rao Garg is an artist, writer, and academic based in Baltimore. She is a former Associate Professor of English at DA-IICT in Gandhinagar, India. She is the recipient of Fulbright doctoral fellowship and has published in the area of Indian women's writings, Bollywood, and food and cultural studies. Her book of poems, *Of Goddesses and Women*, was published by Sahitya Akademi, the Indian National Academy of Letters, in 2021. She has written a graphic novel on sensitizing Indian undergraduate students to diversity, *The Tales from Campus: A Misguide to College*. She has coedited *The English Paradigm in India: Essay in Language, Literature and Culture* (Palgrave, 2017) and *Quicksand Borders: South Asia in Verse* (Macmillan, forthcoming). Some of her works can be found at https://shwetaraogarg.com.

Nishat Haider is Professor of English at Jamia Millia Islamia, New Delhi, India. She is the author of *Tyranny of Silences: Contemporary Indian Women's Poetry* (2010). She has served as Director of the Institute of Women's Studies, University of Lucknow. She is the recipient of many academic awards, including the Meenakshi Mukherjee Prize (2016), the C. D. Narasimhaiah Award (2010), and the Isaac Sequeira Memorial Award (2011). Her academic essays have been included in a variety of scholarly journals and books, such as *South Asian Review, Postcolonial Urban Outcasts: City Margins in South Asian Literature* (Routledge, 2016), and *Premchand in World Languages: Translation, Reception and Cinematic Representations* (Routledge, 2016). She has worked on various projects funded by the Ministry of Women and Child Development, UNICEF, (University Grants Commission) UGC, and other agencies. She has lectured extensively on subjects at the intersection of cinema, culture, and gender studies. Her current research interests include postcolonial studies, translation, popular culture, and gender studies.

Shubhra Ray is Associate Professor of English in Zakir Husain Delhi College (Evening) of the University of Delhi and has a Ph.D. in English Literature from the Centre for English Studies, Jawaharlal Nehru University. She has published articles in edited books and international journals brought out by Duke University Press, Zubaan, and Routledge, among others, in her areas of interest, which are book history, gender studies, and autobiographical studies. She has been the recipient of the Nehru Memorial Museum and Library Fellowship (2018–2020) and the Charles Wallace India Trust Research Grant (2016–2017). She also translates from Bengali and won the Katha Award for Translation in 2005.

Sucharita Sarkar is Associate Professor of English, DTSS College of Commerce, Mumbai, and invited member of the Faculty of Humanities, Dr. Homi Bhabha State University, Mumbai. Her doctoral thesis investigated mothering narratives in contemporary India. Her current research focuses on intersections of maternity with body, religion, cultures, self-writing, and media, usually from South Asian perspectives and with a matricentric feminist focus. She participated in an international collaborative project, New Directions for International Scholarship on Motherhood in Religious Studies, which can be accessed at https://beyondmg.study/. Her recent publications include articles in *Current Sociology* (2021), *Qualitative Inquiry* (2020), and *Open Theology* (2020), as well as chapters in edited anthologies such as *The Palgrave Handbook of Reproductive Justice and Literature* (2022), *Representing Abortion* (Routledge, 2021), *Food, Faith and Gender in South Asia* (Bloomsbury Academic, 2020), and *Thickening Fat* (Routledge, 2020), among others. Her research is documented at https://mu.academia.edu/SucharitaSarkar.

Shailendra Kumar Singh is Assistant Professor at Indian Institute of Technology Tirupati, India. He has published several articles in internationally acclaimed journals such as *Fat Studies, Journal of Lesbian Studies, Women's Reproductive Health*, and *Girlhood Studies*. He is the youngest winner of the Meenakshi Mukherjee Prize for the Best Published Academic Paper in a Calendar Year (2016–2017), sponsored by the Indian Association for Commonwealth Literature and Language Studies.

Samrita Sinha is an alumnus of St. Xavier's College, Calcutta, and the University of Calcutta, India. Samrita is currently Assistant Professor in the Department of English at Sophia College for Women (Autonomous), Mumbai. Her doctoral research is in the domain of Northeast Indian Anglophone literatures. Her article "Narrative Strategies of Decolonisation: Autoethnography in Mamang Dai's The Legends of Pensam" was published by *Rupkatha Journal on Interdisciplinary Studies in Humanities*, which is indexed by Web of Science, Scopus, ERIH PLUS, and EBSCO. She has contributed to several journals and has written book chapters. She is currently coediting a book on *Female Protest Narratives* *from South Asia* that is to be published by Routledge in 2023. She has also been selected for the Charles Wallace Research Grant for the academic year 2022–2023 to pursue research at libraries in School of Oriental and African Studies (SOAS).

Swatie holds a doctoral degree from the University of Delhi. She is the author of *The New Normal: Trauma, Biopolitics and Visuality after 9/11* (Bloomsbury, 2021). Her research interests include violence studies, gender and feminism, visual culture, and, most recently, the intersection of law and literature. She has presented her research at institutes and at conferences hosted by Dartmouth College, the University of Pennsylvania, Jamia Millia Islamia and the University of Heidelberg, the University of California Irvine, and the National Law University, Delhi, among others. She is Assistant Professor at Lady Shri Ram College for Women in the Department of English, University of Delhi, India.

Annika Taneja holds an M.Litt. from the University of St. Andrews, United Kingdom, in modern and contemporary literature and culture, with a minor in postcolonial theory. Her research interests include Indian feminisms, gender theory (gender and the body, gender and labor, etc.), Dalit-Bahujan-Adivasi literature and cultures, Indian speculative fiction, utopian studies, critical urban theory, ecocriticism, and partition literature. Taneja has worked as Creative Copywriter with Wieden + Kennedy in the Delhi and Amsterdam. Currently she is a freelance copywriter, editor, and translator.

Tanupriya is an Assistant Professor with the Department of English and Cultural Studies, CHRIST (Deemed to be University), Delhi NCR campus. She is an awarded gold medalist for her MPhil English in 2017. She was awarded a JASSO (Japan Student Services Organization) fellowship for attending a conference at Kumamoto University, Kumamoto, Japan. She has published her works in peer-reviewed Scopus-indexed journals. Her book chapters are published with Springer, Palgrave Macmillan, and Routledge. She is an editorial board member for the Routledge Handbook of Descriptive Rhetorical Studies and World Languages. Her research interests are Queer visual culture, Female and Queer Body Image, Trans sexualities and writing the self, and varied aspects related to frameworks of gender and sexuality.

Sukshma Vedere is a Ph.D. student in the English Department at George Washington University. She is interested in postcolonial and disability studies. Her dissertation focuses on the representation of disability in Indian fiction and film. Her work has been published in the *South Asian Review* and the *College Language Association Journal*, among others.

Index

www.ingramcontent.com/pod-product-compliance
Lightning Source LLC
Chambersburg PA
CBHW020342270326
41926CB00007B/286